Over the Horizon

Over the Horizon

*Time, Uncertainty, and the
Rise of Great Powers*

Davɪᴅ M. Eᴅᴇʟsᴛᴇɪɴ

Cornell University Press

Ithaca and London

First published 2017 by Cornell University Press
First paperback printing 2020

Library of Congress Cataloging-in-Publication Data

Names: Edelstein, David M., author.
Title: Over the horizon : time, uncertainty, and the rise of great
    powers / David M. Edelstein.
Description: Ithaca : Cornell University Press, 2017. | Includes
    bibliographical references and index.
Identifiers: LCCN 2017004752 (print) | LCCN 2017005598 (ebook) |
    ISBN 9781501707568 (cloth) | ISBN 9781501712081 (epub/mobi) |
    ISBN 9781501709449 (pdf) |
    ISBN 978-1-5017-4845-5 (pbk.)
Subjects: LCSH: Great powers—History. | World politics. | Time
    perception—Political aspects. | Uncertainty—Political aspects.
    Classification: LCC D31 .E34 2017 (print) | LCC D31 (ebook) |
    DDC 320.9—dc23
LC record available at https:// lccn.loc. gov/2017004752

To Levi and Gabriel

Contents

Preface

This book is about how varying time horizons affect international politics. The completion of this book has itself required long time horizons. I am grateful to all of those who have supported this project through the years, starting with my mentors at the University of Chicago—Stephen Walt, John Mearsheimer, Charles Glaser, and James Fearon. Though this book barely resembles the draft that I wrote years ago, its origins nonetheless lie in the remarkable intellectual environment of the University of Chicago.

I could not imagine a better place to have written this book than at Georgetown University. The Center for Security Studies, under the directorship of Bruce Hoffman, has provided both financial and intellectual support, and the center's terrific staff enables faculty to do their best teaching and research. The Edmund A. Walsh School of Foreign Service, led by the late Carol Lancaster, James Reardon-Anderson, and now Joel Hellman, is home to an inspiring group of faculty, staff, and students that makes me excited to go to work every day. The Mortara Center for International Studies has been my physical home. All who visit the Mortara Center are impressed by not only the physical space but also the intellectual excitement it generates. I am grateful to its director, Kate McNamara, during the time I was writing this book, as well as to its small but extremely capable staff.

Beyond the institutions, my colleagues at Georgetown have supported and provoked me. In particular, I am grateful to Andy Bennett, Marc Busch, Dan Byman, Christine Fair, George Shambaugh, Bruce Hoffman, Charles King, Keir Lieber, Robert Lieber, Kate McNamara, Abe Newman, Dan Nexon, Erik Voeten, and James Vreeland. Georgetown's smart and inquisitive students have pushed to make this project better. Rebecca Lissner, Paul Musgrave, Dani Nedal, and Michael Weintraub have been not only students but trusted colleagues. The students in my spring 2016 international security Ph.D. seminar read the entire manuscript and provided invaluable feedback as the project was nearing its conclusion. Finally, from among the students in the Security Studies Program at Georgetown, I benefited from the research assistance of Patrick Calabro, Hannah Byrne, and Michael Sexton. Translations of primary source documents cited throughout the book are mine, with the assistance of colleagues and research assistants.

I have had the good fortune to present parts of this book at a number of conferences and institutions. I am grateful for the invitations and feedback from Cornell University, the George Washington University, the University of California at Berkeley, the University of Chicago, the University of Minnesota, the Ohio State University, and Texas A&M University. I am especially grateful to Jonathan Kirshner for an invitation to present a portion of this book at a conference on classical realism that he hosted at Cornell. In addition, the argument benefited from a presentation at the D.C. area International Relations Workshop. At these various presentations, Matt Fuhrmann, Gene Gerzhoy, Elizabeth Saunders, Ron Hassner, Ron Krebs, Randy Schweller, and Josh Shifrinson provided particularly valuable comments and questions. Other commentators at annual meetings of the International Studies Association and the American Political Science Association, including Jeff Legro, Norrin Ripsman, and Jack Levy, also helped this book become better than it otherwise would have been. David Gill of Nottingham University was kind enough to read the entire manuscript and provided insightful feedback.

The most important opportunity I had to present this manuscript was at a book manuscript workshop at Georgetown, organized and supported by the Mortara Center. I cannot express how grateful I am to the participants who so carefully read the manuscript and provided quite simply the single most important day in this project's formation: Jasen Castillo, Alex Downes, Nuno Monteiro, Kate McNamara, Paul Musgrave, Abe Newman, Dani Nedal, Dan Nexon, and Keren Yarhi-Milo.

At Cornell University Press, Roger Haydon has been a consistent advocate of this project. I am grateful for the care with which he handled the manuscript, the trenchant comments that he offered at various stages, and, perhaps most of all, his wry and sarcastic sense of humor when it was most (or sometimes least) needed.

All scholars have their "inner circles"—those people whom they most trust not only with the intellectual challenges of this business but also with the personal and emotional ones. At Georgetown, Kate McNamara and Abe Newman have been colleagues as well as remarkably supportive friends. Whenever I thought I might never get to the end, it was often Kate and Abe who bucked me up and got me back to work. Beyond Georgetown, nobody has believed more in this project than Jasen Castillo. Even when he was undoubtedly tired of doing it, he always reminded me of why this book would be important. Similarly, Alex Downes has a ruthless intellect, so his faith in this project always reassured me when I had my doubts. Finally, Ron Krebs continues to inspire me through the consistently high quality of his own scholarship, and his friendship, encouragement, and pointed critiques have made me a better scholar and this a better book.

The debts one accrues in writing a book are not, however, just intellectual. I am thankful to the family and friends who have tolerated my more-than-occasional grumpiness as I have completed this book. In particular, I am grateful for the love and support of my immediate family as well as my wife's. I have not always been eager to answer questions about this book, but please know that had everything to do with the book and nothing to do with you.

It is perhaps odd to acknowledge a hobby as contributing to the completion of a book, but in this case, it is appropriate. A few years ago, I discovered the sport of triathlon. Since then, training and racing have provided a necessary outlet for excess energy and anxiety and also a new community of friends that I have come to cherish. Those workouts and those friends provided much-needed relief when I confronted the most challenging aspects of completing the manuscript. In particular, I am grateful to Sara Colangelo, my teammates in Speed Sherpa Nation, and especially Dave Henkel. Dave has been my triathlon coach since shortly after I took up the sport. As much as he has taught me about swimming, biking, and running, he has taught me an equal amount about pushing myself to achieve ambitious goals not just in triathlon but also in life.

Finally, none of this would have been possible without my wife, Robin Peck. Her love, support, and faith have been unrelenting, and I will forever be grateful. As I have been writing this book about time horizons, I have frequently been amused by the invariably short time horizons of our boys, Levi and Gabriel. In recent months, they have asked with increasing volume, "When is the book going to be done, Dad?" Well, it's done now, and they deserve as much credit as anybody. With apologies for the patience it has asked of them, this book is dedicated to them.

Over the Horizon

Introduction

Competition, Cooperation, and the Rise of Great Powers

What explains variation in the levels of cooperation and competition between existing great powers and the emerging potential threats they face? In this book, I answer this question with a temporal theory of great power politics. I argue that how states weigh threats and opportunities in a knowable present as opposed to an uncertain future is a significant and underappreciated influence on the policies that their leaders pursue. Contrary to prominent existing arguments in international relations, I contend that attention to the future often leads to more competition than cooperation but that uncertainty about that future opens the space for cooperation rather than foreclosing it.

Consider what could be the most important international political development of the twenty-first century: the emergence of the People's Republic of China as a global superpower. The continuing rise of China could transform the international system, revolutionize the international economy, and, if history is any guide, result in devastating conflict. Yet while bookshelves are filled with breathless studies speculating on the future of China, less research has put the rise of China in historical and theoretical perspective. This book seeks to remedy this shortcoming.

Despite persistent warnings about China's growing capabilities and uncertain intentions, U.S. leaders of all political persuasions have pursued a largely cooperative, rather than a competitive, strategy toward China since the end of the Cold War.[1] Indeed, it is fair to say that if the United States does one day confront a powerful China, then Washington and the U.S. consumer will have played a sizable role in fueling the growth of that threat. If China is indeed a long-term threat to U.S. interests, then this cooperation would seem unwise and poses a puzzle. It would presumably be easier to constrain China while its capabilities are still nascent than decades from now when it will have even more capability to resist the coercive tools available to the United States. And it certainly would make little sense for the United States to be contributing to China's growth into a peer competitor.

Yet Sino-U.S. cooperation has also not been a constant. Warnings of a looming Chinese threat increased in the immediate aftermath of the Cold War, were replaced by more cooperation after the attacks of September 11, 2001, and have picked up again in response to provocative Chinese behavior in the waters surrounding East and Southeast Asia.[2] What explains this variation, and what might it tell us about both where Sino-U.S. relations have been and where they might be going in the future?

More broadly, cooperation between existing powers and potential long-term threats to those states is a recurrent pattern in the history of great power politics. Existing powers have aided, either passively or actively, the growth of the states that they eventually find themselves fighting. They do not "strangle the baby in the cradle" but instead help that baby grow up big, strong, and oftentimes threatening. Why would states do this, especially when they can anticipate the growth of another state and when they may later come to regret this cooperation?

The central argument of this book is that such behavior results neither from downplaying an emerging potential threat nor from misplacing optimism about transforming a possible threat into a reliable friend. Rather, it is a product of the recurrent dilemma that state leaders face in taking costly action now or deferring that action until later. The short-term rewards of cooperation combine with uncertainty about the future to make cooperation not only possible but likely. Such cooperation is not naïve, nor is it irrational. It is, instead, a by-product of the incentive that state leaders face to capture short-term rewards despite the long-term risks of doing so.

The Puzzle

Temporal considerations are central to international politics. In chapter 82 of book 1 of his *History of the Peloponnesian War*, Thucydides records an address by the Spartan king Archidamus: "No one can blame us for securing our own safety by taking foreigners as well as Greeks into our alliance when we are, as is the fact, having our position undermined by the Athenians. . . . If [the Athenians] pay attention to our diplomatic protests, so much the better. *If they do not, then after two or three years have passed, we shall be in a much sounder position and can attack them, if we decide to do so.*"[3] Like Archidamus, political leaders regularly weigh the options available now versus those that may be available a few years down the road. Such calculations are inherently complicated, as there is usually greater certainty about both the costs and the benefits of acting now as opposed to waiting until later. Procrastinating could prove to be beneficial, but it also could turn out to be extremely costly.

Centuries later, Niccolò Machiavelli, in chapter 3 of *The Prince*, writes with a similar attention to temporal dynamics: "The Romans did just what every wise ruler ought to do. . . . You have to keep an eye, not only on present troubles, but on those of the future, and make every effort to avoid them." "That is how it goes in affairs of state," Machiavelli continues. "When you recognize evils in advance, as they take shape . . . you quickly cure them; but when you have not seen them, and so let them grow till anyone can recognize them, there is no longer a remedy."[4]

In explaining his decision to sell the Louisiana Territories to the United States, Napoleon Bonaparte dismissed concerns about the long-term threat potentially posed by the United States. "Perhaps it will also be objected to me, that the Americans may be found too powerful for Europe in two or three centuries," Napoleon explained. "But my foresight does not embrace such remote fears."[5] Napoleon, like so many other political leaders, viewed the potential threats to his country in a temporal context.

More recently, in 1989 as the Cold War was ending, Chinese premier Deng Xiaoping suggested that China should "hold our ground" and "be cool-headed." China must not be "impatient" and instead should "hide our capacities and bide our time."[6] Even as Chinese material capabilities increased, it would not, in Deng's view, behoove China to draw attention to itself and its growth. More than twenty-five years later, China continues to weigh the wisdom of this approach.[7]

Even more recently, in his 2015 National Security Strategy, U.S. president Barack Obama argued that the challenges the United States faces require "strategic patience and persistence."[8] Whether it is religious extremism, climate change, or the continuing rise of China, in Obama's view, short-term solutions are either unavailable or prohibitively costly. Success will require a commitment to the achievement of long-term gains despite the temptation to focus on short-term opportunities.

In fact, temporal dynamics are everywhere in international politics.[9] State leaders constantly need to make decisions in which they evaluate the costs and benefits of acting in the short term versus deferring action until later.[10] Consider some examples: When a state launches a preventive war, it concludes that it is better to pay the costs of fighting a war now rather than waiting until later.[11] A state that values its reputation is willing to pay short-term costs to generate the long-term benefits that it believes come from having a desired reputation.[12] Similarly, hypocritical state behavior may reflect state myopia depending on the costs imposed for that hypocrisy.[13] Trading sensitive technology to a potential adversary may promise short-term economic reward, but at potentially significant long-term risk.[14] Whether the United States pursues military intervention unilaterally or multilaterally may depend on the relations that U.S. leaders anticipate having with other states in the future.[15] States may create independent central banks to limit the ability of myopic political leaders to act in ways that advantage those leaders in the short term but for which the state will literally pay the price later.[16] Decisions about foreign direct investment and foreign aid may depend critically on both the time horizons of the donor state and the perceived time horizons of the leaders of recipient states.[17] Leaders with short time horizons may be willing to make insincere commitments to human rights treaties when they know that they will not be around to pay the price for long-term noncompliance.[18] Finally, perhaps no issue captures the dynamics of intertemporal trade-offs better than climate change, where the decision to sign on to any treaty today reflects a state's willingness to pay short-term costs to produce long-term benefits for the environment.[19]

Temporal considerations, then, have played a critical role in how states consider the opportunities and challenges before them. Surprisingly, theory that explicitly addresses these trade-offs remains scant.[20] I focus, in particular, on how temporal dynamics affect the interaction between existing and rising great powers during power transitions: Do states address emerging potential threats now or later? And do rising powers assert their interests sooner rather than later? A power transition describes a situation in which one great power threatens to overtake the capabilities of another. The most extreme competitive response to a rising great power is a preventive war initiated by a declining power to keep a rising power from becoming stronger. Preventive wars involve a temporal trade-off: it is worth paying the cost now to prevent a transition from taking place in the future. Though the prevalence of preventive war has been much debated, conflicts from the Peloponnesian Wars through World War I and the Iraq War have all been interpreted as preventive wars.[21]

But states certainly do not always launch preventive wars. Rather than adopt competitive strategies that seek to foreclose the growth of an emerging threat, existing powers sometimes kick the can down the road, adopting strategies that, in fact, make their rise more likely. Evidence of this strategy appears in cases as varied as European reactions to the rise of Germany in the late nineteenth century to U.S.-Soviet relations at the onset of the Cold War to contemporary Sino-U.S. relations.[22] In most cases, states hedge their bets, combining elements of competitive and cooperative strategies, or evolve from one approach to another. For example, in the case of imperial Germany, much of Europe was initially willing to cooperate with Chancellor Otto von Bismarck's Germany before eventually turning to more competitive strategies.

The existing international relations literature offers explanations for preventive war as well as alternatives like engagement, but what it does not provide is an argument accounting for variation in these strategies: Why do existing powers sometimes cooperate with emerging threats, and why do they sometimes compete? And, in some cases, what explains the transition from one strategy to another? Robert Gilpin's account in *War and Change in World Politics* of the challenges facing declining powers in international relations is perhaps best known.[23] But while Gilpin provides the menu of options available to such states, he gives less sense of how states choose from that menu, other than to suggest that wars are commonly a result: "The first and most attractive response to a society's decline is to eliminate the source of the problem."[24] But the evidence suggests that this is not always the option chosen by great powers, nor does it explain when states choose to act more or less assertively.

The Argument

I argue that the time horizons of political leaders are critical to understanding why leaders prefer certain strategies over others. A leader's time horizon refers to the value that leader places on present as opposed to future payoffs, or, as it is often called, the rate of intertemporal discounting. Time horizons can also be conceived of as the temporal context within which states make decisions. Do leaders consciously consider the future implications of present behavior, or are they myopically focused on the short term? Time horizons might conceivably belong to leaders, but they may also be attributes of a state in a particular context, regardless of who the leader is at any given moment.

Specifying "long" and "short" time horizons as a certain length of time would be arbitrary. Some studies in political science have equated a leader's time horizons with the expected duration of time in office, but it is not clear that all leaders frame their time horizons this way rather than relative to some other development in the world.[25] Instead, throughout this book, I consider short and long term as proxies for different states of the world. Leaders with short time horizons are focused on the immediate future in a general state of affairs that they do not expect to change dramatically. Leaders with long time horizons are more focused on a world that emerges after some predictable, but not necessarily certain, transformation of the underlying structure within which they operate. For some democratic leaders, looking beyond their time in office could constitute long time horizons. For others, it may have to do with an anticipated change in the international system.

For example, in the context of a rising great power, a leader with short time horizons would be focused on the period of time before the rising power has achieved parity with existing great powers in the international system. Such leaders discount the future heavily, paying less attention to the consequences of another state's long-term rise. Alternatively, a leader with longer time horizons would be more attentive to a possible future in which a rising power is as capable as or even more capable than other existing great powers.

Leaders with short time horizons are less concerned with the effects of their current behavior in the long term. Leaders with long time horizons are more conscious of the ways in which current behavior affects long-term developments. Fundamentally, I am concerned with which of these two states of the world leaders focus on and with what consequences.

The trade-off between short and long time horizons represents what I call a "now or later" dilemma. Political leaders face a recurrent dilemma between acting now to address some issue or choosing to defer action until later. On one horn of this dilemma, leaders might choose to act now to address some threat, but that means paying a certain cost in the short term to address that long-term threat. On the other horn of the dilemma, leaders might opt to put off dealing with the threat. This might conserve resources in the short term, but they may then have to pay more in the long term to deal with the threat should it emerge.

The time horizons of great powers in the face of emerging potential threats are determined by three considerations: other realized threats that they face in the short term, the opportunities for short-term gains through cooperation with the emerging threat, and their level of concern about the long-term intentions of an emerging potential threat. How leaders of these states resolve their now-or-later dilemmas is influenced directly by these three considerations.

Rising powers face their own now-or-later dilemma involving how assertively to seek their interests in the international system. Acting provocatively too soon could generate balancing efforts by other states, whereas waiting too long could mean forgoing opportunities for substantial benefit. The time horizons of emerging threats are a product of the balance between the incentives to be patient and the pressures to be assertive sooner rather than later.

Cooperation or competition emerges out of the interaction of existing and rising powers' time horizons. Cooperation is likely to emerge when (a) existing powers are focused on the short term, preferring to defer addressing any long-term threats, and (b) rising powers prefer to maintain cooperation that fuels their rise rather than acting in ways that raise concerns about their long-term intentions. When the leaders of existing powers are more focused on the long-term threat posed by another actor, then the prospects for cooperation in the short term diminish. Rather than facilitate cooperation, the so-called shadow of the future can be foreboding when it comes to great power politics.

Critical to how existing powers respond to rising great powers are the beliefs they hold about the rising power's intentions. The long-term intentions of a rising great power are characterized by true and unmeasurable uncertainty. In fact, the further into the future that one projects, the more uncertainty is likely to be present. That is, the evolution of those intentions is likely to be affected by so many different variables that estimating those intentions in a probabilistic manner is difficult if not impossible. This true uncertainty only reinforces the incentives that state leaders have to focus on the short term, as uncertainty makes it impossible for states to accurately assess long-term threats and opportunities. Rather than make a costly gamble on long-term uncertainty, states are inclined to procrastinate until uncertainty is transformed into measurable risk as indicators of a state's intentions reveal themselves. The costs of assuming the worst about long-term intentions are prohibitively high for most states.

To be clear, states may later come to regret this cooperation with a rising great power, but that is precisely what makes explaining such cooperation so important. In retrospect, existing great powers may be misguided in cooperating with a rising great power, but that does not negate the notable pattern of such cooperation repeatedly occurring, nor does it mean that such cooperation is "irrational." This book seeks to explain precisely why such cooperation persists even when states may later come to regret it.

The Contribution

Explaining this puzzle contributes to at least three major debates in international relations. First, I offer an account of threat perception with a novel consideration of temporal dynamics. Whereas conventional accounts focus on shifting relative power or perceptions of a state's intentions, I emphasize that time is an integral part of how threats are perceived and also share the belief that perceptions of intentions are critical to the process of threat perception. The rise of China and the United States' reactions to it cannot be understood fully without attention to how U.S. leaders have weighed present opportunities against the potential long-term risks of cooperation.

Second, I offer an alternative understanding of the role that uncertainty plays in international politics. Uncertainty is not necessarily a source of conflict, nor do states automatically assume the worst about uncertain intentions. Instead, uncertainty about future intentions can create the space for short-term cooperation. It is time—the unavoidable delay between the present and the future—and uncertainty about the future that allow for outcomes that other theories of international politics would not expect. I borrow from the work of two of the twentieth century's most important economists—John Maynard Keynes and Frank H. Knight—to introduce a different and more compelling understanding of uncertainty that distinguishes what is truly unknowable about future threats from measurable risk.

Third, though the book seeks to explain any case in which an actor is faced with an emerging threat, it offers, in particular, a richer understanding of both past and present great power transitions. Power transitions are, in fact, more interesting and complex than the commonly depicted linear model of state levels in which relative capabilities pass each other on a graph. The politics of power transition determine whether such transitions end in conflict or cooperation. Only through the account offered in this book do we come to understand the recurrent historical pattern in which declining states facing a rising power with uncertain intentions have nonetheless aided and abetted that power's rise.

Implications for the Rise of China

In the final chapter, I develop the implications of the argument for the contemporary rise of China. I do not come at this issue from the perspective of an expert on China, and this book is not intended to join the stack of insightful books that have focused on China's rise. Instead, I aim to enhance our understanding of that rise by bringing a new theoretical lens and comparative historical evidence to bear.[26] By doing so, the book will explain the past and present pattern of cooperation between China and its interlocutors as well as anticipate the dynamics that are likely to determine how those relationships evolve in the future. I will explain why the United States has abetted the rise of a possible competitor. I will also explain the conditions under which we ought to expect the nature of that relationship to change. Finally, I will offer suggestions on how the Sino-U.S. relationship might be managed in the coming years to minimize the possibility of conflict.

In terms of the past, the argument helps us understand the willingness of the United States to aid the rise of China. Despite consistent warnings about the potential power of a growing China, the United States has continued to engage in vast amounts of economic exchange profitable to China. In 2014 alone, the U.S. trade deficit with China was nearly $350 billion.[27] In turn, those profits have been invested in military capabilities that could one day threaten U.S. interests. The origin of this cooperation does not lie in U.S. Pollyannaish hopes for transforming Chinese intentions in a benign direction, though there has certainly been hope of China becoming a "responsible stakeholder."[28] Instead, this cooperation has been primarily the product of Washington's now-or-later dilemma in the face of uncertain future Chinese intentions and the appreciable economic benefits of present cooperation. The United States has valued short-term economic benefits more than it has been scared off by the long-term risks posed by a rising China. At the same time, China has mostly refrained from behavior that would raise concerns about its intentions and provoke a response in the short term. How we have gotten to the current state of Sino-U.S. relations cannot be understood without an appreciation of these dynamics.

That said, one of the puzzles about Chinese behavior is the increase in provocative Chinese actions. Most notably, the effort to create and claim territory in the South China Sea has aggravated relations with the Philippines and Vietnam, while island disputes with Japan have rekindled tension in that relationship. Meanwhile, partly out of concern for its allies in the region, the United States appears to have become increasingly concerned with the threat posed by China and has moved to "rebalance" its grand strategy toward Asia.[29]

But why would China assert itself now despite the likelihood that this would push the United States away from cooperation and toward competition? In the next chapter, I explore this issue theoretically. In this specific case, China has been moving away from the heavily export-led economy that fueled its initial growth, and the result has been less short-term value in cooperative relations with the United States.[30] Moreover, Chinese leaders have sought international successes to placate domestic audiences. Thomas J. Christensen writes, "Chinese leaders worry increasingly about domestic stability and regime legitimacy as the distribution of income grows more stilted, more people lose their land in eminent domain cases, urban housing becomes unaffordable, and widespread corruption remains largely unchecked."[31] Finally, some have labeled Chinese behavior as "reactive assertiveness," in that it has often been prompted by the actions of China's smaller neighbors with contending claims.[32] In short, China's leadership has placed more value on short-term opportunities for gain despite the possible adverse consequences for relations with the United States.

As for the future, current Sino-U.S. tension does not ineluctably need to lead to conflict. U.S. reactions to China in the coming years will be based not only on concern about the continuing growth in its military capabilities but also on indications of its long-term intentions as well as the costs and benefits of present cooperation and competition. If Beijing can quiet its own nationalist elements, then it may be able to continue to grow with the assistance of the United States or at least unimpeded. The United States may one day regret having provided that assistance, but short-term incentives for cooperation can be powerful. To be clear, growth in Chinese capabilities will surely be consequential, and the stronger China becomes, the less room it will leave U.S. leaders to cooperate in the face of uncertain intentions. If uncertainty about Chinese intentions resolves in the direction of relative certainty about malign intentions, then the likelihood of a Sino-U.S. cold or even hot war will increase. Transitions in relative material capabilities do not, however, speak for themselves in the absence of information about how those capabilities are likely to be used in the future.

This book brings to the fore an understanding of the role that time and uncertainty about the future play in international politics. Cooperation in the face of future uncertainty is more common than many expect. Neither uncertainty nor reactions to uncertainty are constant and unchanging, but rather they depend on the manipulation of indicators of intentions and the value that political leaders put on present benefits as opposed to the costs of acting to prevent the emergence of a future threat.

In the next chapter, I develop the logic of my argument and present the book's research design. In the subsequent four chapters, I explore the role that these dynamics have played in consequential cases over the past two centuries. In the concluding chapter, I return to the case of contemporary China.

Time Horizons and International Politics

In this chapter, I develop a theory explaining variation in the relationships between great powers and the emerging potential threats they face. I argue that the time horizons of political leaders—the extent to which those leaders focus on and value the long or short term—influence the strategies they adopt. The balance of long- and short-term opportunities and threats determines the time horizons of states, which in turn affects the grand strategies that they pursue. Cooperation or competition between existing powers and emerging potential threats is a product of the interaction of the two states' time horizons.

Four scope conditions are noteworthy. First, I focus here on threats that are long-term and potential rather than on the acute, short-term threats posed during crises.[1] When states face acute threats, their inclination to respond immediately does not pose much of a puzzle. Second, in laying out the logic of my argument, I focus on potential power transitions in which a rising power threatens to overtake an existing power. The potential threat is identified by increasing material capabilities that could constitute it at as a threat. The logic of the argument is not limited to power transitions, but they are important instances of the dynamic I explain in this chapter. Third, I develop my theory to explain the relationship between one existing great power and one rising great power, but international politics is obviously rarely so simple. While the addition of more actors does not undermine the logic of the argument, in the empirical cases that follow, I explore how the interaction of more than two great powers complicates the strategic calculations that states must make. Fourth, my primary unit of analysis is states themselves rather than individual leaders. Leaders inevitably make decisions and must have their own personal time horizons, but my argument suggests that the temporal pressures affecting grand strategies exert themselves primarily on states regardless of who their particular leaders are at any given time.

Time in International Politics

Attention to temporal dynamics in international politics is not entirely new, though explicit theorizing of the role of time has been uncommon.[2] Rather than view international politics in fixed temporal snapshots, I emphasize the temporal processes that shape and define relations between states. How leaders think about the future and weigh uncertain futures versus the relatively certain present ought to be a significant element in our theories of international relations.[3]

To be fair, the scholarly literature has not completely ignored temporal factors, though their inclusion has often been implicit rather than explicit.[4] Dale C. Copeland assumes that states have long time horizons when he argues that whether or not economic interdependence leads to peace or war depends on leaders' expectations of future trade.[5] In their study of the interwar period, Norrin M. Ripsman and Jack S. Levy argue that British leaders were "buying time" before confronting Germany, again implying lengthier time horizons.[6] Anne E. Sartori argues that states may acquiesce in disputes now to build a valuable reputation for the future.[7] As with all arguments about reputation, Sartori implies that states attach value to their reputations such that they are willing to pay some cost in the short term to generate a long-term benefit.[8] Relatedly, how concerned states are with impressions of their resolve depends fundamentally on how much they weigh the present versus the future.[9] What these arguments fail to explore is the potential variation in time horizons and its consequences.

Some theoretical arguments have been more explicit in their temporal claims. Neoliberal institutionalist theory contends that cooperation among states becomes more likely as the "shadow of the future" grows longer, and international institutions complete with mechanisms for reciprocity are a particularly effective tool for lengthening that shadow.[10] High degrees of institutionalization lead to lengthy time horizons, and institutions can help solve the problem of time inconsistency (i.e., an actor may say now that it is going to do one thing in the future but change its mind as that date approaches).[11] Thus, the creation of institutions itself reflects long time horizons and also induces them by increasing the certain future rewards for cooperation.

But the logic of these shadow-of-the-future claims has been questioned. Robert Powell notes that the logic depends on the sequencing of benefits and costs. In neoliberal institutionalism, cooperation is possible because highly valued benefits are available in the short term, with threatened costs existing only in the long term (i.e., the costs of forgone future cooperation). One can imagine situations in which the converse is true. When great benefits are expected in the future and that future is highly valued, then leaders may be more inclined to cheat in the short term if it helps them achieve those long-term goals. As an example, Powell notes that both Japan and Germany cheated in building up arms in the 1930s, but they were willing to do so because the expected long-term benefits exceeded any costs of cheating.[12]

James D. Fearon offers another critique, suggesting that a longer shadow of the future will make the initial negotiation of any international agreement that much more difficult. If states expect that an agreement will have far-reaching and long-standing consequences, then they are likely to hold out for a more favorable deal.[13] Knowledge that an institution may persist for a lengthy period may actually inhibit the consummation of an agreement. If all of this is true, then the shadow of the future may actually make cooperation more difficult to generate.[14]

More broadly, attention to time is also not new to social science.[15] Social scientists have written extensively on the temporal calculations of political leaders, though less so in theoretical accounts of international politics.[16] Conventionally understood, time horizons reflect an actor's inclination to make intertemporal trade-offs.[17] That is, how willing is a person or government to pay some short-term cost for the possibility of an even greater long-term benefit? Myopic individuals would rather capture a short-term reward even if the possibility exists that such a choice will prove detrimental over the long term. More farsighted individuals forgo the temptation of a certain short-term reward for the possibility of the long-term payoff.[18] Yet still, in his seminal book on the role of time in politics, Paul Pierson writes that "we know relatively little about the time horizons of different political actors" even though differences in time horizons have, in his words, "profound consequences."[19]

This book, therefore, is an effort to better and more explicitly explicate the role of time horizons in international relations. An understanding of the role of time horizons begs the question of what explains variation in the time horizons of political actors. Existing efforts at analyzing variation at the individual and state level to understand how states assess present versus future options have thus far failed to account for the observed level of variation.

At the individual level, psychologists and behavioral economists have found that people almost always value the short term over the long term.[20] Individuals are myopic, and the question is just how shortsighted they are.[21] Initial economic models suggested that people discount exponentially, but subsequent work has argued that individuals discount hyperbolically, placing even more value on the short term as opposed to the long term.[22] One explanation for this myopia focuses on the cognitive ability of people to manage the overwhelming amount of information that they receive.[23] Faced with more information than they can effectively process, people are psychologically attracted to what they can address in the short term rather than to uncertain long-term developments.[24]

While the research in this literature has almost always found that state leaders have short time horizons, there are some exceptions. For example, experienced leaders may have longer time horizons, as their seasoning encourages the patience to wait for long-term rewards.[25] Alternatively, though, older leaders may have shorter time horizons as they become concerned about their legacies.[26] Other experimental work has examined how long-term concerns influence individuals' short-term behavior but has little to say about the conditions under which leaders have such longer time horizons.[27] Ultimately, the difficulty with individual-level explanations of time horizons is that they struggle to explain variation in the observed time horizons of individuals, including political leaders.

Explanations that focus on regime type face similar difficulties in accounting for variation. The most prominent domestic political explanation for time horizons focuses on electoral pressures within democracies.[28] Such pressures induce short time horizons in political leaders who must be concerned with the next election.[29] As George F. Kennan lamented of the U.S. political system, "A good deal of our trouble seems to have stemmed from the extent to which the executive has felt itself beholden to short-term trends of public opinion in the country and from what we might call the erratic and subjective nature of public reaction to foreign-policy questions."[30] Elsewhere, Randall L. Schweller attributes "underbalancing" to domestic political dynamics that compel shortsighted behavior and impair the ability of states to respond to long-term potential threats.[31]

The absence of elections in nondemocratic regimes would presumably allow for longer time horizons, but there may be good reason to doubt this claim.[32] The paranoia that is typical of tyrannical and authoritarian regimes may induce an unwillingness to make intertemporal trade-offs.[33] Moreover, studies point out that it is not just democracies that face audience costs.[34] Just like their democratic counterparts, authoritarian leaders have to be concerned with the security of their office. In fact, given the absence of regular, peaceful elections in authoritarian regimes, such leaders may have even more reason to be concerned with keeping their supporters happy in the short term, as the penalty for angering a domestic audience may be more severe in a nondemocratic state.[35]

Meanwhile, others have argued that domestic politics may allow for longer time horizons in certain contexts, but such arguments either lack convincing evidence or apply to relatively unusual situations. For example, Alexis de Tocqueville argued that democracies imbue their citizens with concerns for the welfare of future citizens, though the evidence for this claim is unclear.[36] Alternatively, short-term pressures might be felt less by lame ducks in democratic systems, though even lame ducks may worry about the fate of their party after they leave office.

Beyond regime type, time horizons may also be a product of the ideological commitments of a state. If a state is deeply committed to a certain ideology, then it may place less value on the short term as it sees itself engaged in more of a long game.[37] The problem with this argument is that most modern nation-states are committed to some ideology, whether liberalism, communism, or a particularistic nationalism. Like individual-level or regime-type explanations, arguments that find time horizons rooted in ideology have difficulty accounting for variation with what appears to be a constant.

In short, the problem with individual- and domestic-level accounts of time horizons is that neither can explain variation in the choices that states make between now and later. In this book, I add a strategic dimension to our understanding of time horizons, pointing to how leaders weigh the temporally immediate and distant threats that their states face, the uncertainty about those threats, and the benefits of short-term cooperation.

The Argument

My argument focuses on how uncertainty about the future reinforces the pressures on state leaders to focus on the short term. Leaders of existing great powers are disinclined to expend considerable resources on an uncertain long-term threat. When existing powers focus on the short term, mutually beneficial cooperation with rising powers becomes more likely. Conversely, the more state leaders become alerted to the potentially threatening long-term intentions of a rising power, the less likely cooperation in the short term with a rising great power becomes. In this way, the argument shares Fearon's skepticism about the cooperation-inducing effects of the shadow of the future, but it also develops the argument in novel directions. Whereas Fearon's concern is about the long-term lock-in effects of an agreement negotiated today, my contention is that true uncertainty about the future makes short-term, pragmatic cooperation more likely and sizable future risk makes cooperation less likely. Whereas Fearon does not consider how state time horizons vary, I investigate precisely how concerned state leaders are with the long-term future and with what consequences.

THE DEPENDENT VARIABLE: GRAND STRATEGIES
OF COOPERATION AND COMPETITION

The dependent variable in this study is the grand strategies that states pursue toward each other. These strategies vary along two dimensions. First, they are arrayed along a spectrum from most cooperative to most competitive, with a variety of less cooperative or competitive strategies in the middle. Existing power strategies that offer substantial gains—either relative or absolute—to a rising power can be considered cooperative, while those meant to impede the growth of a rising power are competitive. Cooperative existing power strategies include policies that facilitate economic exchange, allow for arms transfers, or involve political commitments on the rising power's behalf. Competitive policies include, but are not limited to, explicit internal or external balancing. Denying a rising power access to markets might also constitute competition. In addition, and apart from this spectrum of strategies, states could pursue strategies of indifference toward each other. That is, a state might neither cooperate nor compete with another state.

Second, strategies of cooperation and competition vary from more active to more passive. Committing to defend another state through an alliance is active cooperation, while allying against that state is active competition. Existing powers may not seek actively to promote the continuing growth of a potential long-term threat, but they may nonetheless do so passively through regular economic exchange. Similarly, the pursuit of general international diplomatic agreements that limit a rising power's freedom of movement qualifies as more passive competition.

To compare more concrete examples, the economic instruments employed by Europe in an attempt to manage Germany immediately after World War I are distinct from the diplomatic approach adopted by Britain toward the United States at the turn of the twentieth century, and both examples are distinct from the Franco-Russian military alliance consummated in 1893. As I discuss throughout the empirical chapters that follow, all were in ways competitive, though none exclusively so, and they varied in the intensity of competition and the tools they employed.

In reality, few great powers pursue exclusively cooperative or competitive strategies toward other great powers. Adversaries trade with one another, and even friends develop military capabilities that can be redirected from one state to another if necessary.[38] States hedge their bets, protecting themselves in case another state turns out to be either friendlier or more adversarial than they expected. The critical question is the balance between these different types of strategies. Under what conditions do states pursue predominately cooperative or competitive strategies, and what might lead states to change the balance between these different strategic approaches?

Consider the U.S. trade deficit with China, which has enriched China and allowed it to develop military capabilities that could threaten U.S. interests. Nobody would argue that the United States' goal has been to transform China into a peer competitor, but the predominately cooperative strategies it has pursued may nonetheless have such an effect. As Robert D. Blackwill and Ashley J. Tellis write, "Integration, the prevailing U.S. approach toward China and the one followed assiduously since the 1970s, has undoubtedly contributed to China's rise as a future rival to American power."[39] At the same time, there is no denying that the United States is also preparing for the prospect of conflict with China in the future. The United States' strategy is neither exclusively cooperative nor exclusively competitive, so strategies are best assessed by gauging how these different elements are balanced.

EXPLAINING COOPERATION AND COMPETITION

Cooperation or competition is the product of the interaction of the temporal frames of a rising power and a declining power. Rising powers tend to be focused on realizing their long-term potential and therefore avoid provocations in the short term. Existing powers tend to be more focused on the short term as they fear their own acute decline and therefore are both more interested in beneficial short-term cooperation and less willing to pay the high immediate costs of competition.

My argument has two critical implications that diverge from much existing literature. First, contrary to popular shadow-of-the-future arguments, I contend that longer time horizons can lead to competition, not cooperation, in the context of rising great powers. Second, uncertainty about intentions does not necessarily lead to competition. Instead, that uncertainty can create the opportunity for pragmatic cooperation until that uncertainty is resolved.

Existing Powers: Respond Now or Later? Addressing a long-term potential threat poses what I call a now-or-later dilemma for an existing power. The state must decide whether to address such a threat now, when there is still uncertainty about how that threat will look in the long-term future, or later, when it is possible that the threat will have either failed to come to fruition or become much more dangerous than imagined. When the leaders of an existing power opt for the later horn of the dilemma—that is, choosing essentially to procrastinate—then cooperation between an existing power and the potential future threat is more likely.

Choosing the now horn of the dilemma means committing to addressing a long-term threat now rather than later. The existing power will adopt more competitive strategies with the goal of, at a minimum, stalling the rise of the emerging power. At a maximum, the now horn of the dilemma might lead to preventive war intended to eliminate the potential for a long-term threat altogether. Addressing a threat now, rather than later, is costly, both to the emerging state and to an existing power that must forgo beneficial trade or conceivably pay the price of war. Still, those costs of addressing a threat now may be considerably less than the costs of addressing a threat later when it has become more powerful and is less vulnerable to economic, political, and military tools of coercion.

By adopting the later horn of the dilemma, state leaders allow for the possibility of continuing short-term cooperation. Economic exchange may be beneficial to the emerging potential threat as well as to existing great powers and their leaders responsible for maintaining a productive economy. Economic interest groups within a state may push particularly hard to capture economic gains from cooperation. In the short term, friendship with a rising power may also be useful in addressing other more pressing threats. A government that chooses to defer addressing a long-term potential threat accepts the possibility that dealing with it as a full-fledged threat later will likely be costlier than dealing with it in the short term, but such a trade-off may be acceptable to myopic political leaders, especially when there is uncertainty about whether the threat will come to fruition.

Neither choice is attractive, making it a true dilemma. Dealing with the threat now is costly in the short term and also more likely to guarantee that a potential adversary becomes a real adversary over time.[40] If successful, though, confronting a future threat in the short term can eliminate that threat at lesser cost than addressing it later. Coping with the threat later avoids those short-term costs, but at the risk that the threat that ultimately emerges may be difficult to manage.

What determines whether states choose to focus on short-term opportunities or act to prevent the emergence of long-term threats? I contend that states assess what they know about the short and long term in relation to the threats and opportunities that are before them. In general, the more certain states are about a long-term threat, the more likely they are to focus on doing something about that threat in the near term. Offsetting such pressures, however, are (a) the value of short-term cooperation with the potential threat and (b) the presence of more immediate threats that must take priority over a long-term potential threat.

For existing powers, the short-term benefits of cooperation often provide a significant incentive to put off dealing with a potential long-term threat. The more economically lucrative such cooperation is, the more attractive it makes short-term cooperation.[41] Under these circumstances, leaders generally will prefer the short-term benefits of cooperation to the costs of competition, even if such cooperation may have detrimental long-term consequences. Take the extreme example where two states have no diplomatic, political, or economic relations. In such a case, there is little to be lost by acting now as opposed to later (other than the conceivably significant costs of taking any action itself).

Whether a state focuses on the long term also depends on whether it faces other more immediate threats that demand its attention. More temporally distant threats are less likely to be addressed than more immediate threats. More immediate threats are also likely to be addressed in concrete and specific ways, while longer-term threats might be considered more abstractly.[42] Great powers cannot afford to expend scarce national resources addressing a possible long-term threat when a real threat is before them and seems more immediately dangerous.

One can also imagine situations in which an existing power views an emerging power as an ally in managing a more immediate threat. The United States and China found common cause in confronting perceived Islamic extremism in the wake of the attacks on the United States on September 11, 2001, despite long-term concerns about the continuing rise of China.[43] Conversely, when no immediate threat is present, it is more likely that a state will begin to prepare its national security resources for dealing with a long-term threat on the horizon. States that face less acute threats to their security can be more forward-looking, while states with immediate security threats will generally be more myopic. States that enjoy more geopolitical "slack" can better afford the luxury of thinking about the long term.[44]

If this argument is correct, then structural factors may affect whether states are more inclined to focus on the short or long term. In multipolar systems where potential short-term threats are generally more abundant, states are compelled to focus on the short term. Though the argument in this chapter is modeled around two states interacting, multipolarity inevitably introduces the dynamics of multiple great powers simultaneously weighing short- and long-term threats and opportunities against each other, and the tendency in such a situation will be to discount the future relative to the complex present. In a bipolar system, the two poles see each other as short-term threats, but they may also be more comfortable anticipating that today's threat will also be tomorrow's threat. By addressing each other, they confront both short-term and long-term threats. Whether a unipolar power is more focused on the long or short term depends on whether a rising peer competitor has begun to realize its potential. The more apparent such a competitor is, the more likely the unipolar state is to focus on the threat it poses over the long term.

The case study presented in chapter 3 of British reactions to the emergence of the United States at the turn of the twentieth century draws particular attention to this aspect of the argument. The United States' aggressive behavior raised some concern in London about U.S. intentions, but Britain did not have the assets to protect its interests around the globe. Given a seemingly more dangerous and imminent threat from Germany, London opted to cede control over the western hemisphere to the United States in order to turn its attention to interests endangered by the simultaneous rise of Germany.

Short-term threats and opportunities put long-term concerns out of sight and out of mind. In the absence of compelling short-term threats and opportunities, states are more likely to look to the long term. And the more threatening a rising power appears over the long term, the more likely an existing power is to act in the short term to address it. The less certain a threat from a rising power appears, the more likely an existing power is to prefer cooperative short-term strategies. Finally, leaders are also cognizant of potential long-term benefits of cooperation. State leaders assess the benefits they might expect to gain from future trade knowing that they cannot be certain that those gains will materialize.[45]

Assessing a long-term potential threat involves two important but distinct challenges: risk and uncertainty. The economist Frank H. Knight famously drew a distinction between these two concepts nearly a century ago. "Uncertainty must be taken in a sense radically distinct from the familiar notion of risk, from which it has never been properly separated," Knight wrote. "The essential fact is that 'risk' means in some cases a quantity susceptible of measurement. It will appear that a measurable uncertainty, or 'risk' proper, as we shall use the term, is so far different from an unmeasurable one that it is not in effect an uncertainty at all."[46] Risk can be assessed using probabilistic estimates that some event will occur. Examining the evidence before them, actors can evaluate a probability and act accordingly.[47] Uncertainty captures the notion that some things may be truly unknowable and therefore probability estimates are impossible to generate.[48]

Imagine a situation in which the outcome of some game ranges from zero to one hundred. If an actor could estimate the probability of different outcomes occurring along that spectrum, then one could talk of risk. If, however, the actor is unable to assess whether an outcome of eighty is more or less likely than any other outcome, then the game would include true uncertainty.[49] In international relations literature, the distinction between risk and uncertainty has been employed to make sense of reactions to the global financial crisis in 2008. Stephen C. Nelson and Peter J. Katzenstein argue that the crisis involved true uncertainty, not just risk, and that actors at the time employed social conventions to generate responses to that uncertainty.[50]

Now consider how true uncertainty might affect a discounting model of international politics. In the logic of discounting, future payoffs are discounted by some factor between zero and one. Discounting captures the notion that future payoffs are not as valuable as current payoffs due largely to the costs of having to wait for a future payoff. In the financial realm, for example, interest rate expectations may lead actors to discount future payoffs. Using a discount factor allows one to assess whether an actor would prefer a current or a future payoff at any given moment. The more an actor discounts the future, the more attractive a current payoff is. Risk can easily be incorporated into such a model. Future payoffs become the product of various probabilities of different outcomes, including a probability that captures any risk. Uncertainty, however, renders such a model indeterminate, as one cannot generate expected payoffs for the future if probabilities cannot be assigned to different outcomes. Whereas uncertainty renders strategic considerations indeterminate, risk makes them manageable.

Transfer this abstract logic to the issue of rising great powers. The more uncertainty there is about the threat posed by a rising great power, the more difficult it is for an existing power to calculate the trade-off between acting now and acting later to address a potential long-term threat. As states become clearer about the threat posed over the long term—as uncertainty becomes risk—it is easier for a state to calculate whether it ought to direct its efforts against a short-term immediate threat or toward a longer-term emerging threat.[51]

Thus the assessment of rising great powers is characterized by both risk and uncertainty. The further one looks into the future to assess a long-term threat, the more uncertainty is likely to be present. The future is fuzzy, and predicting or even assigning probabilities to different outcomes is difficult. Any number of complex factors influence whether a long-term threat comes to fruition, including domestic political change, economic transformations, and international developments. Under conditions of long-term uncertainty, states are reluctant to act in ways that may make some unfavorable outcomes more likely than others. Unable to determine how severe a threat they actually face, great powers are inclined to wait for that uncertainty to resolve itself, addressing short-term concerns and capturing immediate opportunities while procrastinating on long-term potential threats. Long-term uncertainty reinforces any other instincts that state leaders may have to focus on the short term.

Key to my argument is that uncertainty can become risk. States go from a condition of being unable to assess how best to respond to an unknowable future to being able to assign probabilities to whether a state is a threat or not. In particular, it is knowledge about a state's intentions that allows the transformation from uncertainty to risk. The potential of a state to generate threatening capabilities is often, in the realm of risk, easier to estimate given knowledge of a state's underlying resource capacity. Intentions, however, can be much more difficult to estimate, and long-term intentions in particular are likely to be the source of true uncertainty.

The distinction between risk and uncertainty and the process by which uncertainty becomes risk ties my argument together in three ways. First, it explains why states may be puzzled about how to respond to a long-term potential threat. If that threat could simply be estimated, then how a state responds to either a short- or long-term threat may be less of a puzzle. Second, it makes clear why beliefs about intentions, rather than assessments of capabilities, are so critical to the assessment of long-term threats. Whereas estimates of capabilities are more likely to be characterized by risk, assessments of intentions involve more uncertainty. Third, the transformation from uncertainty to risk accounts for why even incremental information about intentions is so critical. Any information about intentions helps states begin to transform uncertainty into risk.

By intentions, I mean simply how a state plans on using the material capabilities available to it. Intentions do not exist independent of capabilities but rather reflect how a state plans to use the capabilities available to it. Such intentions range from aggressive, offensive behavior to plans only to act defensively.

If an existing power is certain that a rising power has malign long-term intentions, then it becomes more inclined to act in the short term to address that long-term threat.[52] Conversely, cooperation becomes more likely as certainty of benign intentions grows. In cases where intentions remain uncertain, I maintain that the likely state response is not to assume the worst about those intentions but rather to kick the can down the road, capture the short-term benefits of cooperation, and look for opportunities to update any beliefs the state may have about the rising power's intentions. As Robert Jervis argues, "National leaders . . . generally hesitate to take strong actions in the face of such uncertainty. While one common motive for war has been the belief that the situation will deteriorate unless the state acts strongly, and indeed this kind of fear drives the security dilemma, leaders usually put off decisions if they can." Jervis continues that leaders are "predisposed to postpone, to await further developments and information, to kick the can down the road."[53] If a rising power's long-term intentions are uncertain, existing powers will more likely defer addressing until later any potential threat posed by that state.[54]

This argument is contrary to conventional international relations arguments that suggest that uncertainty ineluctably leads to competition in international politics.[55] I contend that the leaders of existing great powers may welcome the short-term benefits from cooperation if the alternative is paying the likely exorbitant costs of "assuming the worst" about an emerging power's long-term intentions. Moreover, immediately adopting competitive strategies in the face of uncertainty only makes it more likely that the potential threat will become a real threat.[56] Rather than expend valuable resources on an uncertain and potential future threat, states prefer to procrastinate until they are more certain of the severity of the threat they are facing. These incentives are only further compounded to the extent that competitive behavior, such as preventive wars and aggressive arms races, may be "irrevesible."[57] If competitive behavior is easy to ratchet up but difficult to reverse, then it only increases the reluctance of leaders to pursue expensive competition under conditions of long-term uncertainty. This is especially true when leaders expect that they may ascertain more and better information in the future that will allow them transform uncertainty into risk. Leaders would prefer to put off irreversible decisions until they have sufficient information to justify such behavior.[58]

Why do states try to discern intentions rather than choosing the seemingly safer course of assuming the worst about how a potential competitor's capabilities will be used? First, precisely because intentions can always change, leaders are particularly attentive to them over the long term. The malleability of intentions provides an opportunity to adopt strategies, including cooperative strategies, that might shift intentions in a more benign direction. Existing powers hedge their bets and remain prepared to shift strategies when necessary in the face of changing intentions. The alternative of "assuming the worst" promises to be exceedingly costly. It amounts to the equivalent of former U.S. vice president Richard Cheney's "1 percent doctrine" (i.e., if there is even a 1 percent chance that something dangerous to the United States is happening, then it must be met with an aggressive response), and consistently applying such a doctrine would be difficult, if not prohibitively expensive.[59]

Second, capabilities can be hard to project into the future and, in any case, are indeterminate of state behavior. While developments in capabilities are generally easier to anticipate given that they are rooted in material resources, a state's future military capabilities are still dependent on technology and also on the economic might to pay for those capabilities. Even more importantly, capabilities do not speak for themselves. They can be used in multiple ways, as offensive realists themselves have repeatedly argued in criticizing the literature on the offense-defense balance.[60] If states are to avoid the exorbitant costs of assuming that all capabilities will be used in aggressive, offensive ways, they must devote, assess, and then respond to intentions, not just to capabilities.[61] To be clear, states remain cautious about taking a risk on a rising power's intentions. The danger of divining incorrect intentions is greater with a more powerful state than with a less powerful one. Capabilities matter, but they are not all that matter.

To assess long-term intentions, states rely on a composite of all available indicators at their disposal.[62] States examine enduring characteristics, like regime type and ideology. They also consider behavior that might indicate more or less aggressive intentions. Such behavior includes provoking crises, but it also may include the acquisition of certain capabilities that signal intentions.[63] Such behavior need not be fully "costly" to affect state beliefs.[64] It provokes concern about the long term, which then leads to more immediate efforts to address the threat. Again, uncertainty is transformed into risk. The motive behind a state's behavior may be unclear, but states are likely to err on the side of concern about the long-term implications of aggressive behavior. As indicators of benign or malign intentions mount, the overall composite image shifts in one direction or the other.

As the evidence I present below suggests, states also frequently attempt to craft litmus tests of other states' intentions. By forcing a rising power into a decision, other states can gather potentially valuable information about its intentions. Testing intentions is difficult. States may or may not recognize that their long-term intentions are being tested in any particular situation, and, either way, this may make it difficult for states fairly to interpret behavior as a credible indication of long-term intentions. If a state realizes it is being tested, it may have incentives to misrepresent its long-term intentions. If a state does not realize it is being tested, then its behavior may be motivated by shorter-term concerns not meant to convey information about long-term intentions. Despite these limitations, the historical record reveals the repeated use of such litmus tests. Importantly, if states were simply assuming the worst about others' intentions, these tests would be unnecessary.[65]

Importantly, this notion of how states evaluate likely intentions departs from the "costly signaling" framework that has become predominant in the study of international politics. Costly signaling implies that states only update their beliefs about another state's intentions when they issue signals that only a non-bluffing state would take. Either states sink costs or they tie their hands in a way that backing down would be unacceptably costly.[66] In contrast, I argue that even evidence short of costly signals can add to the accumulated weight of the evidence in support of a probabilistic argument. As John Maynard Keynes argued, "As the relevant evidence at our disposal increases, the magnitude of the probability of the argument may either increase or decrease, according as the new knowledge strengthens the unfavourable or the favourable evidence, but *something* seems to have increased in either case—we have a more substantial basis upon which to rest our conclusion. I express this by saying that an accession of new evidence increases the *weight* of an argument."[67] Essentially, the weight expresses the confidence one has in the probability estimate that has been generated. Even non-costly signals can add to the weight of a belief about a state's long-term intentions. As such evidence accrues, the confidence in the probability increases. Put differently, beliefs about intentions are compound and complex. At root, a state has a belief about another state's intentions, but it also then has a varying degree of confidence in that belief.

In the fourth and final empirical chapter below, I examine relations between the United States and the Soviet Union at the outset of the Cold War. I emphasize how the critical shifts in relations between the two sides turned on assessments of Soviet intentions made evident by Soviet behavior, not measurements of Soviet capabilities. While bipolarity certainly created the context for tension between the two great powers, the primacy of intentions accounts for the timing of the origins of the Cold War.

Emerging Powers: Patience Is a Virtue Whether or not an existing power pursues more cooperative or competitive strategies depends, of course, on how the potential threat itself behaves. Emerging, rising powers face their own now-or-later dilemma. On the one hand, these states benefit from patience that allows them to grow stronger before they assertively pursue their interests. Rising powers often recognize that their brightest days lie ahead, so they seek to avoid anything that might prevent them from recognizing their potential. Regardless of whether or not they harbor ultimately aggressive ambitions (or whether they even know at the moment if they will eventually seek expansion), rising powers have an interest in cooperation that fuels their growth. Trade with richer powers can make them wealthier, and the absence of diplomatic or military efforts to inhibit their rise is beneficial. If others adopt competitive strategies, that may make it more difficult for them to continue to grow and reach their potential. In short, patience is a virtue for rising powers.

On the other hand, the leaders of rising powers may face pressures both domestically and internationally to be more assertive. The longer they wait to claim certain interests, the longer they must wait to enjoy both the material benefits and the prestige of holding those interests. By acting aggressively, however, rising powers are likely to elicit concern about their long-term intentions that may lead to costly and dangerous competitive strategies.

I contend that the leaders of rising powers are generally inclined to put off any aggressive behavior. Uncertainty about their future intentions is beneficial for rising great powers. The benefits of patience are significant, while the costs of premature aggression are potentially significant. In turn, states that choose to defer acting more aggressively until later have an incentive to try to influence the level of uncertainty others have about their long-term intentions. States that actually have benign intentions, states that are uncertain about their intentions, and states that have malign intentions all have this same incentive. It is exceedingly difficult for states to prove that they have benign intentions over the long term, so uncertainty may be the best they can do. Thus rising powers typically abstain from behavior that clearly signals intentions that are threatening, even if they cannot credibly signal that they have benign intentions. To be clear, this is not about rising powers simply being nice. To the contrary, the maintenance of uncertainty about intentions in the service of promoting cooperation is ruthless realism. If capabilities are viewed as inherently threatening, indicators of intentions can be used to alleviate a perceived potential threat and thereby allow beneficial cooperation to continue.

Rising powers often find a receptive audience for any reassuring indicators of benign intentions that they can offer. Leaders of existing powers who would prefer to focus on the short term or who must focus on other threats appreciate behavior that does not force their hand into addressing a long-term potential threat at significant short-term cost. The key logic here is that the more provocative rising powers are in the short term, the more questions that raises about their long-term intentions, turning uncertainty into quantifiable risk to which existing powers can and will respond. Uncertainty serves rising powers well.

But the decision to refrain from provocative behavior is not always easy for rising powers. The leaders of rising powers may choose the now horn of the dilemma for two reasons. First, it might be the case that an emerging power reaches the limits of its growth given the resources available to it. In such cases, political leaders may conclude that any loss in cooperation from others is more than offset by the benefits of acquiring additional territory or resources. Emerging threats may act opportunistically to capture territory or resources, especially if they sense that no other state is inclined to oppose them. As Adam J. Tooze brilliantly details in his economic history of Nazi Germany, by the mid-1930s Germany had reached the limits of what its indigenous resources could support, necessitating expansion into other territories. Tooze writes that "by 1936 at the latest it was abundantly clear that even with the most concerted management, it was simply impossible for Germany within the confines of its present territory to achieve anything like self-sufficiency." The solution for Hitler was to expand east, betraying any remaining uncertainty about his intentions.[68]

Second, other states may act in ways that lure an emerging power into aggressive behavior, seeding doubts about its long-term intentions. If other states claim territory that an emerging power believes rightfully to be its own, then it may be difficult for the emerging power to refrain from a reaction that is interpreted as a provocation. One can imagine smaller powers poking a rising power precisely to draw attention to its long-term intentions and thereby perhaps capturing the attention of others.[69] Such provocations serve as useful litmus tests, and the reaction to those tests may be difficult to ignore.

Interactions between China and its smaller neighbors in Southeast Asia suggest the interests of states like Vietnam and the Philippines in drawing attention to Chinese ambitions. China might have benefited by biding its time, but nationalism and the possibility of losing claims in the South China Sea forced Beijing's hands. The respected International Crisis Group has labeled Chinese behavior in these situations as "reactive assertiveness," whereby "Beijing uses an action by another party as justification to push back hard and change the facts on the ground in its favor."[70] Such situations pose a dilemma for rising powers that must either relent to lesser powers or respond assertively. Choosing the former may have undesirable domestic and international consequences, but opting for the latter is likely to raise questions about long-term intentions, leading to more assertive short-term reactions.[71] More generally, nationalist sentiments might generate domestic political pressure for an emerging power to react aggressively to perceived slights. As Jessica Chen Weiss has persuasively argued, nationalist protests play an important role in shaping how Chinese leaders respond to international crises.[72]

In the first empirical chapter that follows this chapter I focus on the rise of Bismarck's Germany in the late nineteenth century. I pay particular attention to the manner in which Bismarck sought to preserve uncertainty about Germany's long-term intentions. Despite clear evidence of Germany's military might and its potential power as a unified country in the center of Europe, Europe's other existing great powers refrained from active, competitive strategies toward Germany until after Bismarck left office in 1890. By manipulating and reinforcing uncertainty about Germany's intentions, Bismarck was able to maintain cooperative relations with the rest of Europe.

In sum, my explanation for varying levels of cooperation and competition between existing and rising powers depends most basically on the interaction of the two states' time horizons. In general, I hypothesize that rising powers are more focused on the potential long-term opportunities of continuing their rise. This leads them to avoid short-term provocations. Maintaining uncertainty about their intentions is beneficial to them.

Existing, declining powers are more likely to have short time horizons. Precisely because they are in decline, they are more likely to be sensitive to short-term threats and opportunities and therefore also more likely to discount any long-term threats to their security. Uncertainty about the long-term intentions of a rising power provides these states with the space to focus on the short-term while allowing long-term uncertainty to resolve itself. If states are truly uncertain about the magnitude of a potential long-term threat, their inclination is to wait until that uncertainty resolves itself. The more certain threats become, the harder it is to resist acting to stop their emergence. A growing belief that a rising power harbors malign intentions accounts for the change away from cooperation to more competitive strategies.

Of course, there is variation in these prevailing patterns. As I explained above, there are reasons why rising powers may become more focused on the short term, and existing powers that are secure and wealthy in the short term may have the luxury of focusing more on the long term. To the extent that the existing and rising powers are both embedded in the global economy, additional incentives will exist for both sides to prefer continued fruitful economic exchange, regardless of any potential long-term risks.

This is not an account of cooperation that relies on gullible states that are taken in by the benign proclamations of rising great powers. Instead, it is about the temporal pressures that induce rational states to welcome opportunities for cooperation despite the risks. States do not make assumptions about intentions; instead, beliefs about intentions are a political tool subject to manipulation, sometimes sinisterly so, by all sides.

The contemporary case of Sino-U.S. relations illustrates well the logic of the argument. Since the end of the Cold War, scholars and pundits alike have paid much attention to the possible long-term threat posed by a growing China with uncertain intentions. Consider the now-or-later dilemma confronting U.S. policymakers. On the one hand, the United States could act in the short term (or could have acted already) to attempt to forestall the emergence of a powerful China that threatens U.S. interests. Though military options such as war have been largely unrealistic, economic and diplomatic tools arguably could have impaired China's growth.[73] But such tools, including limiting U.S. trade with China, would conceivably have done as much damage to the U.S. economy as to the Chinese economy, and they almost certainly would have damaged the short-term political fortunes of any U.S. president who adopted such a strategy.

On the other hand, the United States could defer any competitive strategies with China until later (as it mostly has done so far). While U.S. preparations for a Chinese threat have accelerated, the United States mostly has opted for a more cooperative short-term approach with China. The danger of choosing to defer until later is that China may grow powerful enough that the United States will have limited options to constrain it in the future. Not only may China emerge as a powerful threat to U.S. interests, but the United States will have contributed greatly to that power. Neither option is an attractive one: the short-term costs of competing with an uncertain future threat versus the prospect of dealing with a much more powerful country in the future. For the most part, the United States, like many existing powers before it in similar situations, has opted to procrastinate. Importantly, neither choice—acting now or later—is inherently preferable or more rational than the other. A rational state leader weighing a variety of costs, benefits, and crosscutting pressures may choose either horn of this dilemma.

In the chapter examining European reactions to interwar Germany, I pay particular attention to the now-or-later dilemmas that European leaders confronted. If there was ever a situation in which European powers ought to have been inclined to address a threat now rather than later, it was interwar Germany, given the evident dangers posed by a powerful, revanchist Germany in the center of Europe. Yet even in this situation, cooperation was more prevalent than many would expect, and the logic of now-or-later dilemmas helps explain why.

How Time Horizons Generate Conflict and Cooperation Table 1.1 summarizes the ways in which the time horizons of existing and rising powers interact. Before analyzing this table, a note on the number of states interacting in the model. For simplicity, I have explicated the theory in this chapter in terms of two states interacting—an existing great power and a rising great. In reality, of course, international politics often includes more than two great powers. The cases presented in the chapters that follow vividly demonstrate this. That said, states tend to consider their relations with other states sequentially and as a series of dyadic relationships. While the introduction of additional actors certainly complicates the way in which states consider their reactions to long-term threats, it does not fundamentally change the logic of the argument presented in this chapter.

Back to table 1.1, when an existing power prefers short-term cooperation and a rising power avoids provocation, then cooperation between an existing and a rising power becomes likely. As I argued above, I expect this particular configuration of time horizons to be relatively common.

Competition becomes more likely in any of the other scenarios. When the rising power and the existing power converge on long time horizons, then competition and hegemonic war become more likely as the two states identify opportunities to establish themselves as the dominant state in the system. Hegemonic war is distinguished by a rising power's effort to assert its role as a leading power over the long term.[74] As I discuss in the example of Anglo-U.S. relations below, it is not necessarily the case that the intersection of long time horizons leads to competition, but it is more likely. In the unusual case that a great power reaches confident conclusions about the benign long-term intentions of a rising great power, then cooperation is possible.

When the two states converge on short time horizons—that is, focus on short-term opportunities for gain—then skirmishes between the rising and existing power become more likely as each side seeks opportunities for short-term benefit. In some cases, however, common myopia may create opportunities for pragmatic marriages of convenience, as in the case of Sino-U.S. cooperation in the period after September 11, 2001. Such short-term

Table 1.1 The interaction of rising and declining power time horizons

		Rising Power	
		Long	Short
Declining Power	Long	Increased possibility of hegemonic war	Increased possibility of preventive war
	Short	Conditions conducive to cooperation	Mixture of skirmishes and pragmatic cooperation

cooperation benefits both sides, but especially the rising power over the long term.

Finally, when a rising power has a short-term focus and the declining power has a long-term focus, then the likelihood of preventive war increases. As opposed to hegemonic wars that begin with a rising power asserting itself, preventive wars are initiated by a declining power seeking to prevent its relative descent to a secondary status.[75] If a declining power is concerned about the long term and a rising power acts in provocative ways intended to produce short-term benefits, then the declining power becomes concerned about the rising power's long-term intentions and is tempted to launch a preventive war.

The significance of this argument lies in part in its skepticism about the impact of the shadow of the future on cooperation. Conventional liberal arguments claim that the shadow of the future—the promise of future cooperation—incentivizes states to cooperate in the short term.[76] Here I contend that the more leaders of existing powers focus on the long term, the less inclined they are to cooperate as they grow increasingly worried about the threat they may face. When existing powers examine the long-term intentions of a rising power, they are more likely to be concerned. They do not assume the worst, but it is difficult for rising powers to offer credible reassurances about their long-term intentions. Leaders often see short-term incentives to cooperate, so cooperation becomes more likely as long as states are focused on the short term. The more states become concerned about the long-term intentions of others—the more uncertainty becomes risk—the more reluctant they will become to engage in cooperation. The shadow of the future is often ominous, casting doubt on the wisdom of cooperating with a potential threat.

Alternative Arguments

My argument stands in contrast to two major alternative explanations for the strategies that existing powers pursue toward rising powers. The first of these arguments, buck-passing, offers a different understanding of how states manage emerging threats and expects competition to be the dominant strategy. In this argument, cooperation results when either the emerging power does not yet possess sufficient capabilities to be threatening or an effort is made to pass the buck to others to respond to that threat. The second explanation, engagement, accounts for cooperation as an effort by declining states to enroll emerging threats in a stable institutional order and to shape a rising power's intentions in a benign direction.

BUCK-PASSING

Offensive realists argue that in an anarchic international system, states can never be certain of other states' intentions. Even if a government thinks it knows another's intentions at any given moment, those intentions can easily change. As a consequence, states must assume the worst about others' intentions and respond to capabilities alone. "In an anarchic international system, where there is no ultimate arbiter," John J. Mearsheimer claims, "states that want to survive have little choice but to assume the worst about the intentions of other states and to compete for power with them."[77] The result is the gloomy and tragic world of international politics that Mearsheimer depicts.

When it comes to identifying long-term threats, Mearsheimer argues that a state's latent power is a good predictor of the threatening military capabilities that it will one day possess, so states ought to be able to anticipate future threats and act presently to hinder the emergence of those threats. As Mearsheimer writes, "Great powers also pay careful attention to how much latent power rival states control, because rich and populous states usually can and do build powerful armies. Thus, great powers tend to fear states with large populations and rapidly expanding economies, even if these states have not yet translated their wealth into military might."[78] Prudent states must assume both that rising powers will easily translate potential capabilities into real capabilities and that they then will have the worst possible intentions for using those capabilities.

Mearsheimer's logic is simple and clear, but it also suffers from three flaws that my argument seeks to correct. First, it ignores the temporal dimensions of international politics to which I draw attention. Mearsheimer assumes that state leaders appreciate long-term threats and will want to do something about such threats in the short term. In the concluding chapter of the 2001 edition of *The Tragedy of Great Power Politics*, Mearsheimer contends that the United States will (and should) stop abetting China's rise. In contrast, I argue that addressing such long-term possible threats poses a dilemma for state leaders. States may choose to act now, but they may also have compelling reasons to defer action until later.[79]

Second, Mearsheimer argues that uncertainty about intentions leads to worst-case assumptions about intentions, but there is no logical reason why this necessarily ought to be the case.[80] As Mearsheimer writes, "Because a state's intentions are difficult to discern, and because they can change quickly, rival great powers will be inclined to assume the worst about the potential hegemon's intentions, further reinforcing the threatened states' incentive to contain it and maybe even weaken it if the opportunity presents itself."[81] In contrast, I draw a distinction between true uncertainty and measurable risk.[82] Worst-case assumptions lead to costly behavior that states would rather avoid, so instead they often choose to let uncertainty resolve itself into risk before they take costly actions to confront a potential adversary.[83]

Third, it is not at all clear what it means to "assume the worst" about intentions if capabilities could conceivably be used in a variety of harmful ways. And a state's capabilities certainly cannot convey *when* a state is likely to take aggressive action if in fact it is planning such action. Simply put, capabilities do not and cannot speak for themselves.

Still, offensive realists have an explanation for observed cooperation with rising great powers. Such cooperation is attributed to so-called buck-passing—when a state "attempts to get another state to bear the burden of deterring or possibly fighting an aggressor, while it remains on the sidelines." Importantly, the buck passer "fully recognizes the need to prevent the aggressor from increasing its share of world power but looks for some other state that is threatened by the aggressor to perform the onerous task."[84] If this argument is correct, then we would expect to see states recognizing the threat posed by a rising power but doing their best to get others to pay the cost of responding to that threat.

But this buck-passing argument, too, has critical flaws. First, while buck-passing might be able to explain the absence of balancing, it cannot explain cooperative behavior that enriches the rising power. In other words, buck-passing might be able to explain why the European great powers did not immediately balance against a resurgent Germany in the interwar period, but it has more difficulty explaining why those states actually aided Germany in its recovery. The logic of buck-passing misses the short-term opportunism that drives cooperative declining powers.

Second, buck-passing presumes that states recognize a rising power as a threat. If, however, a declining power does not even recognize the emerging power as a threat warranting attention, then this undermines the buck-passing argument. In contrast, my argument suggests that great powers often choose to capture short-term benefits precisely because what the long term holds is uncertain. The great powers of late nineteenth-century Europe did not see Germany as a threat for which they were passing the buck. In contrast, they saw cooperation with Germany as something that could advance their national interests, despite and indeed because of long-term uncertainty about its intentions. Uncertainty can lead to cooperation, not just to competition.

Third, it is unclear why rational states would ever expect buck-passing to succeed. If one state chooses to pass the buck, then why would they not expect all other states to pass the buck as well? While Mearsheimer contends that such cooperation is meant to create even more pressure for others to catch the buck, there is little reason to expect such a tactic to succeed.[85] If one state seeks to pass the buck, then so should they all. If a state's leaders are concerned with the threat posed by another state, then they should not be satisfied with a buck-passing strategy that leads to an absence of balancing. Consider the multipolar European system in the century before the Cold War. Why would any of the states in the system at the time have expected buck-passing to succeed as a strategy? At a minimum, states attempting to pass the buck should still be seen as balancing internally, on the probability that their efforts at buck-passing will fail, but such internal balancing is often difficult to detect. Geography may account for some of the variation here—more geographically proximate powers may be compelled to catch the buck passed by others—but a geographical explanation only begs the question of why proximate Continental powers would ever take a chance on buck-passing or why insular powers would ever be moved to respond to an emerging Continental threat.

Fourth, the logic of buck-passing suggests that states would shift to more competitive strategies when the rising power becomes sufficiently threatening and no effort has been made to counter that threat, but offensive realism does not specify when this shift ought to take place. As I demonstrate below, the leaders of declining powers do not appear to respond simply to shifts in the material capabilities of rising powers. Rather, they are driven by indicators of worrisome long-term intentions. For example, the Cold War finds its origins less in ominous developments in Soviet capabilities and more in alarming warnings about Soviet intentions. Explanations based on capabilities alone have difficulty accounting for the timing of transitions from cooperation to competition. Significant inflexion points in relative capabilities that could account for these transitions are difficult to identify in retrospect, let alone in real time.[86]

While my argument relies on the logic of procrastination—to delay addressing a potential threat until later to capture present benefits—offensive realism depends on the logic of buck-passing—finding somebody else to pay the price of balancing against an emerging threat. There are two major observational differences between these arguments. First, if buck-passing were occurring, a threat would be recognized, but a state would attempt to push the cost of addressing that threat onto some other state. If procrastination were occurring, states would defer more competitive and costly strategies until later when the nature of the threat they are facing is clearer. Second, whereas the attempt to get others to pay the costs of balancing is critical to the logic of buck-passing, it is not so to the logic of my argument. My argument expects states to procrastinate with no expectation that they attempt to find somebody else to pay the costs.

More generally, the offensive realist understanding of uncertainty about intentions is underdeveloped. Not being completely certain about another state's intentions is not the same as being completely uncertain about those intentions. Uncertainty about intentions varies continuously along a spectrum; it is not dichotomous.

Moreover, offensive realists fail to recognize the distinction between true uncertainty and risk. There are elements of international politics that are truly uncertain, and a rising power's intentions may be one of them. Over time, however, as states gain increasing evidence of a another state's intentions, uncertainty transforms into risk, and states are then able to make probabilistic estimates that allow for more calibrated responses to a rising power.

By treating uncertainty dichotomously—as if any uncertainty is equivalent to complete uncertainty—offensive realists rely on an impoverished and unrealistic conception of uncertainty that ignores the process by which states use their intelligence assets to assess what is truly uncertain and what can be effectively estimated.

ENGAGEMENT

Another alternative explanation for cooperation between existing and rising powers is engagement. In the logic of engagement, cooperation is a strategy for shaping the interests of a rising power such that over time it chooses a more peaceful path. Engagement is an argument that takes temporality seriously: cooperation in the short term is thought to beneficially shape intentions over the long term.

G. John Ikenberry provides one example of the logic of engagement.[87] Ikenberry examines how victorious powers create stable international orders in the wake of war. In his theory, a victorious power enjoys a dominant position in the international system but worries about its eventual decline from that status. Meanwhile, less powerful states fear exploitation by the victorious state. Ikenberry argues that the concerns of both the dominant state and less powerful states have historically been solved through the creation of stable and legitimate orders. In these institutionalized orders, the dominant state binds itself in the short term with the expectation that any order created will persist over the long term even after it has declined.

Institutions thus provide insurance against the uncertain intentions of a powerful state. In return, smaller powers are provided some degree of protection by the dominant state's interest in creating a stable and predictable international order. Therefore, such an institutionally based bargain satisfies both the long-term concerns of the dominant state and the short-term concerns of less powerful, but rising, states. Ideally (for the existing dominant power), the institutions create a lock-in mechanism whereby even rising powers come to see sustaining the international order as in their interest. In this argument, cooperation does not simply reflect preferences. It can also transform interests in a way that engenders future cooperation.

Ikenberry's argument, representative of liberal arguments more generally, has three logical flaws. First, he assumes that great powers have long time horizons and act to create orders that will be the most impactful over the long term. Dominant powers forgo short-term opportunities in order to create a presumably stable long-term order. Cooperation creates a shadow of the future in that states will cooperate now out of the expectation of further valuable cooperation later. How an existing power acts relative to long-term threats, however, is an example of a now-or-later dilemma, and states may opt to capture short-term rewards regardless of the long-term implications. Second, Ikenberry ignores the possibility that once rising powers become more capable they will choose to upend the international order, and there is little an existing power can do to prevent that. Once a rising power has accrued enough power, there is little reason for it to be bound by the rules created by a former dominant power now in decline. Third, while arguments focused on engagement offer an explanation for cooperation, they do not explain when such efforts are abandoned and more competitive strategies adopted instead. In short, they have difficulty accounting for variation.

Applied to the case of emerging, long-term potential threats, engagement theorists would expect to see existing powers engaging rising powers in an effort to enmesh them in a stable international order. Such cooperation ought to look different than the cooperation that my argument expects. Engagement expects deep and embedded cooperation, often instantiated through formal international institutions. If a rising power buys into such an international order, then presumably there is less to fear from such a state over the long term.

My argument expects pragmatic, mutually beneficial cooperation that may be as fleeting as it is valuable. Whereas Ikenberry sees the crafting of stable international orders, I see pragmatic and opportunistic cooperation that is in states' mutual interests. Such cooperation is only sustainable as long as uncertainty about intentions, the relative threat environment, and a state's choice to act now or later favors cooperation. There is no stable, institutional or norm-based international system that rests beyond.

To summarize:

- In my account, variation in competition and cooperation is a product of the interaction of rising power and existing power time horizons. The evidence should reveal short-term-oriented pragmatic cooperation as well as shifting strategies in response to beliefs about long-term intentions.
- In the logic of buck-passing, how an existing power responds to an emerging threat will depend solely on the relative capabilities of that threat—both actual capabilities and potential capabilities. Cooperation is a product of buck-passing. The evidence should reveal that existing powers assume the worst about the intentions of a rising power and react to changes in capabilities alone.

- If states cooperate with rising powers in an attempt at engagement, the evidence should reveal that existing powers seek to institutionalize constitutional orders that serve the existing power's interests in the short term and protect those interests in the long term. Other emerging powers ought to welcome institutional orders that protect them from exploitation by the existing great powers.

Ultimately, I contend that my argument is logically more compelling and better explains the empirical evidence. Most importantly, whereas buck-passing overpredicts competition and engagement overpredicts cooperation, my argument can more effectively account for variation on the spectrum of cooperative and competitive strategies.

In doing so, the argument makes three important contributions. First, it highlights the significance of temporal considerations in international politics. Until now, time has literally been a missing dimension in the study of international politics. Second, it introduces a more sophisticated understanding of uncertainty into the study of international politics. By distinguishing between true uncertainty and measurable risk, the argument better accounts for the way that states examine and react to potential long-term threats. Third and finally, by consciously addressing time and uncertainty, the argument provides a bridge between rationalist arguments like realism, constructivist arguments that emphasize the importance of ideas, and insights from behavioral economics that explain departures from rationalist models of behavior. The argument relies on states rationally assessing potential threats and opportunities and also acknowledges that there is variation in the way that individuals value the future as opposed to the present. By acknowledging that not just costly signals but also identities and beliefs affect perceptions of intentions, the argument links together with prominent constructivist arguments.

Research Design

The case studies in the following four chapters were selected to test various aspects of my argument against alternatives. The four cases capture most of the modern cases of rising and resurgent great powers with the exceptions of early twentieth-century Russia and Japan in the interwar period.[88] From a historical perspective, power transition and great power politics, in general, have been greatly studied, but work that compares individual cases is surprisingly rare.[89] The cases are not meant to come together in one integrated test of the argument, but rather each case focuses on particular aspects of the argument.

The first case, the rise of late nineteenth-century Germany, is a challenging test of the argument that states procrastinate, rather than assuming the worst, about rising great powers with uncertain intentions. If there was ever a case in which a rising great power's neighbors ought to have been immediately concerned with the threat posed by the rising power, it was Bismarck's Germany. In the decade prior to its unification, Germany had decisively defeated three of its neighbors and established itself as a powerhouse at the center of Europe. By examining three of Germany's interlocutors during this period—France, Great Britain, and Russia—I provide three different reactions to Germany's rise as well as capture the complexity of late nineteenth-century European multipolarity.

The chapter focuses, in particular, on the ways in which the leaders of rising powers attempt to manipulate uncertainty about their own intentions and thus others' resolutions of their now-or-later dilemmas. What is remarkable about this period is the level of cooperation between Germany and other European states even after Germany had consolidated its position in the center of Europe and demonstrated its material strength through three decisive military victories. Bismarck worked consistently during this period to assuage concern about Germany's intentions, allowing cooperation to continue despite uncertainty about the long term. When Bismarck's successors opted for a different resolution of their now-or-later dilemma, the nature of European diplomacy also shifted. The combination of Bismarck's long time horizons and the short time horizons of other European powers sustained cooperation until Bismarck's successors acted in provocative ways that raised questions about long-term German intentions.

The next case, British reactions to the rise of the United States, is noteworthy because it provides unusual variation on the dependent variable. Namely, this is one of the few cases in modern history in which a rising great power, the United States, overcame an existing power, Great Britain, without conflict. Beyond that, Washington and London proceeded to form one of the closest great power relationships in modern history. This chapter asks how this happened, focusing in particular on both the threat that Washington genuinely posed to British interests and the manner in which Britain successfully transformed uncertainty into manageable risk. While the emergence of Anglo-U.S. friendship may be clear in retrospect, at that time there was considerable hesitancy about the implications of a powerful United States and the threat it might pose to British interests.

The chapter draws particular attention to the way in which the presence of an alternative threat can lead an existing power to defer dealing with threats deemed less severe and less imminent. Interestingly, in this case, a series of crises certainly brought attention to long-term U.S. intentions, but this only led to more cooperation, not competition. In examining why this might have occurred, I focus on how common identity and ideology may lead to more confidence in benign long-term intentions. Despite short-term-oriented behavior by both sides, cooperation emerged because of unusual British confidence in U.S. long-term intentions.

The third case returns to the German threat in the center of Europe. In this case, the focus is on interwar Germany. Again, I focus on the reactions of three different European states to Germany's rise at a time when there ought to have been immediate concern about Germany's long-term intentions, and, again, the states surrounding Germany had every reason to be suspicious. Despite these potential long-term concerns, short-term economic opportunities took priority. Other European great powers sought ways to put off addressing an uncertain German threat in order to capture short-term rewards. This case provides a test not only of the offensive realist argument that states assume the worst about a rising state's intentions but also of the liberal argument that cooperation with a rising power is intended to shape that country's intentions in a more favorable direction by embedding them in international institutions. Again, I illustrate how the eventual changes in strategy toward Germany were motivated by the process by which indicators of German intentions transformed uncertainty into risk that needed to be addressed.

While the 1930s have been much studied, I focus more attention on the 1920s when cooperation with a recovering Germany was more prevalent than one might expect. Interestingly, though, this cooperation also varied among different European states, and the chapter explores the sources of that variation. Unlike the first two cases, this one examines great power relations in the wake of war (as well as before it). European powers did not behave as if they were assuming the worst about German intentions, even though they had every reason to do so, and uncertainty helps explain why. Here again, for as long as Germany avoided short-term provocation, cooperation was sustainable as European powers had to focus on other short-term threats. Only when Germany's behavior raised questions about its long-term intentions did European leaders extend their time horizons into the future, leading to more competition.

The fourth and final case, U.S. reactions to the rise of the Soviet Union in the wake of World War II, tests a different dimension of the argument. In this case, it is not surprising that the United States and the Soviet Union found common cause in defeating the immediate threat posed by Nazi Germany. Instead, what I focus on in this case is explaining what precipitated the transition from friends to enemies following the war. While the initial U.S. inclination was to withdraw from Europe in the aftermath of the war, the emerging Soviet threat necessitated a continuing U.S. presence. Critically, it was U.S. beliefs about Soviet intentions, not Soviet capabilities, that drove this change. The United States did not simply assume the worst about uncertain Soviet intentions. Rather, U.S. reactions to the Soviet threat shadowed increasingly ominous indicators of Soviet intentions that added weight to the belief that Soviet intentions were malign. In short, this case is less about the temporal dimension of the argument than it is about the focus on uncertainty about intentions and the reactions it produces.

I trace how Soviet-U.S. cooperation evaporated in the transition from World War II to the Cold War. With the German and Japanese threats vanquished, the United States had few other threats to distract it from the potential long-term Soviet threat as Moscow acted to stake its claims in the postwar order before it was too late. The conclusions reached about Soviet intentions, not Soviet capabilities, drove U.S. strategy as it transitioned into the Cold War. This case is of particular interest because of the possible parallels with the contemporary Sino-U.S. case.

Together, these cases present an effective test of my own argument about time horizons and uncertainty and the buck-passing and engagement alternatives. Moreover, beyond testing the arguments as a whole, each case focuses on an important dimension of the argument. In the case of Bismarck's Germany, the efforts by Bismarck to distract attention from any long-term malign German intentions are noteworthy. In the case of the rise of the United States, the role of a shared Anglo-Saxon identity in cementing British beliefs about U.S. intentions highlights the different ways in which states transform uncertainty into manageable risk. The case of interwar Germany highlights the short-term incentives that states have to cooperate even in the face of possibly ominous long-term intentions. Finally, the Soviet case demonstrates that beliefs about intentions, not just assessments of capabilities, are critical to understanding how states evaluate long-term threats.

The Arrival of Imperial Germany

From 1871 until 1890, Europe's great powers refrained from any active effort to balance against the newly unified and increasingly powerful Germany. Over the course of the 1860s, German unification emerged out of decisive military victories over Denmark, Austria, and France. There was no mystery about the implications of Germany's rise or its enormous power potential. Yet a strong, unified Germany was met with more cooperation than competition. In this chapter I seek to explain this pattern of behavior. I also seek to explain why the pattern changed in 1890, leading to the consummation of the Franco-Russian alliance in 1893.[1]

This chapter illustrates, in particular, the value to rising powers of maintaining uncertainty or, even more ideally, positive impressions about their intentions. Bismarck succeeded in persuading others to defer aggressive action against Germany by sustaining a sufficient degree of uncertainty about Germany's long-term intentions. Such uncertainty provided the space for other European powers to pursue more cooperative strategies that were less costly for them in the short term and held out the possibility of shifting German intentions in a more benign direction. Acting sooner to constrain German growth promised to be costly, but postponing action until later might have meant waiting until Germany was too powerful to balance against effectively. Cooperation persisted until 1890 as a product of the overlap between German preferences for deferring aggression and European preferences for deferring balancing. Only when Bismarck's successors signaled more aggressive intentions and started to transform true uncertainty into manageable risk did other European powers begin to balance, including the Franco-Russian alliance.

Bismarck took advantage of various crises in Europe that served to shorten the time horizons of the other European great powers. As long as these states needed to attend to the short term, they could not focus on the potential long-term threat posed by Germany. As expected, the multiple potential short-term threats in the multipolar system of late nineteenth-century Europe induced shorter time horizons. While multipolarity complicates the dyadic theory presented in the previous chapter, this chapter demonstrates that even in multipolarity, states tend to deal with each other sequentially in a series of dyadic relationships. Meanwhile, Bismarck was all too happy to reinforce this short-term focus by mostly avoiding behavior that would raise questions about Germany's long-term intentions.

In the remainder of this chapter I review further what each alternative explanation would expect to observe in this case. Next I sketch a focused history of the period under study. I pay particular attention to the different strategies available to Germany and other great powers at various critical moments. Then I consider the implications of the evidence for the alternative arguments. Which theory better accounts for the observed pattern of interaction between Germany and its neighbors?

Alternative Arguments

My argument expects that cooperation is a product of the interaction of existing powers' and an emerging potential threat's time horizons. If the relationship shifts in a more competitive direction, as I contend occurred in 1890, then this is most likely a result of a shift in time horizons. In the case of Germany, I will explain how Bismarck's successors had shorter time horizons, which led to more provocative German behavior and to concern about long-term German intentions. As a consequence, the time horizons of other European powers elongated, leading in turn to more competitive strategies.

One alternative explanation for cooperation with a rising Germany would attribute such behavior to buck-passing. In the logic of offensive realism, states assume the worst about others' future intentions and balance against capabilities alone, including the potential capabilities of a rising power like Germany. Preferably, however, states can find some other state to do the difficult work of balancing. Even if states prefer to pass the buck, they still ought to refrain from cooperation that aids the emergence of such a threat. In the case of Germany, offensive realism expects that states would have recognized the potential future threat posed by a growing Germany but hoped that another would pay the price of balancing. Any shift toward more competitive strategies would be a clear indication that there was nobody left to pass the buck to in dealing with increasingly threatening German capabilities.

Another explanation would account for cooperation with a rising Germany as an attempt to engage Germany in the hope of shifting its intentions in a benign direction. Any observed cooperation ought to be aimed at the socialization of Germany rather than simply at capturing short-term benefits. Such cooperation should look qualitatively different, and the evidence should reveal leaders viewing cooperation as intended to craft such an order. This long-term-oriented cooperation is intended to develop a shadow of the future that is conducive to continued cooperation.

The evidence presented in this chapter provides more support for my temporal theory than for either alternative. First, the logic of buck-passing fails to explain the cooperation with Bismarck's Germany. Europe's great powers did not simply assume the worst about German intentions and consider ways to counter the emerging threat. Nor did they attempt to pass the buck to other European powers (or have reason to think such a strategy would succeed). Instead, Bismarck used uncertainty about his intentions to Germany's advantage, sustaining cooperation until his successors adopted a more aggressive posture. Second, engagement also fails to explain the development of European politics in the second half of the nineteenth century. There is little evidence to suggest that Europe's great powers were attempting to use cooperation to shape long-term German intentions. Cooperation between Germany and its neighbors was pragmatic and instrumental, not deeply felt or institutionalized.

In focusing on two decades that have received insufficient attention in the study of great power politics, this chapter makes a novel contribution. While the years immediately prior to World War I have certainly been studied extensively, this earlier, more formative period in Germany's rise has not, despite the remarkable absence of balancing against a new great power in the heart of Europe. To the extent this period has been studied it has often been in the spirit of acknowledging Bismarck's supposed diplomatic genius, but such a focus misses the strategic dynamics in this case that are by no means exclusive to the rise of Germany. Explaining both the sources of cooperation in this period and the reason for that cooperation's demise represents an important contribution.

The Unification of Germany and Great Power Politics in Europe

There can be little doubt about the implications of German unification for the European balance of power. On May 10, 1871, the Treaty of Frankfurt formally ended the Franco-Prussian War.[2] It granted the newly unified Germany the provinces of Alsace and Lorraine and allowed German troops to occupy portions of France until a war indemnity of F5 billion was paid. The decisive German victory, on the heels of similar victories over Denmark and Austria, signaled Germany's arrival as a European great power.[3] Benjamin Disraeli, leader of the British Conservatives, declared, "This war represents the German revolution, a greater political event than the French revolution. . . . Not a single principle in the management of our foreign affairs, accepted by all statesmen for guidance up to six months ago, any longer exists. . . . You have a new world, new influences at work, new and unknown objects and dangers with which to cope."[4] Yet, in the years that followed, the response of other European great powers was not to pursue assertive, competitive strategies against Germany.[5] Instead, Europe's great powers pursued more cooperative strategies with Germany. While Germany's partners were reluctant to endorse any aggressive German behavior, the following two decades were characterized by economic and political cooperation.

As I will demonstrate, as German chancellor, Bismarck understood the need to avoid provoking others and the value of maintaining uncertainty about his long-term intentions. Bismarck saw that Germany's brightest days were ahead, so he did his best to avoid behavior that might raise questions about Germany's intentions. Meanwhile, other European great powers, enmeshed in a competitive multipolar system, were compelled to focus on a variety of short-term crises that crowded out any consideration of Germany's long-term intentions. The interaction of long-term German intentions and short-term European intentions led to cooperation. Only when Bismarck's successors behaved more provocatively did Europe's other leaders recognize a long-term threat from Germany that needed to be addressed.

Bismarck's foreign policy was designed to keep other European great powers focused on opportunities for short-term gain rather than on more aggressive efforts to curtail German growth. His goal was to create conditions under which Germany could continue to grow and realize its potential power. Most fundamentally, the German chancellor understood that in a European system of five great powers, it was critical that Germany be in the group of three if the Continent divided into two rival alliances. As Bismarck told Russian diplomat Peter Saburov, "All politics reduces to this formula: to try to be one of three, as long as the world is governed by an unstable equilibrium of five powers."[6] Bismarck consistently maneuvered to ensure that Germany remained among the three.

Bismarck also recognized, however, that a powerful Germany at the center of Europe was inherently a threat to others, so to remain in the coalition of three, he would refrain from behavior that would lead others to question Germany's long-term intentions. Uncertainty about German intentions was a potential asset to Bismarck, and he would work assiduously to try to convince others that Germany did not harbor malign intentions. Not only did Bismarck reject further expansion, but he also questioned the acquisition of Alsace and Lorraine precisely because of the deleterious consequences it could have for long-term relations with France.[7]

Convincing others that Germany was satiated—or at least that its intentions were genuinely unknown—would take some work. Even before Germany's unification, Hans Lothar von Schweinitz, the northern German envoy to Austria-Hungary, reported that Vienna feared that Prussia was intent on destroying the Hapsburg monarchy. Bismarck replied, "The suspicion that northern Germany could have the inclination or interests to destroy the Austrian monarchy is an absurdity that I have often exposed."[8] As historian Otto Pflanze summarizes, "The task of German foreign policy was to shield the Reich from external danger during a period of internal consolidation. The moment had arrived to switch from a revolutionary to a conservative foreign policy. In Bismarck's opinion Germany no longer had any objective that could profitably be attained by war."[9] Though Germany might have benefited from further short-term aggression (and its military power was demonstrably unmatched), Bismarck understood that this was likely to generate an anti-German coalition that would interfere with Germany's long-term growth potential.

As the rest of this chapter unfolds, it will detail the evolution of European strategies toward Germany in the 1870s and 1880s. Contrary to the common hagiography of Bismarck, his grand strategy was not perfect. In fact, the narrative history reveals a series of missteps followed by efforts to correct those missteps before they generated adverse consequences for Germany's continued growth. The missteps are critical because they raised questions about German intentions, and Bismarck consistently felt the need to reassure others in the wake of those missteps.

Bismarck's Instinct to Cooperate: The Utility of Uncertainty

The two decades following German unification may be best understood as an extended effort by Bismarck to allay concerns about German intentions. As a first attempt, in October 1873, Wilhelm joined Alexander II and Franz Joseph in the Schönbrunn Convention, creating the League of the Three Emperors. The league did not call on the signatories to do much other than consult with one another.[10] Still, it alleviated Austrian concerns about further German expansionist aims.[11] Anything that served to convince European powers to defer more aggressive balancing until later was in Germany's interests. Of course, the League of the Three Emperors did not satisfy everybody. France feared that Bismarck was crafting a monarchical bloc with which to conquer Europe.[12] As we shall see later in this chapter, however, Bismarck recognized these French fears and sought ways of keeping France, too, focused on opportunities for mutually beneficial short-term cooperation.

BISMARCK'S MISSTEP: THE WAR IN SIGHT CRISIS

Even as Bismarck attempted to allay concerns about his intentions, he also inevitably took some missteps. In 1875, Bismarck stepped awkwardly into the War in Sight crisis, provoking suspicion around Europe.[13] The crisis emerged out of Bismarck's desire to keep France isolated.[14] If Germany could not win over France, then it was critical to prevent France from allying with other European powers. In January 1875, Bismarck was alarmed to learn that France intended on printing F600 million and acquiring nine thousand battle horses.[15] In response, the chancellor announced that he was prohibiting the export of any additional horses to France and dispatched Joseph von Radowitz, the German ambassador to Greece, to St. Petersburg as a temporary ambassador. Paris feared that Radowitz was sent to receive a guarantee that Russia would not intervene if Germany launched a war against France. In response, on March 13, the French assembly approved the Law of the Fourth Battalions, adding a fourth battalion to each French regiment.[16]

Between the French warhorses, the Radowitz mission to St. Petersburg, and the Law of the Fourth Battalions, tensions between Germany and France reached their highest point since the conclusion of the Franco-Prussian War.[17] The crisis gets its name from an editorial that appeared in the Berlin *Post* on April 8 titled, "Is War in Sight?" The editorial cited the growth in French armaments as heightening the prospects for conflict between France and Germany. Across Europe, the belligerent tone of the editorial raised concerns, especially since many assumed that Bismarck had either written or explicitly approved it.[18]

On April 15, the French ambassador to Germany, Élie Gontaut-Biron, returned to Berlin from a vacation. He met with both the German foreign secretary, Bernhard von Bülow, and the German emperor, Wilhelm, in an effort to reassure them that neither the horse acquisition nor the Law of the Fourth Battalion presaged French aggression.

Tension, however, hardly abated. Less than a week later, Gontaut-Biron found himself seated next to Radowitz at a dinner at the British embassy in Berlin. Radowitz, perhaps after a glass or two of wine, shared his thoughts with the French ambassador: "But if revenge is the inmost thought of France— and it cannot be otherwise—why wait to attack her until she has recovered her strength and contracted her alliances? You must agree that from a political, from a philosophical, even from a Christian point of view, these deductions are well grounded and these preoccupations are fitted to guide the policy of Germany."[19] The ambassador immediately reported this ominous conversation to the French foreign minister, Louis Decazes.

The crisis drew attention to uncertain German intentions. Seeing an opportunity to awaken others to the threat posed by Germany, Decazes distributed Gontaut-Biron's report to French ambassadors throughout Europe with instructions to share with European leaders Radowitz's provocative words. The report alarmed both the British and the Russian governments. Disraeli bluntly remarked, "Bismarck is really another old Bonaparte again, and he must be bridled."[20]

In Russia, the crisis generated concerns about the potential for immediate conflict and also what it foretold about long-term German ambitions. While the tsar was reluctant to challenge his uncle, Kaiser Wilhelm, the Russian foreign minister, Alexander Gorchakov, saw an opportunity to diminish Germany's growing stature in the center of Europe. St. Petersburg conveyed its unhappiness with German behavior through Peter Shuvalov, the Russian ambassador in London. Visiting Berlin during the first week of May, Shuvalov warned both Wilhelm and Bismarck that Russia would not react favorably to a German preventive war against France.[21]

The War in Sight crisis reached its denouement the following week when Tsar Alexander and Gorchakov visited Berlin. During the course of their visit, Bismarck, Wilhelm, Gorchakov, Alexander, and Odo Russell, the British ambassador to Germany, met several times.[22] The German chancellor sought to assuage concerns about the crisis and its larger implications. When the meetings concluded, Gorchakov and Alexander assured Gontaut-Biron that they were satisfied that Germany did not harbor malign intentions toward France. Departing Berlin, Gorchakov sent a dispatch to Russia's ambassadors: "The emperor is leaving Berlin convinced of the pacific dispositions that reign here and that assure the maintenance of peace."[23]

Though the war scare had passed by the end of May, the first major crisis in Europe since German unification had the effect of elongating time horizons, causing others to ponder the long-term implications of a more powerful Germany.[24] The shadow of the future loomed, but not in a way that generated cooperation. The effect of the crisis was to reduce apparent uncertainty about German intentions and incline Europe's great powers to consider more active efforts to restrain Germany.[25] Bismarck, however, had little interest in war, nor did he wish to see efforts to constrain German growth. As he related, "I would rather have resigned than lent a hand in picking a quarrel, which could have had no other motive than preventing France from recovering her breath and her strength. A war of this kind could not, in my opinion, have led to permanently tenable conditions in Europe, but might have brought about an agreement between Russia, Austria, and England, based on mistrust of us, and leading eventually to active proceedings against the new and still unconsolidated empire."[26]

Bismarck acknowledged that the War in Sight crisis had not served Germany well. In the wake of the crisis, the chancellor submitted his resignation, which Wilhelm refused to accept. Pflanze calls the crisis the "greatest diplomatic defeat of [Bismarck's] career."[27] And Bismarck himself reflected that 1875 was "a bad year."[28] Perhaps most importantly, Bismarck learned from the crisis that it would be harder to isolate France than he had hoped. Russian and British interest in France's security surprised him, and the crisis had the effect of pushing France and Russia closer together. "The key to the expunging of the humiliation of the Franco-Prussian War, to the recovery of lost provinces, to the restoration of France's lost leadership in Europe, and, along with that, of her pride, her self-confidence, and her belief in herself and her future . . . lay with Russia, and nowhere else," concludes George F. Kennan in discussing the implications of the crisis for French attitudes.[29] Finally, the crisis and the tension between Bismarck and Gorchakov undermined the League of the Three Emperors, which was central to Bismarck's vision of Germany's place in Europe.[30]

In short, the War in Sight crisis threatened to weaken the core tenets of Bismarck's foreign policy. It challenged Germany's position as "one of the three," and it did anything but isolate France. While Germany stood to benefit from short-term cooperation with other European leaders, the crisis raised concerns about further German aggression in the short term as well as over the long term. By elongating European time horizons, it presumably made competitive strategies toward Germany more likely.

Yet, even after the War in Sight crisis, Europe's great powers remained passive in their approach toward Germany. While Bismarck was greatly concerned about the crisis, the European response was more muted. Information on military expenditures and military personnel from the National Material Capabilities data set reveals no evidence of anything other than a secular rise in capabilities in the period studied in this chapter.[31] There is little evidence of any movement toward an alliance against Germany even in the wake of the crisis. In the next section, I seek to understand why cooperation between Germany and its neighbors persisted.

BISMARCK'S STRATEGY OF REASSURANCE

As expected, Bismarck reacted to the War in Sight crisis by trying to alleviate any concerns the situation raised about Germany's intentions. For example, in 1876, Bismarck attempted to befriend Britain, but London declined any formal relationship.[32] The financial secretary to the war office, Frederick Stanley, the Earl of Derby, remained concerned with long-term German intentions in the wake of the War in Sight crisis: "[An agreement with Germany] is one, however, which, desirable as it may be in principle, cannot be definitively adopted without a clearer knowledge than we now possess of the motives which have led to [Bismarck's] recent overtures, and of the expectations which he, and the government which he represents may have formed of the results of the understanding proposed by him." Derby also reminded Russell, "It is unnecessary to point out . . . that England desires no exclusive alliances, nor do the principles of English policy admit of such being contracted."[33]

A year later, Bismarck reiterated the basic principles of his foreign policy in the Kissingen Diktat of June 15, 1877.[34] Bismarck emphasized the importance of the relationship between Britain and Russia. This relationship had both sources of potential friendship and sources of potential enmity, and, for Bismarck, it was critical to keep them neither allied nor at war. If they were allied, then the addition of France would place Germany in the smaller coalition of European great powers. The chancellor returned to his familiar fear of a balancing coalition against Germany, "le cauchemar des coalitions."

The Kissingen Diktat proposed ways of addressing both the Anglo-Russian relationship and the position of Germany in Europe. First, Bismarck suggested that British and Russian insecurity could be addressed by recognizing both Britain's interests in Egypt and Russia's desire to control the Black Sea. He stopped short, however, of calling for an Anglo-Russian rapprochement out of his concern that it might grow into a coalition against Germany.[35]

Second, Bismarck noted the importance for Germany of befriending as many European states as it could. While relations with France might be difficult to reconcile, the best way to prevent an anti-German coalition was to make Germany useful in the short term and to avoid any provocation that raised longer-term concerns. Bismarck wrote, "[The picture I have in mind is] not one of gaining territory, but of a political situation as a whole, in which all the powers except France [have] need of us and would thus be deterred as far as possible from coalitions against us by their relations with each other."[36] It would not be long before Bismarck found an opportunity for Germany to be useful and needed.

EUROPE'S SHORT TIME HORIZONS: THE CRISIS IN THE BALKANS

When he was not at the center of situations like the War in Sight crisis, Bismarck made good use of other crises that kept other European powers focused on the short term and allowed him to reassure them about German intentions. Crises have the effect of compelling leaders to focus on the short term, and such a crisis in the Balkans in the late 1870s again distracted Europe's leaders from concern about the rise of Germany.

European diplomacy in the late 1870s was dominated by the first of many crises in the Balkans prior to World War I.[37] The crisis was precisely the type from which a rising power with uncertain intentions like Germany could benefit: Germany was not a central antagonist in the crisis, but it could play a useful role in resolving it. Such behavior would keep other powers focused on more immediate threats while allowing Germany to act in ways that suggested it did not have malign intentions.

Tension between Russia, Austria-Hungary, and the Ottoman Empire over the fate of Serbia, Bosnia, and Bulgaria was a near constant in nineteenth-century European diplomacy.[38] Though it had no direct interests in the region, Britain found itself supporting the Ottoman Empire out of concern for unfettered access to British colonies in central and southern Asia.[39] Bismarck's main concern was to prevent the Balkans from destroying the relationship between Russia and Austria-Hungary and the League of the Three Emperors with it. Such a development might push Russia toward Britain and eventually a coalition including France. Berlin was willing to sacrifice the Ottoman Empire, if it prevented war, salvaged the league, and kept Europe's attention away from Germany.[40]

In the summer of 1875, Christian communities in Bosnia and Bulgaria rose up against Ottoman rule. Various diplomatic efforts to resolve the crisis followed. In December 1875, Austro-Hungarian foreign minister Julius Andrassy issued a note calling for religious freedom and taxation reforms in the Ottoman Empire.[41] When that did not succeed, the Berlin Memorandum, issued by the emperors of Germany, Russia, and Austria-Hungary, called for other Ottoman domestic reforms, but that too failed.[42] Finally, on June 30,

1876, Serbia declared war against the Ottoman Empire. Russia joined Serbia's war effort at the end of April 1877.[43] The Ottoman forces were no match for Russia's intervention, and despite Osman Pasha's famous effort to defend Plevna, Slavic victory appeared inevitable by the end of 1877.[44]

In early March of the following year, with victory in sight, St. Petersburg proposed the draconian Treaty of San Stefano, which called for large Ottoman territorial concessions in the Balkans, a sizable war indemnity, and the creation of an ostensibly autonomous Bulgaria that Russian troops would be permitted to occupy for two years after the war.[45] Aside from obvious Ottoman dissatisfaction with such terms, the proposed treaty also offended both Britain and Austria-Hungary. From London's perspective, the treaty would do little to protect its access to the Black Sea, while Vienna rejected the Russian occupation of Bulgaria. This dissatisfaction created an opportunity for Bismarck to play peacemaker.

The Congress of Berlin, convened on June 13, 1878, offered Bismarck the chance simultaneously to resolve a dangerous crisis in Europe and to reassure others about Germany's intentions.[46] The agreement eventually reached repudiated the Treaty of San Stefano. It guaranteed the survival of an independent Ottoman state while also offering London the option to occupy Cyprus, satisfying Austria-Hungary by creating only a weakened, divided Bulgaria, and even placating France by inviting it to occupy Tunis.[47]

Russia was the most dissatisfied participant leaving Berlin. As William L. Langer summarizes, "The Berlin Treaty was the complete negation of Pan-Slav aspirations as expressed in the Treaty of San Stefano."[48] To St. Petersburg, it appeared that it had fought a war against the Ottoman Empire only to see the benefits go to Britain and Austria-Hungary. Russian leaders stood by as Germany defeated France in 1871, but now Bismarck had done little to advance Russia's interests in the aftermath of the Russo-Turkish War.

I return to the Russia question below, but first it is worth reviewing the role that Bismarck played in negotiating this peace agreement. "I do not conceive peace negotiations as a situation in which, faced by divergent views, we play the arbitrator and say: it shall be thus, and it is backed by the might of the German empire," explained Bismarck. "But I imagine a more modest role . . . more that of an honest broker, who really intends to do business."[49] Bismarck recognized that he could rectify any damage that had been done by the War in Sight crisis by refocusing European leaders on short-term opportunities for cooperation. A European crisis in which Germany was not directly involved focused European powers on greater threats in the short term and away from any long-term concerns about German intentions that had emerged in 1875.

Bismarck's strategy appears to have worked. It is worth quoting historian Lothar Gall at length: "In the eyes of St. Petersburg, London, Vienna, and even Paris, [Bismarck] now increasingly became the man who was not only prepared but was probably alone in a position to keep within bounds, for the sake of peace in Europe and an order acceptable to all the powers, German demands for power and prestige and the forces of German nationalism. . . . The troublemaker of Europe . . . had in the space of a few years become a kind of guarantor of the European order."[50] This was a remarkable shift from the concern about Germany only a few years earlier.

The pressure that other European powers faced to focus on other threats raised by the crisis in the Balkans precluded efforts to address any potential long-term threat posed by Germany. There is little evidence that cooperation with Germany was motivated at this point by either buck-passing or engagement; rather, it was motivated by short-term pragmatic concerns.

REASSURING RUSSIA

Bismarck's maneuvering at the Congress of Berlin dissuaded other European powers from choosing to act sooner rather than later to balance against Germany more actively. While other states were not necessarily allying themselves with Germany, diplomatic and economic cooperation was continuous. Trade among these powers continued as if there was no threat to worry about, and there was little effort to hedge cooperative economic relations with more competitive military or diplomatic policies.[51]

Bismarck was, however, concerned about having alienated Russia.[52] As a remedy, he sought to rebuild the League of the Three Emperors, indirectly by pursuing an Austro-German alliance. Such an alliance would isolate Russia, motivating it to seek better relations with Germany. The kaiser was skeptical of isolating Russia in this way, but Bismarck eventually convinced him to go along.[53] In October 1879, Germany and Austria-Hungary agreed to a defensive alliance that required each signatory to assist the other in the case of a Russian attack.[54] As Bismarck instructed Schweinitz, the German ambassador to Vienna, "We must strive for a closer understanding with Austria that will lead to an organic relationship that cannot be dissolved without approval by the parliamentary bodies of both countries."[55]

Across Europe, reactions to the alliance and what it foretold about German intentions were mixed. France feared that the alliance would give Germany a free hand to attack it. In response, Bismarck labored to convince Paris that the alliance was not directed at France. He assured the French ambassador to Vienna, Charles Raymond de Saint-Vallier, that the alliance was motivated by Russian hostility. Surprisingly, given its unhappy history with Germany, the French government seemingly accepted Bismarck's explanation, and, as I will detail below, a period of Franco-German détente followed.[56]

Reassured that the alliance was not directed against France, Britain offered its informal support of the pact. Disraeli wrote, "I believe that an alliance between [Austria-Hungary, Germany, and Britain], at this moment, might probably be hailed with something like enthusiasm by the country."[57]

Though British perfidy ultimately prevented such an alliance, Bismarck now knew that he need not fear British participation in an anti-German coalition.

Russia, of course, was most displeased by the alliance. If it was not directed against France, then it could only be directed against Russia. St. Petersburg faced two strategic alternatives. It could seek a countervailing alliance, most likely with France, or it could attempt to repair its relationship with Germany, as Bismarck had hoped it would. Actively balancing against Germany in the short term promised to be costlier than postponing such behavior into the future. St. Petersburg chose the more cooperative approach. "A friendly Prussia places us in the privileged position of being the only power in Europe," leading Russian diplomat Peter Saburov wrote to the tsar, "which need fear no attack and which can reduce its budget without risk, as our August Master did after the Crimean War."[58] Facing the choice of costly competition or beneficial, short-term cooperation, Russia chose cooperation. Russia's leaders were relieved to be able to focus on immediate threats rather than the long-term threat potentially posed by Germany.

COOPERATION CONTINUES: THE RETURN OF THE LEAGUE
OF THE THREE EMPERORS

In my argument, it is the intersection of a rising power's longer time horizons and existing powers' short time horizons that creates conditions conducive to cooperation. Thus far, the evidence has illustrated this logic at work: the more European powers focused on the short term, the less concerned they were with the long-term rise of Germans.

Bismarck continued to seek methods of reassuring other European great powers, including reviving the League of the Three Emperors. This idea gained additional momentum following the Liberal party victory in British parliamentary elections in April 1880. The new Liberal prime minister, William Gladstone, advocated a return to the Concert of Europe, an idea that was anathema to Bismarck.[59] The British ambassador in Berlin, Odo Russell, reported that Gladstone's election caused "a perfectly ridiculous panic in Berlin" because of "the terror Mr. Gladstone inspires Bismarck and the German court with."[60] The election of Gladstone simultaneously meant that Britain became less interested in advancing its relationship with Germany while Germany became more interested in reinvigorating its relationship with Europe's conservative monarchies.

On June 18, 1881, the League of the Three Emperors was renewed in Berlin.[61] The renewal of the league represented a return to the three principles that had guided German foreign policy since 1871. It kept Germany in the coalition of the three in Europe. It isolated France. And it unified the three monarchical empires in Europe. All the while, it reassured other states of Germany's long-term intentions, allowing Europe's leaders to focus on short-term threats and opportunities.

For Austria-Hungary and Russia, the short-term benefits of cooperating outweighed any long-term risks introduced by such a strategy. Had German intentions been more clearly malign, the agreement would have been harder to reach, especially for Russia, but continuing uncertainty actually made this cooperation possible. Russia, now led by Alexander III, had been left isolated, alone, and fearful by the Austro-German alliance. St. Petersburg was even further concerned that Britain would join with Germany and Austria, threatening Russian interests in the Black Sea region.[62] While the initial league in 1873 had been mostly symbolic, the renewed league addressed the very real short-term security concerns of Europe's conservative powers, especially Russia.

The final piece of Bismarck's intricate web of pacts and alliances was the Triple Alliance of 1882, which joined Germany, Austria-Hungary, and Italy together in apparent opposition to France.[63] For Italy, the alliance provided a valuable short-term guarantee against its colonial rival. For Austria, the pact alleviated any concern about Italian irredentism, allowing Austria to concentrate on the Balkans. For Germany, it provided further insurance against the possibility that France and Russia might come together to oppose it.[64] Again, little concern was expressed about the potential long-term threat posed by Germany as other more immediate threats demanded attention.

THE INTERSECTION OF LONG AND SHORT TIME HORIZONS: THE FRANCO-GERMAN DÉTENTE

Great power cooperation with Germany during this period was mostly passive. That is, it was not necessarily designed to make Germany more powerful, but by continuing to eschew balancing alliances and by maintaining economic and diplomatic relations, it facilitated Germany's continued rise.

Germany's efforts to reassure others about its intentions even included its perpetual adversary, France. If any country ought to have been expected to adopt more assertive competitive strategies toward Germany in the late nineteenth century, it was France. Yet France did not balance against Germany during this period; instead, it enjoyed a cooperative détente with Berlin. Bismarck sought to manage a fine line of keeping France isolated but not feeling threatened. Especially in the wake of the War in Sight crisis, the chancellor understood that threatening behavior toward France could backfire by drawing attention to Germany's uncertain long-term intentions. Conveniently for Bismarck, domestic economic and political issues as well as colonial ventures gave France incentives to focus on the short term rather than concerning itself with long-term German intentions.

Bismarck worked hard throughout the 1870s to distract French attention from any revanchist goals in Alsace and Lorraine. Nothing about German behavior constituted "costly signals" that only a friendly Germany would have undertaken, but as long as Berlin refrained from aggressive behavior, it seemingly allowed cooperation to continue. Only a year after the War in Sight crisis, former French president Louis-Adolphe Thiers observed, "Hitherto France and Germany have been like two greyhounds coupled to one leash and pulling in opposite directions. Things have now changed. We are gradually coming to pursue the same course and can arrive at an understanding."[65] Four years later, this sentiment only seemed to have strengthened, even if it did come with some reservations. "But if England is hostile to us, if her hostility encourages that of Italy," the French ambassador to Germany, Saint-Vallier, argued, "then the friendship of Germany becomes indispensable to our security. I stand for this; that we have the friendship of Germany, not her protection. I wish to be a friend, not a vassal."[66] An important determinant of how states resolve now-or-later dilemmas is the nature of the other threats that a state faces both in the short and long term. Given short-term uncertainty about France's relationship with England and Italy, the space was opened for it to engage in pragmatic short-term cooperation with Germany.

Bismarck was only too happy to reciprocate.[67] Explaining his support of the French occupation of Tunis to Saint-Vallier, Bismarck concluded, "The interests of my politics commands this policy, because, not only does the Emperor wish to die glorious and tranquil, but because I do not wish to have another war on my hands . . . I give up adventure and I stand for calm and security, guaranteed by friendly relations with our neighbors, especially with you."[68] On a different occasion, Bismarck again sought to strengthen ties with France through Saint-Vallier: "I am convinced that a great country like France needs to find satisfaction in her foreign policy, and as I cannot unhappily give it to you in Alsace-Lorraine, I desire to make it somewhere where no German interests conflict with French interests. . . . I prefer to tell you frankly, I desire and hope to turn your thoughts from Metz and Strasburg in aiding you to find some satisfaction."[69]

On the one hand, these were empty words that even a German leader with malign intentions would have issued. On the other hand, however, they reinforced a French preference for cooperation during this period. France faced a choice of short-term opportunities for colonial gain supported by Bismarck or a longer-term aggressive balancing strategy against Germany that would have been costly (and likely unsuccessful) in the short term. It chose the cooperative approach to the benefit of both France and Germany.

ELONGATING TIME HORIZONS: THE EFFECT OF BISMARCK'S EXPERIMENT IN COLONIALISM

As with the War in Sight crisis, not everything Bismarck did advanced his foreign policy goals. In the mid-1880s, Bismarck's newfound interest in colonialism generated concern about Germany's long-term intentions. Up until that point, Bismarck had enjoyed the colonial competition between other European powers, which only made them less likely to balance against Germany. For example, he welcomed the dispute between France and England over Egypt. In Egypt, the chancellor supported Paris but attempted to do so in a way that would not fully alienate London.[70] All of this served Germany well: the dispute prevented any alliance between Britain and France against Germany while also keeping them focused on the short-term threat from each other rather than on any long-term threat from Germany. In Egypt, Bismarck had accomplished his goal: "a political situation in which all the powers except France would need us, and would be deprived of the coalition against us by their relations with each other."[71]

Bismarck, himself, had strenuously avoided any colonial endeavors. Germany's priorities lay in Europe, and German colonialism would only draw unwanted attention to German intentions by placing Germany in competition with other European powers.[72] Looking back in 1888, Bismarck told a German advocate of colonialism: "Your map of Africa is very fine, but my map of Africa is here in Europe. Here is Russia and here is France and here we are in the middle. That is my map of Africa."[73]

Surprisingly, then, Bismarck began to explore opportunities for German colonies in the summer of 1883.[74] As much as leaders like Bismarck may want to avoid behavior that provokes a more competitive response, they also are responsive to other pressures that push them in that direction and lead them to be less patient than might behoove their long-term interests. In this case, a combination of domestic and international factors motivated Bismarck's interest. Paul M. Kennedy summarizes the domestic benefits: "A successful colonial policy might well increase exports, assist the economy and help— to a greater or lesser degree—to reduce the prospects for social unrest. . . . These successes would enhance Bismarck's own position, identifying him yet again in the public's eye as the great national hero."[75] Leaders of the German manufacturing sector sought sources of raw materials as well as potential new markets at a time when Germany and the rest of Europe were mired in a deep recession.[76] Internationally, Bismarck sensed that European preoccupation with the situations in Egypt, the Balkans, and the Near East provided a permissive international environment in which he could respond to domestic imperatives without necessarily provoking an international reaction.[77]

German tobacco entrepreneur Adolf Lüderitz led the German charge into Africa. As German exploration expanded in southwestern Africa, it inevitably butted up against British imperial interests.[78] Such tension made Bismarck skittish, but German business interests prevented him from abandoning Germany's search for colonies.[79]

In December 1884, the British Parliament approved an extraordinary expenditure of £5.5 million to protect British colonial interests in response to

Germany's increasing imperial behavior. In response, Bismarck dispatched his son Herbert to London in an effort to reassure the British. Herbert told Gladstone, "We only hope to do [colonialism] in a very small and humble manner, and we are in doing it giving to you the strongest proof of confidence in the future friendship of the two countries."[80]

Germany and England eventually reached an agreement in October 1886 to carve up southwestern Africa, but for Bismarck, Germany's foray into colonialism had hardly been worth it. Later, in his famous 1907 memorandum on Anglo-German relations, Sir Eyre Crowe highlighted Bismarck's "disregard of the elementary rules of straightforward and honorable dealing" during this period.[81] Rather than keep others focused on short-term opportunities for cooperation with Germany, Bismarck's emerging interest in colonialism drew attention to long-term German intentions. Elongating European time horizons was counter to Bismarck's general strategy during this period. As historian Hans-Ulrich Wehler concludes, "German imperialism can be seen on the one hand as a defensive strategy in domestic politics. On the other hand, it introduced an aggressive component into Germany's foreign relations."[82]

In the end, German colonialism was an important hiccup in Bismarck's grand strategy of deflecting attention from his long-term intentions. At the same time, once again, there was no concerted balancing effort against Germany in response. While Berlin's relationship with London was wounded, it was not so damaged that London sought ways to curtail Germany's continued emergence as a great power. Even as he stuck his toe into the waters of colonialism, Bismarck again turned to reassuring others about long-term German intentions.

BISMARCK'S PATIENCE: KEEPING FRANCE ISOLATED

"We are surrounded by friends in Europe," Bismarck told the Reichstag in January 1885.[83] Despite his foray into colonialism, Bismarck's goal of convincing the rest of Europe that Germany did not necessarily harbor malign intentions appeared to be succeeding. The Franco-German détente continued, Anglo-German tension over colonial issues was subsiding, and the League of the Three Emperors had been renewed in March of the previous year. During 1885, however, the complexion of European politics began to change, and by 1887 Bismarck faced a far more challenging foreign policy environment.

The transformation began with the fall of Jules Ferry's government in France at the end of March 1885. Ferry had been the primary French advocate of détente with Germany, and the success of royalist parties in October elections indicated a resurgence of revanchist sentiment in France.[84] As a government came to power that was more skeptical of both the benefits of short-term cooperation and future German intentions, the pressures increased to do something sooner rather than later about the continuing rise of Germany.

The new prime minister, Charles de Freycinet, supported a foreign policy that would shift focus away from colonial ventures and back to the Continent. "The experience of 1882 [in Egypt] taught me; I knew we could not count on the cabinet at Berlin," Freycinet observed on taking office. "[Bismarck] did not foster any black designs with regard to France, but he was pleased to see her isolated, weakened; to keep her so, any means was good to him. He watched jealously to see that we did not concert with Russia and he used the Egyptian question to create distrust between England and us."[85] Unlike his predecessor, Freycinet understood Bismarck's motives for seeking détente with France. Simultaneously, other developments, including the appointment of "General Revanche," Georges Boulanger, as minister of war, signaled a desire to reclaim France's lost provinces.[86] The Franco-German détente was effectively over, and Bismarck again faced the challenge of how to keep France isolated and others dissuaded from acting sooner rather than later to counter Germany's growth.

Surprisingly, then, Bismarck's response to renewed revanchism in France was to present a new military bill to the Reichstag on November 5, 1886. The bill, known as the Septennat, proposed a seven-year military budget plan beginning on April 1, 1887. The new budget included a roughly 10 percent increase in the size of the military by 41,135 men to a total of 468,409 as well as an annual budget allocation of M24 million to the military. The extant military appropriations bill was not due for renewal until the following year, so Bismarck's proposal seemed both precipitous and threatening.[87]

The Septennat produced both domestic and international opposition. Domestically, the Reichstag expressed reluctance to approve the expense of the new bill, but Bismarck made it clear that if it refused, he would simply dissolve Parliament and reconstitute it with members more amenable. Internationally, Bismarck well understood that the seven-year bill would raise fears about Germany's longer-term intentions.

Addressing the Reichstag on January 11, 1887, the chancellor attempted to placate domestic audiences while reassuring international audiences. Bismarck argued that it was French aggression that had driven the need for the new bill. "Is this epoch of frontier warfare with France at an end, or is it not?" Bismarck asked. "I can only voice my own suspicion in this regard, and say that it is not at an end; this would need a change in the entire French character and the whole frontier situation."[88] Despite Bismarck's plea, the Reichstag initially refused to approve the new budget, after which Bismarck carried through on his threat to reconstitute the Reichstag.[89]

Internationally, Bismarck sought to renew and reorient a variety of Germany's relationships in an effort to keep France isolated and alleviate concern about the new military bill. The Triple Alliance between Germany, Austria, and Italy was renewed for an additional five years.[90] Bismarck also encouraged Britain and Italy to join in the First Mediterranean Agreement, which sought to reinforce the status quo in the Mediterranean while opposing any further French colonial ambitions. Austria-Hungary eventually acceded to the accord, and Italy and Spain reached their own agreement. The sum total of these agreements, all encouraged by Bismarck, was to solidify in Europe and in the Mediterranean a status quo that was very much in Germany's interests. While Germany was positioned to continue its growth unhindered, Bismarck had managed to create a network of agreements that primarily constrained French freedom to respond to Germany.

Importantly, the First Mediterranean Agreement included a rare British agreement with a Continental power. Concerns about access through Russia to its colonies in southern and central Asia and continuing problems in Egypt convinced the new, Conservative prime minister, Lord Salisbury, that such a commitment could further British interests. Salisbury advised the queen: "If, in the present grouping of nations, which Prince Bismarck tells us is now taking place, England was left out in isolation, it might well happen that the adversaries, who are coming against each other on the Continent, might treat the English Empire as divisible booty. . . . The interests of Italy are so closely parallel to our own that we can combine with her safely."[91] Once again, short-term opportunities to benefit from cooperation trumped any concerns about long-term German intentions. Faced with a strategic choice of how to protect its interests, London chose to reach an agreement with Italy, an ally of Germany, primarily out of concern for Russia. The potential long-term dangers of joining together with an ally of Germany's took a backseat to more immediate concerns, especially other relative threats.

REASSURANCE AND MYOPIA: THE REINSURANCE TREATY

The one piece of the European puzzle remaining for Bismarck was Russia. Unstable Austro-Russian relations undermined the League of the Three Emperors, which was allowed to lapse in June 1887.[92] Advisers to Alexander III were divided in their views of Germany. Some, like prominent journalist Mikhail Katkov, did not trust Germany and preferred to seek a relationship with France. Others, like Foreign Minister Nikolay Giers, saw value in maintaining friendly relations with Berlin.

The more pro-German faction eventually prevailed with the tsar. In May and June, Bismarck and Peter Shuvalov, the Russian ambassador to Germany, negotiated a secret agreement now known as the Reinsurance Treaty. Signed on June 17, the treaty committed both signatory powers to maintain for three years a policy of "benevolent neutrality" should the other power become involved in a war with a third power. This commitment would not be binding if either power started a war with France or Austria-Hungary. The agreement also recognized the historic interests of Russia in the Balkans and "the European and mutually obligatory character of the principle of the closure of the Straits of the Bosphorus and Dardanelles." Russia was also granted a free hand in Bulgaria to establish "a regular and legal government."[93]

For Russia, the treaty guaranteed three important short-term interests. First, Russia was assured that it would not face an opposition coalition that included Germany. Second, it protected the territorial status quo in the Balkans while recognizing Russian influence in Bulgaria. Third, it appreciated Russian interests in controlling the straits.[94] Once again, the benefits of short-term cooperation with Germany outweighed any concern about long-term German intentions. The treaty simultaneously satisfied Russia's short-term security needs while allowing Germany to continue to grow toward realizing its long-term potential.

The Reinsurance Treaty was yet another piece of the intricate web that Bismarck famously created. Germany still maintained its alliance with Austria, but the Reinsurance Treaty with Russia complemented that commitment. The First Mediterranean Agreement among Britain, Austria, and Italy served Bismarck's interests in maintaining the status quo in the Balkans and the Near East. Finally, in December 1887, Austria, Italy, and Britain signed the Second Mediterranean Agreement, which guaranteed the integrity of the Ottoman Empire against Russia (thereby offsetting the commitment Germany had made in the Reinsurance Treaty).[95] The short-term machinations of European diplomacy left little room for considering the long-term threat posed by Germany.

By the end of 1887, then, Bismarck had managed to accomplish his goal of preventing any effort to impede Germany as it continued to grow more powerful. Despite various domestic changes in Britain and France and despite an ill-conceived exploration of colonialism, Germany remained unencumbered by any balancing alliance. Throughout, Bismarck sought to satisfy the short-term interests of other European powers, which effectively distracted their attention from any threat posed by Germany. Even if Bismarck could not credibly signal outright benign intentions, he could maintain enough uncertainty about those long-term intentions to allow short-term cooperation to continue. As Pflanze concludes, "Whatever may be said of faith and honor, [the Mediterranean Agreements and the Reinsurance Treaty] served not only Germany's interests but also Europe's by keeping France and Russia apart for the time being."[96] As the short-term interests of the declining powers continued to be satisfied, the rising power benefited and sought to prolong that cooperation.

The Decaying of Bismarck's Order: How Beliefs about Intentions Explain the Demise of Cooperation

Not all trends were in a positive direction for Bismarck. On November 10, 1887, the German government instructed the Reichsbank to stop using

Russian securities as collateral, in what is known as the Lombard-Verbot. Predictably, a complete sell-off of Russian securities in the German exchange markets followed, and the price of those securities plummeted as a consequence. There is some debate over the motive for the Lombard-Verbot. Pflanze argues that Bismarck ordered it out of concern for a possible Russian military buildup, while Kennan points to more direct economic motives.[97] Either way, the effect of the Lombard-Verbot was to compel Russia to look for other economic partners, including France. As expected, when the emerging potential threat seeks short-term advantage, it is likely to draw the attention of existing powers. By encouraging economic ties between St. Petersburg and Paris, the ban on Russian securities provided a foundation for closer political ties.[98] In short, the Lombard-Verbot undermined much of the benefit for Russo-German relations that the Reinsurance Treaty had created and opened the possibility that Russia would look elsewhere for diplomatic and economic partners.

At the same time, the stability of Bismarck's order was also challenged by yet another crisis in southern Europe. On July 7, 1887, the Bulgarian Parliament elected as its prince Ferdinand of Coburg—the favored candidate of Vienna—against the wishes of Russia. As tension grew, Bismarck reassured Vienna, London, and Rome and warned St. Petersburg that he intended to support Austrian interests in Bulgaria. "German policy will always be obliged," asserted the German chancellor, "to enter the line of battle if the independence of Austria-Hungary were to be menaced by Russian aggression, or if England or Italy were to be exposed to invasion by French armies."[99] While the crisis continued to keep Europe focused on the short term, it was also an additional source of tension between Germany and Russia.

Meanwhile, rumors began to circulate that Russia was preparing to attack Poland. The Russian Thirteenth Cavalry Division was transferred from Moscow to the Warsaw military district, while St. Petersburg's rhetoric became increasingly anti-Austrian. In response, Bismarck's principal military adviser, Helmuth von Moltke, suggested that Germany consider launching a preemptive war against Russia.[100] By early 1888, the crisis over the fate of Bulgaria had raised the probability of war in Europe to the highest it had been in a decade.[101]

But Bismarck understood that a war in Europe would disrupt the balance of power in Europe and would also likely resolve the uncertainty about German long-term intentions in a way detrimental to German interests. If Bismarck's goal was to prevent assertive balancing against Germany, then any conflict involving Germany would be counterproductive. The chancellor worked both to assuage Austrian fears and to calm Russian outrage over the election of Ferdinand. To reassure Russia, Bismarck made public the defensive terms of the Austro-German alliance. And to satisfy Austria, Ferdinand was permitted to stay in power, and the crisis in Bulgaria passed peacefully.[102]

On February 6, 1888, while still trying to get the Reichstag to pass the Septennat, Bismarck delivered one of his most well-known speeches. "We Germans fear God, and nothing else on Earth!" Bismarck proclaimed. But Bismarck also had a more conciliatory message to deliver: "And so I declare that the ill-feeling which has been voiced against us by Russian public opinion and particularly in the Russian press will not deter us from supporting any diplomatic steps which Russia can take to win back her influence on Bulgaria, as soon as Russia makes her wishes known."[103] Once again, Bismarck appears to have understood that the key to the continued success of his foreign policy was maintaining Russia's, as well as others', preference to defer active balancing against Germany until later.

WILHELM II'S IMPATIENCE: THE TRANSFORMATION OF EUROPEAN POLITICS BEGINS

On March 8, 1888, the ninety-two-year-old German emperor Wilhelm I died in his palace in Berlin. His immediate successor, Frederick III, lasted only three months before succumbing to cancer of the throat. Wilhelm II, Wilhelm I's grandson, then became kaiser.

The new kaiser and his advisers did not share Bismarck's view of the value of maintaining good relations with Russia. Unlike his grandfather, Wilhelm II had little affection for Russia. Military leaders like Moltke and Alfred Waldersee, who had both advocated for preemptive war against Russia and supported a closer relationship with Austria-Hungary, had great influence over Wilhelm II.[104] Less than a month after ascending to the throne, the new kaiser was persuaded by Bismarck to visit Russia, but the visit did little to dispel Wilhelm's distrust.[105] Bismarck's commitment to avoiding overly provocative actions was left in doubt with the change in German leadership.

While Wilhelm's advisers and Bismarck continued to debate Germany's relationship with Russia, Russia's relationship with France showed continuing signs of improvement. In October 1888, negotiations began that culminated in December with the first of a series of French loans to Russia. Military ties between the two powers also increased. The tsar's brother, Vladimir, visited France and purchased five hundred thousand French-manufactured rifles.[106]

With Franco-Russian relations improving and Bismarck maintaining his goal of being "one of three" in any European coalitions, the only direction for the chancellor to turn next was toward London. In January 1889, Bismarck proposed an Anglo-German alliance to Salisbury: "My idea is that, if His Majesty agrees, a treaty shall be concluded between the English and the German governments, by which each pledges help to the other if France in the course of the next one, two, or three years, as the case may be, should attack either power."[107] Explaining his policy to the Reichstag at the end of

January, Bismarck stated, "I regard England as the old traditional ally, whose interests do not clash with ours."[108]

Simultaneously, Bismarck encouraged Salisbury to push the Naval Defense Act through Parliament. The Naval Defense Act introduced the "two-power standard" into British naval planning: the British navy would strive to maintain superiority over the combined strength of the next two largest naval powers, which, conveniently enough, were France and Russia at this point.[109] If Bismarck was going have a British ally, then he wanted that ally to be as strong as possible.

Ultimately, the Naval Defense Act passed, but Salisbury declined Bismarck's offer of an alliance, leaving it "on the table, without saying yes or no."[110] Combined with traditional British reticence at joining Continental alliances, Salisbury's skepticism of the intentions of both Bismarck and the new kaiser precluded a formal arrangement. Nonetheless, Wilhelm was invited to visit England in the summer of 1889 as a symbol of continuing friendship, and Bismarck succeeded at maintaining at least uncertainty about German intentions, even if the resulting cooperation would fall short of an alliance.

Wilhelm's visit only aggravated tension in the Russo-German relationship.[111] While Bismarck had worked carefully to avoid any provocation that might lead Russia to move even closer to France, the young kaiser was not particularly concerned with salvaging relations with St. Petersburg. During the trip, Queen Victoria named Wilhelm as an honorary admiral of the British fleet. The kaiser left England enthralled: "Should . . . the will of Providence lay the heavy burden on us of fighting for our homes and destinies, then may the British fleet be seen forging ahead side by side with the Germans, and the 'Red Coat' marching to victory with the 'Pomeranian Grenadier'!"[112]

To be clear, Bismarck wanted to pursue a stronger relationship with Britain, but he was more concerned than the kaiser to do it in a way that would not alienate Russia. In October, Tsar Alexander visited Berlin while traveling back to St. Petersburg from a trip to Denmark.[113] Both Bismarck and Wilhelm offered reassurances to the tsar, but this was only a temporary abatement in growing Russo-German tension.

THE TIDE TURNS: BISMARCK'S RESIGNATION
AND THE AFTERMATH

The guiding principles of Bismarck's foreign policy were becoming harder to sustain. Wilhelm II's provocative behavior was prompting others to consider balancing against Germany and leaving Germany with only Austria-Hungary as an ally. Germany had managed to relieve France of its isolation by pushing Russia toward Paris. And Bismarck's battles with the kaiser's military advisers were making his domestic position less tenable. While Bismarck understood the advantages of distracting others from the long-term implications of Germany's continued rise, the provocative behavior of other German leaders would ultimately prompt more concern about Berlin's long-term intentions, transforming uncertainty into risk to which other European powers would respond.

All that said, in late 1889, the Russian ambassador in Berlin, Peter Shuvalov, approached Bismarck about possibly renewing the Reinsurance Treaty, which was set to expire in June 1890. Shuvalov thought it best to act sooner rather than later given the emerging difficulty in Russo-German relations. Wilhelm initially offered surprising support for a renewal of the treaty, but this support was fleeting.[114] On March 15, 1890, the German consulate in Kiev sent a report to Berlin of ominous Russian military preparations. Wilhelm was alarmed: "It is perfectly clear from the reports that the Russians are strategically concentrating their forces and are on the point of declaring war. . . . It is high time to warn the Austrians and take countermeasures."[115]

The divide between Bismarck and Wilhelm over Russia was too much to bear. On March 18, Bismarck submitted his resignation.[116] "I could not retain . . . the ministry of foreign affairs," Bismarck wrote in his letter of resignation, "after the recent decisions arrived at by Your Majesty, for by so doing I should be calling into question all the successes obtained in our Russian policy during the reign of your two predecessors, in spite of unfavorable circumstances."[117] Georg von Caprivi was appointed the new chancellor, and Baron Adolf Marschall von Bieberstein was selected as the new minister of foreign affairs.

The new German leadership was allied with the anti-Russian military influence of Waldersee and Moltke. Only two months after their appointment, Wilhelm II opened a new session of the Reichstag by proposing a new military bill. Moltke followed by advocating an expansion of the German empire. Surely, France and Russia would notice.[118] Bismarck's goal of maintaining enough uncertainty about long-term German intentions to prevent balancing against Germany had been abandoned.

Bismarck's resignation and the appointment of his anti-Russian replacements had dramatic consequences for European diplomacy. This is not to suggest a "great man" argument in which Bismarck himself was critical but rather simply to say that his successors had a different approach to German foreign policy. Given the continued growth of Germany, maintaining the useful uncertainty about German intentions may have proved as difficult for Bismarck as it was for his successors, but what is clear is that Bismarck's successors abandoned any effort to offer reassuring signals about long-term German intentions. As a consequence, Europe's other great powers became more inclined to assertively balance against Germany. As Laurence B. Packard writes, "Bismarck's dismissal early in 1890 removed the last obstacle in the way of Russia's approach to France—not so much because in him, now that the old emperor was gone, the tsar had lost the last German friend in whom he had confidence, as that the new Kaiser was launching an entirely new policy."[119]

France and Britain were uncertain how to react to Bismarck's dismissal. Nobody in France mistook Bismarck for a friend, but at least he was reasonably consistent and predictable.[120] His departure led to concern about long-term German intentions that Bismarck had previously managed to avoid. Langer writes, "By 1890 [the French] had come to believe that Bismarck was a force for peace and that there was little likelihood of his provoking a conflict. But it was generally believed that the 'warlike' young Kaiser, who had chosen a military man as his chancellor, would attempt to emulate Frederick the Great and would initiate his personal rule with a foreign war."[121]

In London, Bismarck's resignation raised similar questions. Instead of considering an alliance with Germany, Britain now considered allying against Germany. Bismarck's dismissal was, wrote Salisbury, "an enormous calamity of which the effects will be felt in every part of Europe."[122] As others became more certain about German intentions, the resolution of the dilemma over whether to balance now or later shifted toward now.

WILHELM'S NEW COURSE: QUESTIONS ABOUT THE FUTURE

The first critical decision facing the Caprivi government was whether to renew the Reinsurance Treaty. Unsurprisingly, the government quickly convinced Wilhelm to allow the treaty to lapse. For the Russians and, in particular, for the pro-German foreign minister Nikolay Giers, this was an ominous development.[123] "The new chancellor's views about our relations are very significant," wrote the tsar after being informed by Giers of the German decision. "It appears to me that Bismarck was right when he said that the policy of the German Emperor would alter the day when he, Bismarck, retired."[124] The Reinsurance Treaty expired on June 18, leaving Russian leaders increasingly concerned about future German intentions. As Langer concludes, "By refusing even to discuss the continuance of the old treaty relation they gave Russia every reason to think that a thorough-going revision of German international relations was intended."[125]

Wilhelm had embarked on his "New Course" foreign policy.[126] As Germany moved away from Russia, it would move toward Britain. In May, Berlin and London began negotiations over the Heligoland Treaty, which granted territorial control of Zanzibar and Witu in Africa to Great Britain in exchange for German control of the North Sea island of Heligoland.[127] Coincidentally and symbolically, Caprivi informed the Reichstag of the treaty on the same day that the Reinsurance Treaty expired.[128]

Wilhelm visited Britain a month later, and the preeminent historian A. J. P. Taylor identifies the summer of 1890 as the "high-water mark of intimacy" in Anglo-German relations.[129] The London *Daily Telegraph* surmised,

"Everywhere in Europe the Treaty is regarded as the prelude of a not formal but nevertheless sound Anglo-German Alliance." Political commentator Gabriel Monod wrote in the *Contemporary Review* in July 1890: "It is difficult to avoid seeing in the treaty a partial accession of England to the Triple Alliance and a design on the part of the two nations to make common cause, in some degree, against France and Russia."[130]

Britain and Germany stopped short of any formal alliance, but the improvement in their relationship was noticed across Europe. Meanwhile, Russo-German relations continued to deteriorate. Wilhelm and Caprivi visited with their Russian counterparts at Narva in late August, but the meeting was unproductive. If anything, concern about future German intentions only scared the Russians further away from Germany and toward France.[131] Unlike Bismarck, Wilhelm and Caprivi failed to distract others, including Russia, from worrying about the future of German foreign policy.

BALANCING AT LAST: THE FRANCO-RUSSIAN ALLIANCE

The final consummation of the Franco-Russian alliance did not come easily. In February 1891, Wilhelm sent his mother, Empress Frederick, to Paris in an ill-fated attempt to salvage Franco-German relations.[132] While the empress's visit generated concern in St. Petersburg, Russia was reassured after the disastrous trip. "The *entente cordiale* which has been so happily established between France and Russia is the best guarantee of peace," Giers observed. "While the Triple Alliance ruins itself in armaments, the intimated accord of the two countries is necessary to maintain a just balance of power."[133]

In May 1891, the Triple Alliance (Germany, Austria-Hungary, and Italy) was renewed with an added protocol recognizing Britain as an associate member of the alliance.[134] London demurred from fuller participation, but even the associate status was enough to raise concern in France and Russia. In early July, Wilhelm again visited London, where mutual expressions of support were offered.[135] After that visit, Antoine de Laboulaye, the French ambassador in St. Petersburg, had a conversation with Giers about formalizing the Franco-Russian relationship.[136]

Five days later, the French naval fleet visited the Russian port of Kronstadt for a successful two-week stay. French foreign minister Alexandre Ribot then instructed Laboulaye to seek an agreement in which it was "understood that if one of the Powers of the Triple Alliance comes to mobilize its forces, France and Russia, without having need of prior consultation, will mobilize theirs immediately and simultaneously."[137]

France and Russia sought different protections from the Franco-Russian alliance. France was most directly concerned with security from a German attack. Russia wanted a more general agreement that would help to protect its interests in the Near East while also offering security on the Continent.

By late August, Arthur Mohrenheim, the Russian ambassador in Paris, and Ribot exchanged formal diplomatic notes.[138]

Despite his skepticism about the young kaiser, Giers continued to try to salvage Russo-German relations, mostly by reinvigorating commercial ties.[139] But unlike their predecessors, the new German leaders evinced little interest in maintaining productive relations with Russia. Three issues, in particular, divided the countries: disagreements over import tariffs, Germany's conciliatory posture toward Poland, and continuing tension in Bulgaria.[140]

The Franco-Russian alliance remained an informal, political agreement for the following year and a half, until the alliance was finally formalized at the end of 1893 as the first instance of active balancing against Germany. Over the course of those eighteen months, Russo-German relations continued to deteriorate.[141] During the summer of 1893, the Reichstag approved a new military bill increasing the size of the German army just as the Russo-German tariff war was intensifying. Simultaneously, a war scare in Asia over the fate of Siam increased tensions between France and Britain, driving France even more toward Russia.[142] Once the tsar was convinced that the alliance would not commit Russia to participating in any French revanchist plans, the two sides reached an agreement.[143] Packard concludes, "France was relieved from her isolation and given some assurance of her national safety, and Russia saved her position in the Eastern Question from isolation and acquired the support of France."[144]

The Franco-Russian alliance was the first concerted effort to balance against Germany since its unification in 1871. It was prompted by the short-term security situation in Europe as well as by the concerns about long-term German intentions that the new leadership generated. German provocations raised long-term concerns that led to immediate balancing efforts. As Taylor succinctly puts it, "The system by which Germany directed the affairs of Europe came to an end in August 1892."[145] Frederick L. Schuman writes, "The diplomatic hegemony of the continent which Germany had enjoyed since 1871 was undermined and the coalition which she had created for the maintenance of the status quo was now faced by another coalition designed to change the existing territorial and political equilibrium."[146] With the abandonment of Bismarck's strategies of distracting other great powers from the potential long-term threat posed by Germany's rise came the alliance that Bismarck had always feared.

Explaining Cooperation and Competition with Imperial Germany

What best explains the pattern of cooperation and competition with Germany in the two decades after its unification? At the end of this period, why did relations shift away from cooperation and toward competition? The evidence best accords with the dynamics that I have argued explain variation in cooperation and competition between rising and existing great powers. Bismarck successfully manipulated others' beliefs about German intentions. Other European powers opted to procrastinate on addressing a potential German threat, in large part because there were more pressing threats to confront during this period and also because the costs of doing so more immediately would have been high. Long-term uncertainty left European reactions indeterminate until that uncertainty became more manageable risk. When Europe's policies toward Germany did change in 1890, it was primarily as a result of a shift in beliefs about Germany's long-term intentions, not its capabilities. As Bismarck claimed, "Germany, like contemporary Austria and England, belonged to the class of satisfied nations, 'saturated' as the late Prince Metternich expressed it, and is therefore pacific and anxious to keep things as they are."[147] Whether or not this was true of imperial Germany is not as critical to my argument as that Bismarck worked hard to convince others it was true. As David Calleo concludes, "Success depended not only upon Germany's remaining the balancing power in so many awkward triangles, but also upon convincing the rest of the world that Germany was a sated power."[148] As long as Germany was focused on long-term gains and other European powers were compelled to focus on the short term, cooperation in Europe was possible. When the new German leadership sought more short-term opportunities for gain, the level of concern about long-term German intentions increased concomitantly.

Bismarck understood that uncertainty about his intentions served him well, and whenever there were indications of more aggressive intentions—such as the War in Sight crisis or Germany's experiment with colonialism—Bismarck worked to alleviate any concern. Bismarck saw each instance of apparent German impatience as a mistake in retrospect. Bismarck's successors saw value in a more aggressive approach to foreign policy. As Germany shifted to capturing more opportunities now, other European powers similarly moved toward balancing against Germany now rather than later.

More specifically, consider the behavior of each of Germany's main interlocutors during this period. Again, even in a period of multipolarity, states tended to approach their relations with each other and with Germany in a sequential, dyadic manner. French cooperation with Germany during this period is perhaps most surprising. France had the most reasons to be fearful of Germany after 1871. It had been decisively defeated in the Franco-Prussian War, and Bismarck's future intentions were uncertain. Surprisingly, then, even France demonstrated a willingness to cooperate with Germany.

French strategy toward Germany during this period was largely passive. It did not actively assist in the rise of Germany, but it also did not actively seek to balance against it. This strategy is best attributed to a combination of German efforts to manipulate beliefs about its intentions and the prohibitive costs of balancing against Germany on its own. For most of the period, Paris had no allies available with which to balance against Germany, and the costs of France pursuing a more unilateral approach to active competition would have been prohibitive.

Bismarck aimed to forestall French efforts to form an anti-German balancing coalition by keeping France satisfied in the short term. He encouraged French colonialism in northern Africa, telling Saint-Vallier, the French ambassador in Berlin, "I think the pear is ripe and it is time for you to gather it. . . . I believe that the French people need some satisfaction for their *amour-propre*, and I sincerely desire to see them obtain what they want in the Mediterranean, their natural sphere of expansion. The more success they find in that sphere the less will they be moved to assert their grievances against us."[149] Satisfy France in the short-term with colonial acquisitions, and France would be less focused on addressing any threat from Germany. Colonial competition had the added benefit of distracting France from addressing any longer-term concerns.

The Franco-German détente came to an end with the rise of the Boulanger movement in 1885. For this patriotic, revanchist movement, reconciliation with Germany was inconceivable. General Jean-Baptiste-Marie Édouard Campenon, the French minister of war, succinctly observed, "What separates the two governments is the memory of the last war."[150] France, however, lacked a partner to ally with against Germany until Russo-German relations started to deteriorate after Bismarck left office and the decision was made to abandon the Reinsurance Treaty. Economic relations between France and Russia developed first, followed by diplomatic and then military relations. The culmination was the consummation of the Franco-Russian alliance.

In this case, there is little evidence to support either a buck-passing or an engagement explanation for French behavior. Offensive realists would explain cooperation as attempts to pass the buck for balancing to some other state. Buck-passing requires an initial recognition of a threat and then a conscious decision to get some other state to balance. While French leaders were ever aware of the danger on their border, there is little evidence of France actively trying to get others to pay the costs of balancing against Germany, and there was no reason for them to be confident that any other state would be willing to pay that cost. Moreover, offensive realism would expect strategies to shift in response to a state's capabilities, but the evidence in this case suggests that the Franco-Russian alliance was a product of changing beliefs about German intentions, not capabilities.

In the logic of engagement, cooperation ought to be aimed at providing short-term rewards and also at enmeshing the rising power in a stable international order. As the established great power facing its decline, France ought to have sought an institutionalized international order that would protect France over the long term. But French time horizons were short, and cooperation was primarily aimed at capturing short-term opportunities. It is unclear what, if any, international order France sought to bring Germany into during this period.

Instead, the French approach is best understood as a pragmatic, short-term-oriented strategy. The rewards in terms of colonialism were not insignificant for France, whereas the short-term costs of further confrontation could have been high. In response, one might argue that France had few options to balance against Germany, but that is, in part, the point. In the absence of any other power that was also concerned about long-term German intentions, it made little sense for France to pursue a more competitive strategy toward Germany. French strategy only began to shift when a government came to power that was more concerned with the historical relationship between France and Germany and an alliance partner that was increasingly concerned with long-term German intentions became available in the form of Russia.

As for Britain, Germany seemed to pose little immediate threat to British interests, especially given the lack of German colonial interests, at least initially. The economic benefits of trade with Germany were potentially substantial, whereas the costs of doing anything in the short term to hinder German growth would have been excessive. Unsurprisingly, then, the dominant British approach throughout this period was passive to active cooperation with Germany. This economic cooperation itself is not particularly surprising (it continued up until World War I), but what is surprising is the lack of any countervailing strategy designed to offset the emergence of a threat from Germany. Doing something now to address a potential long-term threat from Germany held little attraction for the traditionally perfidious British government.

As British historian A. A. W. Ramsay notes, "In 1871 there was no single power that could meet Germany on equal terms in war, nor were there many which equaled her in potential wealth and intellectual development."[151] Britain did not respond by balancing against Germany.[152] To the contrary, as Salisbury wrote in January 1880: "Germany is clearly cut out to be our ally. Matters will, of course, have changed if it should ever enter into Germany's head to desire Copenhagen or Rotterdam."[153] Like French leaders, British leaders were initially concerned by the War in Sight crisis, but within a year of the crisis, London considered seriously an alliance offer from Berlin. Trade with Britain played a considerable role in fostering German growth, and there were few signs of military competition between the two states.[154]

Two developments in the early 1880s prompted increased British concern about German long-term intentions. First, the election of the Liberal Gladstone ministry introduced skepticism about Bismarck's more Realpolitik ways. Second, Bismarck's foray into colonialism awakened concerns about long-term German intentions. Though England and Germany ultimately resolved their issues in Africa, Germany's exploration was worrisome.

Anglo-German relations improved when Berlin found an opportunity to assist Britain in the short term. The benefits of cooperation now led London to put off any need to balance against a continuously growing Germany. The

Mediterranean Agreement offered German support of British positions in the Mediterranean without much in exchange from London. Salisbury was reluctant to pull Bismarck's "chestnuts out of the fire" if a crisis emerged involving Germany, but the Mediterranean Agreement was useful for Britain.[155]

For the majority of the period studied in this chapter, British leaders favored cooperation over competition in relations with Germany. Rather than balance against evident German power, London sought ways that it could help protect its interests in both the Mediterranean and Asia. Though relations grew somewhat stronger as Russo-German relations deteriorated, Britain would not consider a full alliance. As Kennedy concludes, "What 'Bismarckism' had done was make every British government from the 1860s to the 1880s, whether Liberal or Conservative, so distrustful of Berlin's real motives in its external policy, and, in many respects, so disapproving of its domestic-political arrangements, that a firm, public, and binding Anglo-German alliance was out of the question."[156] While this distrust prevented any British alliance with Germany, there also remained sufficient uncertainty to prevent a balancing alliance against Germany. The response to uncertainty was not to assume the worst but rather to hedge one's bets and take advantage of beneficial short-term cooperation.

Again, there is little evidence that the cooperation between Germany and Britain can be explained as either buck-passing or engagement. London was intrigued at several points by the prospect of a relationship with Germany, suggesting that it did not necessarily view Germany as a threat. British strategy varied more with assessments of Germany's intentions than its capabilities. As for engagement, there is again little indication of London attempting to construct a stable international order in which a rising Germany could be embedded. Instead, Britain's concerns about the fate of its empire led it to seek short-term opportunities to shore up that empire against potential imperial competitors. As long as Germany could offer those protections, any long-term concerns about Germany would be discounted.

Finally, the Russian approach to the rise of Germany was also predominately cooperative until the situation deteriorated after Bismarck departed. Russia faced other short-term threats, most notably in the Balkans, that it had to prioritize over confronting a long-term German threat. Not only was it uncertain about future German intentions, but Russia actually seemed reassured at points about those intentions. As long as a reasonable amount of uncertainty remained, Russia was willing to abstain from taking more proactive steps to limit German growth. Like France, Russia viewed the short-term costs of doing anything to hinder German growth as prohibitive. Only when uncertainty about German intentions seemed to dwindle and a French ally was available did more competitive strategies gain favor in Russia.

Russia was initially optimistic about its relations with the newly formed Germany. Tsar Alexander II was the nephew of Kaiser Wilhelm, and beyond familial ties, they shared a fondness for conservative monarchical government. In 1873, Russia, Germany, and Austria-Hungary agreed to the first iteration of the League of the Three Emperors.

The War in Sight crisis, however, also introduced tension into the Russo-German relationship. While Russia sought friendly relations with Germany, it could not support a war against France. Russian concerns only grew a few years later when the outcome brokered by Bismarck at the Congress of Berlin favored Austria-Hungary over Russia. St. Petersburg felt even more isolated when the Austro-German alliance was consummated in 1879.

Bismarck sought to repair relations with Russia by reviving the League of the Three Emperors in 1881, but relations would be strained by periodic tension in Bulgaria. In 1887, however, Russia and Germany agreed to the Reinsurance Treaty. By offering reassuring signals to St. Petersburg, the Reinsurance Treaty convinced Russia to hold off on seeking an alliance with France. Though periodic tension was evident, cooperation predominated in relations between Russia and Germany for the first two decades after German unification.

Russo-German relations only fully collapsed when Bismarck's successors opted not to renew the Reinsurance Treaty in 1890. Cooperation with Germany up to that point had been motivated by the short-term benefits that such cooperation offered Russia. Bismarck sought to prevent a balancing coalition that would curtail Germany's diplomatic freedom. To do so, he placated all the European powers, including Russia, in the short term, which limited the extent to which they considered the long-term potential threat posed by Germany. When the benefits of short-term cooperation with Germany evaporated, the Russians turned to a strategy for balancing Germany over the long term.

My explanation focused on Bismarck's manipulation of others' beliefs about German intentions is superior to either a buck-passing or an engagement explanation. For addressing Germany, Russia did not pass the buck to others; rather, it sought to partner with Germany to protect its interests. Russian cooperation was motivated by short-term concerns about its security and its interests in the Balkans and in Asia. Nor is there evidence to support an engagement argument that would see cooperation grounded in some effort to establish a stable and sustainable international order.

"Bismarck's diplomacy was probably decisive in the preservation of peace among the European great powers during the [two decades following German unification]," Pflanze writes. "He convinced a skeptical Europe that he, and Germany, had no further expansionist objectives. By preventing a major European war over the Balkan question in 1875–1878 and 1885–1888, he restrained for a time the destructiveness of the forces he had earlier unleashed."[157] In this chapter, I have argued that Bismarck worked to persuade others to value short-term cooperation over more competitive strategies. Moreover, he took advantage of short-term crises in Europe both to signal that his own intentions might be benign and to distract others from focusing on a potential long-term German threat. As long as he was successful, Germany could continue to grow for the long term without any efforts made to curtail its growth. European powers consistently chose strategies that maximized short-term benefit rather than paying any short-term cost in order to deal with a potential long-term threat from Germany. To be clear, one should not overstate the degree of cooperation with Germany: it was primarily passive in the form of economic exchange, but nonetheless it is striking that for over two decades after its unification, Germany faced no unified effort to balance against it.

Facing other immediate threats, Germany's potential competitors simply did not have the luxury of addressing the long-term potential threat posed by Germany in the short term. Only when Bismarck's successors provoked concern about Germany's long-term intentions did Europe's leaders begin to react more competitively to Germany's rise. Bismarck capitalized on these short-term threats, playing the honest broker when he could. Meanwhile, on the few occasions when Bismarck took a misstep, such as the War in Sight crisis or colonialism, he worked hard to back away from those crises and reassure others about German intentions. Crises involving a rising great power have an immediate impact on the perceived threat from the rising power, but they also have a potential longer-term impact in extending declining powers' time horizons.

Also as expected, cooperation was a product of the interaction of the resolution to now-or-later dilemmas. Declining powers in Europe valued short-term cooperation as a way of managing their declines. Rising Germany valued short-term cooperation as a way of fueling its long-term rise. Mutually beneficial cooperation was an equilibrium outcome. Economic exchange was important fuel for Germany's rise. As Wilfried Feldenkirchen writes, "As worldwide economic connections grew and Germany itself developed from an agricultural into an industrial nation, world trade became increasingly important as an agent of German prosperity. Between 1850 and 1913 German foreign trade increased on the average of 4% annually, even faster than overall economic production."[158]

Why did this cooperative equilibrium come to an end? Or rather why did the great powers begin to balance against Germany even as they continued to trade with it? Even if one assumes that state leaders were perfectly cognizant of German material capabilities, as illustrated in figure 2.1, there was no shift in those capabilities in 1890 that can explain the change toward competition. Instead, after Bismarck, Germany's leaders shifted in a direction that raised greater concerns about its long-term intentions.[159] By allowing the Reinsurance Treaty to lapse, Germany's leaders sent a signal to Russia that it needed to consider alternative ways of ensuring its security over the long term. Beliefs about Germany's intentions, not its capabilities, led to the shift in Russian strategy.

Figure 2.1. Great power capabilities, 1850–1914.

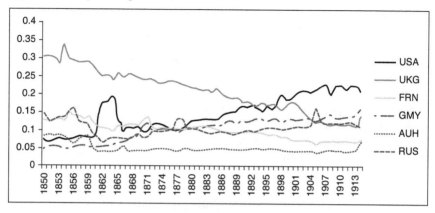

Source: Correlates of War Composite Index of National Capability (CINC). Available at http://cow.dss.ucdavis.edu/data-sets/national-material-capabilities/national-material -capabilities-v4.

In short, this case reminds us that threats are not just two-dimensional— power and intentions. In fact, there is a third critical dimension—time. As states consider ways to respond to various potential threats, how they think about the timing of those threats and how they value the short term versus the long term is critical to understanding the strategies they adopt as a result. It is the interaction of state time horizons that produces cooperation or competition.

In the next chapter, I consider another power transition that ensued shortly after Germany's rise in Europe: the rise of the United States. As opposed to the rise of Germany, the rise of the United States did not result in a world war. In fact, the United States and Great Britain became the best of allies. The next chapter seeks to explain how and why this happened.

The Rise of the United States

In this chapter, I examine the period at the turn of the twentieth century when the United States surpassed Great Britain as the most powerful state in the western hemisphere and, arguably, in the entire international system.[1] By the end of the nineteenth century, the United States had a population greater than all other states except Russia, and it led the world in the production of wheat, led or nearly led the world in the production of coal, iron, and steel, and accounted for almost 30 percent of world manufacturing production.[2] What is unusual about this case of power transition is that it ended without any conflict between the two countries, despite a history of animosity between them and despite considerable uncertainty about future U.S. intentions. As I contend, it was the resolution of that uncertainty, based primarily on a shared Anglo-Saxon identity, that allowed Britain to entrust its interests to the United States. Though the Anglo-U.S. "special relationship" is today taken for granted, that was not the case in the late nineteenth century as Britain was declining and the United States was rising.

I argue that this peaceful transition can be explained by two factors. First, Britain was compelled by international circumstances to focus on the short term and the rising German threat in Europe. Short-term demands did not allow London to expend resources on the potential long-term threat posed by the United States. In the face of uncertainty about U.S. intentions, London confronted a difficult trade-off between addressing the short-term German threat and responding to the potentially significant long-term U.S. threat. Second, and unexpectedly, when a series of crises did arise and could have raised British concern about U.S. long-term intentions, competition was not the result. The United States opportunistically sought advantages in these crises. It eschewed patience. Such behavior ought to have precipitated British concern with long-term U.S. intentions. Instead, the British resigned themselves to withdrawing from the western hemisphere and found comfort in the Anglo-Saxon identity that they shared with the United States.

That Anglo-U.S. relations developed in a friendly rather than an acrimonious direction is well known. This chapter offers two novel contributions. First, the case illustrates that threats are relative in a temporal sense. States in a multipolar system are likely to face more than one potential threat, and temporality explains, in part, how states prioritize those threats. The geographic and temporal proximity of the German threat in Europe meant that London had to focus there rather than on the long-term potential threat posed by the United States.[3] To be clear, Britain had significant reason to be concerned by the rise of the United States, but uncertainty and temporal concerns led it to address the German threat first. Second, the case illustrates again the importance of beliefs about intentions in shaping relations between states. There should be no doubt that the United States acted in an aggressive, expansionist manner as it rose to power, yet there was no effort to balance against it.[4] While structural forces compelled leaders in London to focus on Europe, beliefs about U.S. intentions reinforced their instincts to cooperate with the United States.

I focus in this chapter on three crises that defined Anglo-U.S. relations at the turn of the twentieth century. Each crisis illustrates the assertiveness of a rising United States but also the resignation of Britain to abandoning its interests in the western hemisphere. In addition, I discuss the evolution of British preferences about foreign influence, including the United States, in East Asia.

Alternative Arguments

Some might suggest that the case of the Anglo-U.S. power transition is an easy case that does not require further investigation. The British, the argument goes, had little choice but to abandon their interests in the western hemisphere to the United States and accept a more assertive United States in East Asia. However, I contend that there is more to glean from this case. First, while it is obvious in retrospect that it made sense for London to acquiesce to the United States, the interests at stake were not inconsequential at the time. Understanding British decision making remains important and interesting. Second, it is often underappreciated just how aggressively the United States asserted its interests at the turn of the twentieth century, so it is worth investigating how friendship, rather than enmity, emerged out of that U.S. aggression. It was not immediately apparent that the short-term German threat exceeded the long-term uncertain threat from the United States.

My own argument explains variation in Anglo-U.S. cooperation based on the interaction of the two states' time horizons. In particular, my account in this chapter emphasizes (1) how Britain's time horizons were shortened by the other threats it faced during this period and (2) how, despite aggressive U.S. behavior that should have provoked long-term concern in London, the British were able to find some reassurance in their shared identity with the people of the United States. Uncertainty was transformed into manageable risk by the interpretation of these indicators of intentions. In this case, they were indicators not of behavior—which remained troubling—but of shared identity. In fact, the evidence reveals that the United States did little through its behavior to try to shape British beliefs about its intentions—it saw little danger in acting assertively sooner rather than later. Nonetheless, for Great Britain, the choice to defer addressing a potential long-term U.S. threat emerged as the best way to manage the potential long-term risk posed by the United States. The result was sustained Anglo-U.S. cooperation.

Buck-passing would explain British cooperation with the United States as an attempt to get others to pay the costs of balancing against a rising power. This buck-passing logic, however, has a harder time explaining active cooperation. Presumably, it is the result of a state trying to benefit while it waits for others to pay the price of balancing against the rising power, but as I explained in chapter 2, it is not clear why rational states would ever expect others to pay this cost. Competition presumably replaces cooperation only when it is clear that buck-passing has failed and no other state has assumed the role of balancer. Assessments of capabilities, not intentions, should drive the behavior of states. In this case, British cooperation with the United States would be explained by the British desire to have somebody else pay the price of balancing against the United States, though, as we will see, it would have a difficult time explaining cooperation after U.S. capabilities had grown substantially. Moreover, it is not at all clear who the British could have reasonably thought would accept the buck of balancing against the United States.

Finally, others would see British engagement with the United States as a strategy for influencing U.S. interests as it continued to emerge as a great power. By this argument, the United States and Britain had mutually compatible interests in a stable international order. Cooperation aimed at crafting such an order should be qualitatively different than cooperation aimed at capturing short-term rewards. It should seek to enmesh the rising power in an international system from which it will derive benefits that outweigh those that might be captured by less cooperative behavior. As I will argue below, however, British cooperation was not motivated by any attempt to shape U.S. interests. Instead, it was a pragmatic response to short-term pressures that Britain faced.

Neither buck-passing nor engagement can explain this case as well as an explanation focused on time horizons and intentions. There were no other countries to which Britain could pass the buck for balancing against the United States, and there is no evidence that it expected any other country to balance against the United States. As for engagement, Anglo-U.S. cooperation was not directed at the creation of any type of lasting international order. Rather, it was a pragmatic decision driven largely by the British need to respond to more immediate threats.

The U.S. Challenge to Britain

For most of the nineteenth century, Anglo-U.S. relations were acrimonious.[5] Early in the century, residual tension from the American Revolution culminated in the War of 1812.[6] In the middle of the century, territorial disputes in the Pacific Northwest soured relations.[7] During the U.S. Civil War, British sympathy for the Confederacy raised the prospect of Anglo-U.S. conflict.[8]

During the middle and later parts of the century, British military and political leaders devised plans to defend Canada against a U.S. attack.[9] The plans called for a massive attack against U.S. cities on the Atlantic coast and a blockade of U.S. trade across the Atlantic. The British learned from the Union victory in the Civil War, however, that defending Canada against a U.S. attack would be difficult, if not impossible, and thus began to contemplate alternative ways of responding to the rise of the United States.[10]

At the same time, London became increasingly concerned with threats to its interests in parts of Europe and Asia. As Kenneth Bourne writes, "In the era of Gettysburg and Königgrätz, Britain's sense of military vulnerability in North America and diplomatic weakness in Europe made a withdrawal from Canada and greater concentration at home peculiarly attractive."[11] Starting in the 1870s, London encouraged the Canadian government to consider how it might defend itself against the United States without support from England. The 1871 Treaty of Washington between the United States and Great Britain resolved some remaining disputes and put others before arbitration, but tension persisted.[12]

"There was in 1895 a widespread and deep-rooted feeling of animosity towards Great Britain," writes Marshall Bertram about U.S. attitudes.[13] At the end of the century, British leaders continued to concern themselves with the safety of Canada from a U.S. attack, and it appeared inevitable that a growing United States would further encroach on British interests. Three different crises transformed Anglo-U.S. relations. Perhaps surprisingly, these crises led to less, not more, animosity between the two former adversaries. While all were resolved peacefully, one can imagine a different, more competitive course that could have been taken but was not.

In the end, the crises ought to have led to more and not less British concern about the rise of the United States. The rising United States unapologetically seized short-term opportunities in all three crises, which might have led to concern in London about the long-term implications of the rising power. My argument expects such indications of intentions to extend time horizons, leading to increased competition between the existing and the rising powers. Instead, however, the British found themselves resigned to the rise of the United States and hopeful that a shared Anglo-U.S. identity could sustain friendship between them.

THE VENEZUELA BOUNDARY CRISIS: U.S. ASSERTIVENESS AND BRITISH DISTRACTION

The first crisis that revealed the increasing assertiveness of a rising United States and the passive acceptance of a relatively declining Britain occurred in Venezuela. The crisis emerged in the summer of 1895 as the culmination of a half century of tension between Great Britain and Venezuela over the boundary between British Guiana and Venezuela.[14] The de facto boundary was the so-called Schomburgk Line, which had been established by the British surveyor Robert Schomburgk between 1841 and 1843. The line favored British over Venezuelan interests, and Venezuela had lacked the capability to more assertively stake its claims. The discovery of substantial gold deposits in the disputed territory in the 1870s raised the stakes. In early 1887, Venezuela severed diplomatic relations with Great Britain as an expression of its unhappiness with the disposition of the boundary.

Venezuela initially appealed to the United States for assistance under the Monroe Doctrine, but it received little response. Washington was generally reluctant to risk a further deterioration in Anglo-U.S. relations over a South American boundary dispute. In 1895, however, U.S. interest in the Venezuela dispute increased as a result of two developments.[15]

First, William L. Scruggs published a pamphlet titled *British Aggression in Venezuela, or the Monroe Doctrine on Trial*. Scruggs had previously served as U.S. ambassador in Caracas and had been hired by the Venezuelan government to lobby in Washington in support of Venezuela's boundary claims.[16] Scruggs's pamphlet vigorously argued that the United States ought to intervene on behalf of Venezuela. In the face of this lobbying campaign, in February 1895, the House and Senate approved and President Grover Cleveland signed a resolution calling on Great Britain and Venezuela to submit their dispute to arbitration.[17]

Second, Richard Olney was appointed to succeed Walter Q. Gresham as U.S. secretary of state. Whereas Gresham had generally been cautious and prudent in his practice of foreign policy, Olney was known to be impatient and cantankerous.[18] The new secretary was determined to resolve the Venezuela dispute in an expeditious manner. As Ernest R. May writes, "By naming Olney Secretary of State, Cleveland virtually made ready to force a crisis with Great Britain."[19] On July 20, Olney sent a lengthy and belligerent dispatch to the U.S. ambassador in London, Thomas F. Bayard, with instructions to deliver the message to British prime minister Salisbury.

Cleveland would later refer to Olney's note as a "twenty-inch gun."[20] Olney asserted the rights of the United States under the Monroe Doctrine to intervene in the boundary dispute. He also characterized as "unnatural and inexpedient" any permanent political relationship between a European and an American state. It is worth quoting at length what came to be known as the Olney Corollary to the Monroe Doctrine: "If grounds exist sufficient to persuade the United States that the political or territorial integrity of an American state is threatened by a non-American power, the United States regards the Monroe Doctrine as automatically implicated, and claims the right to intervene between the two disputing states. Termination of the dispute through a settlement reached by the free consent of both states will be considered as satisfying the Doctrine. If, however, no such settlement is reached, the United States may suggest, and impose impartially, such a composition of the dispute as seems in its sole judgment reasonable and just."[21] In perhaps the most famous passage, Olney declared, "Today the United States is practically sovereign on this continent, and its fiat is law upon the subjects to which it confines its interpretation."[22] Olney concluded by insisting that the British agree to arbitrate the boundary dispute, and he requested a response from London before Cleveland's annual message to Congress on December 2. The United States was clearly not inclined to be patient about asserting its interests in the western hemisphere.

The British response was not immediately forthcoming. Threats to its interests in Asia were consuming London's attention, and Salisbury may not have appreciated the seriousness that Olney attached to the situation in Venezuela. In fact, Salisbury's reply did not arrive until after Cleveland further scolded the British for enlarging British Guiana "against the will of Venezuela."[23]

Salisbury's reply finally arrived on December 6. In it, the prime minister vehemently disputed Olney's various claims. Salisbury began by offering the British interpretation of what had transpired in Venezuela. He bluntly rejected any claim that the Monroe Doctrine constituted international law and suggested that it could only be such if the broader international community signaled its assent. Instead, through British eyes, the Monroe Doctrine was a unilateral declaration that had no international standing.

Salisbury indicated a willingness to enter negotiations over the Venezuela boundary, but he was not willing to sacrifice British interests. Any compromise would be unacceptable if it involved "the transfer of large numbers of British subjects, who have for many years enjoyed the settled rule of a British colony, to a nation of different race and language, whose political system is subject to frequent disturbance, and whose institutions as yet too often afford very inadequate protection of life and property."[24] British interests in Venezuela were real, and until an acceptable compromise could be found, the Schomburgk Line would have to stand.[25]

Cleveland was on a fishing vacation when the British response arrived, and Olney had already prepared a rejoinder by the time the president returned. Olney and Cleveland agreed that British intransigence warranted a special message to Congress. On December 17, Cleveland sent an aggressive defense of the U.S. position to Capitol Hill. The president insisted that the United States had attempted to act as an impartial mediator in the boundary dispute. That having failed, Cleveland requested that Congress allocate funds for a special committee that would investigate the boundary dispute and suggest a resolution. The president emphasized that once the committee had settled on an appropriate boundary, the United States would "resist by every means in its power, as a willful aggression upon its rights and interests" attempts by Britain to further alter the boundary. The note ended with an ominous acceptance of "all the consequences that may follow" from the position adopted.[26] Congress endorsed Cleveland's message and quickly approved the funds requested to establish the special investigative committee.

Cleveland's message had both international and domestic audiences. Internationally, Cleveland believed that British behavior in Venezuela was truly unacceptable. May writes, "Cleveland thought the Venezuelans were being robbed of their rightful lands. He felt strongly that international law should be observed by all nations, great and small. He believed himself entitled by the interests and traditional policy of the United States to speak up for judicial settlement of the dispute."[27] Domestically, with a presidential election approaching in November 1896, Cleveland felt the need to demonstrate his resolve in order to resist the rising populist wing of the Democratic Party.[28] As expected, one source of impatience among rising powers is the need to satisfy a domestic audience. Domestic reaction to Cleveland's bellicose approach was, however, mixed. While public opinion applauded Cleveland's stand against British imperialism in the western hemisphere, war with Britain would be costly and unwelcome. The fear of war led to plummeting stock prices, an exodus of gold from the United States, and rising concerns about the state of the fragile economy.[29]

To recap, the crisis over Venezuela brought attention to U.S. intentions in the western hemisphere and did not necessarily augur well for British interests. The United States' assertiveness signaled a shift in its ambitions that might best be explained by a reluctance to validate the British position in the western hemisphere. The impending U.S. presidential election only exacerbated pressures for Cleveland to behave aggressively despite what such behavior might reveal about U.S. long-term intentions. Domestic pressure outweighed any other pressure to attempt to manipulate British beliefs about U.S. intentions. In response to Cleveland's message to Congress, Salisbury wrote to Michael Hicks Beach, chancellor of the exchequer, on January 2, 1896: "A war with America—not this year but in the not distant future—has become something more than a possibility."[30]

Only a day later, however, British attention would be drawn away from Venezuela and toward another colonial interest, South Africa. Despite the potential long-term threat posed by a rising United States, London could not afford to address that concern when more important interests were being threatened elsewhere. All threats are relative, including in a temporal sense, and the U.S. threat seemed more distant, both geographically and temporally.

On January 3, Kaiser Wilhelm II of Germany sent a telegram to the Boer president, Paul Kruger, congratulating him for capturing a group of British subjects in the Transvaal. Berlin hoped the telegram would convince Britain to curtail its imperialist activity.[31] In response to the telegram, London increasingly recognized the need to prioritize the threats to its various interests around the globe. On January 11, over the prime minister's objections, the British cabinet rejected the hard line that Salisbury had been taking on the prospect of arbitrating the Venezuela dispute. The cabinet was now inclined to accept limited arbitration. Though Salisbury continued to reject the legitimacy of U.S. intervention in the Venezuela dispute, problems elsewhere forced London to accept that the United States would have a role in resolving the conflict.[32]

Negotiations between British and U.S. diplomats on an arbitration agreement began shortly thereafter.[33] The most contentious negotiations centered on which territories would be subject to arbitration and which had been occupied for long enough that they rightfully belonged to one party or another. In November 1896, Olney and Lord Pauncefote, the British ambassador to the United States, agreed on a treaty of arbitration that recognized fifty years as the critical length of occupation that was necessary to make arbitration unnecessary. A five-member panel would arbitrate claims over the remaining territory.[34] Under pressure from Washington, Venezuela accepted the terms of the Olney-Pauncefote agreement, and two years later the arbitration panel issued a judgment that, after all that, favored British claims.[35]

"Yet although in retrospect the crisis seems too silly and even too short to have raised any serious prospect of war," Bourne writes, "both sides nonetheless did actively consider the possibility."[36] For the most part, leaders in both Washington and London recognized that it would not be worthwhile to fight a war over Venezuela.[37] Especially after the delivery of the Kruger telegram, Venezuela continued to slide down Britain's list of national priorities. A. E. Campbell observes, "South America was, unlike South Africa, an area in which Britain was willing to abdicate, so far as that could be done without loss of prestige."[38]

At the same time, abandoning Venezuela was not easy for London. The newly discovered gold deposits were potentially of great value. British subjects continued to reside in South America. Leaving Venezuela might also signal a more general abandonment of British interests in the western hemisphere and the decline of the British Empire.

While the relatively small stakes in Venezuela can explain why this crisis never escalated to war, the logic of my argument explains why the British did not more assertively pursue their interests in some other way in Venezuela. Faced with more immediate and greater threats to its security, London could not afford to adopt a strategy that was more aggressive in the short term because of long-term concern about the United States. At the same time, the United States' unapologetic behavior left little doubt about its intentions to be a hegemonic power in the western hemisphere. U.S. leaders acted opportunistically to assert expanded interests and also felt domestic pressure to demonstrate U.S. hegemony. The United States was less patient than a farsighted rising power might ideally be, but the British capacity to respond was limited.

THE ISTHMIAN CANAL DISPUTE: THE ABANDONMENT OF BRITISH INTERESTS

The second significant dispute in Anglo-U.S. relations was over control of the canal to be built across the Central American isthmus.[39] Eventually, the British would again cede to the United States as they attended to more pressing threats elsewhere. The commercial and strategic interests at stake in the canal were significant, and the decision to grant control to the United States was not taken easily. Once again, the United States behaved impatiently, but opportunistically, to assert its interests.

The idea of building an isthmian canal was a familiar one at the end of the nineteenth century. Both U.S. and British policymakers had long recognized the value in building a canal that would obviate the need to circumvent Cape Horn. The 1898 dispute began when President William McKinley called for the United States to begin construction of the canal and also to consider retaining total control over access to the canal once it was built.

The combination of growing U.S. commercial interests in Asia and the result of the Spanish-American War, which granted the United States control over the Philippines, prompted McKinley to address Congress on December 5.[40] The president declared that expansion of the United States into the Pacific demanded that a canal be built and "that our national policy now more imperatively calls for its control by this government."[41]

Great Britain had equally significant reasons for wanting to maintain at least some control over access to the planned canal. The canal offered the most efficient route for British commercial and naval vessels to reach the farthest corners of the British Empire. London's objection was not to McKinley's suggestion that a canal be built, but only to his demand that the United States control access to it. If Anglo-U.S. relations were to deteriorate, Washington would have the unacceptable ability to restrict British access to the canal.

The British ambassador to the United States, Pauncefote, immediately protested McKinley's message to Congress. Pauncefote argued that the United States was obliged to abide by the terms of the 1850 Clayton-Bulwer

Treaty in which the United States and Great Britain had agreed not to seek exclusive control over the canal, to forgo colonization of Central America, and to guarantee the neutrality of the canal and Central America, more generally.[42]

U.S. secretary of state John Hay responded to Pauncefote by offering to revise the terms for which McKinley had called. The revised U.S. proposal, however, still insisted that the United States control the construction of the canal and access to the canal after it was completed. The only apparent concession was a willingness to maintain the neutrality of the canal, but what that meant was unclear if the United States controlled access.[43] Hay presented his proposal to Pauncefote in Washington and asked the U.S. ambassador in London, Henry White, to submit the same to the British cabinet.

Salisbury immediately rejected Hay's proposal for three reasons. First, British naval leaders were concerned that construction of the canal on Hay's terms would endanger British military and commercial interests. Second, the canal dispute emerged at the same time as another dispute over the Alaskan boundary with Canada. British leaders hoped that they could use negotiations over the canal as leverage in negotiations over the Alaskan boundary. Third, members of the cabinet argued that exclusive U.S. control of the canal was unacceptable until all sources of Anglo-U.S. conflict had been resolved. The risk of the United States limiting British access to the canal if Anglo-U.S. relations were to deteriorate was too great.[44] Salisbury telegrammed Pauncefote on February 2, 1899, to inform him of the cabinet's decision: "[Members of the cabinet] are averse to obstructing what may be of value to commerce, but they also fear that if they yield a point so entirely to the advantage of the U.S. without some diminution at least of the causes which might bring the two countries into conflict, there would be serious dissatisfaction here."[45] London still saw the United States as potentially threatening to its interests, even as it hoped for some solution that would allow it to focus its attention elsewhere.

Negotiations over the canal stalled, and when they resumed in December 1899 quickly resulted in British agreement to the revised treaty in February 1900 without any resolution of the three main British objections. There are two explanations for this sudden reversal of British policy. First, the Boer War reminded London how few friends it had in Europe and how valuable friendship with the United States could be.[46] The war was demanding significant resources, and Washington was a lone source of support for London.[47] As Pauncefote summarized, "The national feeling [in the United States] about the canal is almost as intense as that regarding the Monroe Doctrine and the opposition of Britain to its construction would undoubtedly impair very seriously the good relations now existing between the two countries. . . . America seems to be our only friend just now and it would be unfortunate to quarrel with her."[48] British needs in the short term trumped any possible concern about the long-term risk of ceding control of the canal to the United States. For Washington, meanwhile, there appeared to be little cost to the continued aggressive assertion of its interests. With domestic audiences satisfied and little credible international opposition, the United States did not worry about how its long-term intentions were perceived.

Second, Pauncefote warned that if Britain did not agree to Hay's proposals, then the U.S. Congress and president were inclined to act unilaterally to revise the Clayton-Bulwer Treaty.[49] Any agreement was preferable for Britain to unilateral U.S. action, so on February 2, Salisbury instructed Pauncefote to inform Hay of Britain's intent to sign the revised treaty.

Unfortunately for Hay, the Senate had by this point grown dissatisfied with the terms of the treaty. In particular, some senators objected to the neutralization of the canal. After much back-and-forth and a subsequent round of renegotiations between Hay and Pauncefote, a new, revised treaty was agreed to that allowed the United States to police access to the canal but that would not allow the United States to alter control over the canal or prevent other countries from joining the treaty. The treaty was signed in Washington on November 11, 1901, and ratified by the Senate on December 16.[50]

Like the resolution to the Venezuela dispute, the Hay-Pauncefote Treaty signaled British resignation to U.S. ascendance in the western hemisphere.[51] Threats elsewhere constrained the ability of London to contemplate a long-term threat from the rise of the United States, and one way to concentrate resources on other threats was to withdraw resources from lesser interests. As J. A. S. Grenville, a leading historian of the period, summarizes, "The signature of the Hay-Pauncefote Treaty in 1901 marked—and the British cabinet was in no doubt about this—the conscious British recognition of the eventual United States supremacy in the Western Hemisphere and thus entailed a fundamental change in the relations of the two countries."[52] Britain maintained interests in the western hemisphere, including access to the canal, but it was willing to entrust those interests to the United States.

The isthmian canal dispute could have raised questions about long-term U.S. intentions, but London opted to cooperate now and deal with any potential consequences later. The combination of U.S. short-term opportunism along with short British time horizons ought to have generated competition, but London was occupied elsewhere. A more competitive, long-term-oriented strategy would have sought British control over the canal in response to uncertainty about long-term U.S. intentions, but such a strategy would have been costly in the short term. Given the immediate threat posed by Germany and the ongoing Boer War, such a strategy was untenable. Further, as I discuss below, the British came around to the realization that the United States could ultimately help to protect its remaining interests in the western hemisphere.

Uncertainty about U.S. intentions did not reflexively lead to competition. As Lionel M. Gelber concludes, "For now the Monroe Doctrine would preserve rather than menace existing interests in Central America and beyond—a prospect of which the Foreign Office had not altogether been oblivious when the final canal treaty was signed. . . . For in the western hemisphere, by her *rapprochement* with the United States, Great Britain had been reinsuring the status quo."[53]

THE CANADA-ALASKA BOUNDARY: COOPERATION
DESPITE CONCERN

The canal dispute was tied to a third dispute between Great Britain and the United States over the border between Canada and Alaska.[54] Following the same pattern as in the previous two disputes, London eventually decided to back away from its Canadian interests in the face of more immediate and significant pressures elsewhere. The interaction of time horizons— converging on the short term—might have suggested that more competitive relations would result.

Considering the length of the Canadian-U.S. border and the acrimonious nineteenth-century Anglo-U.S. relationship, it is not surprising that the Canadian government viewed the rise of the United States with some apprehension. Canada's claim to territory in the Yukon dated back to an 1825 treaty between Canada and Russia, but that treaty left the boundary between Canadian and Russian territories ambiguous.[55] More precisely, the treaty failed to specify whether the boundary would follow the inlets of the river on which the treaty was based or simply follow a straight line down the middle of the river.[56] The nature of the boundary had consequences for commerce, so when the United States acquired Alaska in 1867, the Russo-Canadian dispute became a Canadian-U.S. dispute.

As mentioned earlier, Canada's concerns about its ability to defend itself against its neighbors to the south intensified in the wake of the U.S. Civil War.[57] A series of raids across the Canadian border by Irish American Fenians only further heightened concern.[58] That said, the United States was also exhausted by its civil war and faced little obvious reason to attack Canada. Through the 1870s and 1880s, Canada sought to build a more amicable relationship with the United States.

But the Canada-Alaska boundary dispute reignited in 1897 when significant gold deposits were discovered in the Yukon territory. "Lured by reports of fabulous gold strikes," writes historian Charles S. Campbell, "thousands of rough and ready prospectors from all over the world, but mainly from the United States . . . were stampeding to the northwest of the Dominion. . . . Almost overnight towns like Circle City, Dawson City, Bonanza, and El Dorado were springing up from a wilderness hitherto unknown to habitation."[59] Since obtaining Alaska, the United States had shown little interest in its boundary with Canada, but this transformation of the territory into a hotbed for prospectors generated a new sense of urgency to clarify the border.

The outbreak of the Spanish-American War also created additional pressure to resolve this and other disputes between the United States and British interests.[60] While other European powers pressured Washington to seek a diplomatic resolution to the crisis following the sinking of the *Maine*, Britain took a more reserved position. London instructed Pauncefote "to be guided by the wishes of the American government before associating himself with any collective action by the foreign envoys in Washington."[61] Accordingly, when war broke out, the British government did not join other European powers in protest.

In the two months preceding the war, Washington learned that its only source of international support was London. As the British valued U.S. support in Africa, the United States appreciated the support of Britain in Cuba. "Each country, at the time of the Spanish-American War, found itself without allies, threatened by several of the European great powers, and needful of the diplomatic support of the other," observed Stuart Anderson.[62] If the United States and Great Britain were to be friends, however, it would be helpful to resolve any remaining disputes, including over the boundary between Canada and Alaska.

Thus, at the end of May 1898, the United States, Canada, and Great Britain created the Joint High Commission to consider any disputes among them. In addition to the Alaska boundary, the commission would consider a range of issues involving fur seals, fisheries, and trade reciprocity.[63] The first meeting of the commission was convened in August and was ineffectual. While the United States refused to cede ground, Canada sought an unrealistic comprehensive settlement of all possible disputes. Great Britain, meanwhile, was caught between its sense of obligation to Canada and its interest in improving relations with the United States. The lobbying efforts of shippers and exporters in the northwestern United States, U.S. and Canadian coal and lumber industries, and gold prospectors seeking to stake their claims all further undermined the negotiations.

The Joint High Commission met for the final time on February 20, 1899, without having reached any agreement on the issues it was created to address. U.S. secretary of state Hay laid blame on the British representative: "By far the worst member of the Commission to deal with is Lord Herschell, who is more cantankerous than any of the Canadians, raises more petty points, and is harder than the Canadians to get along with. In fact, he is the principal obstacle to a favorable arrangement."[64] Campbell concludes that the commission was an "unmitigated failure."[65]

The next month, the governor of Alaska, John Green Brady, reported to Hay that the squabbles between Canadian and U.S. settlers were intensifying. Attention shifted away from a permanent settlement and toward an interim solution that would prevent violent conflict. Negotiations reopened in May 1899 (following the death of the obstinate Herschell), and five months later Hay and Reginald Tower, the British chargé d'affaires in Washington, agreed on a temporary arrangement.[66]

This solution was completely satisfactory to nobody, but it was more than had been accomplished by the Joint High Commission's attempts to reach a comprehensive settlement. The modus vivendi recognized most U.S. claims, but it did so only temporarily. Canada insisted that the agreement could not become permanent unless the United States was willing to offer substantial territorial concessions. Meanwhile, the British government was disappointed that a permanent solution that could remove this sore spot in Anglo-U.S. relations had not been found. With the Boer War under way, London was more interested than ever in strengthening relations with the United States, and any agreement that did so permanently would have been favored by London, regardless of any long-term costs, including the fate of Canadian claims.[67] Other threats distracted London from the western hemisphere, but they also led it to view the United States as potentially a valuable partner and supporter.

With the adoption of the temporary agreement, British and U.S. attention turned elsewhere. The British turned to South Africa, and to the extent that Anglo-U.S. negotiations continued, they were focused more on the isthmus canal dispute than on Alaska. The Canadian government was left hoping that a satisfactory permanent settlement of the boundary dispute would be tied to a resolution of the canal issue, but two events coincided in the fall of 1901 to make such a connection untenable.

First, on September 6, McKinley was assassinated in Buffalo, New York, and replaced by Theodore Roosevelt. Roosevelt had a more aggressive and less compromising attitude toward foreign policy than either McKinley or especially Hay did.[68] Roosevelt envisioned U.S. dominance over the western hemisphere, and, accordingly, he was uninterested in negotiating any compromise on the Alaskan boundary. As Campbell observes, "Roosevelt was determined to take a stand on the Alaska question, which he saw as a challenge to the supremacy of the United States and himself."[69] Roosevelt believed that the United States had the stronger legal case, but he also concluded that the United States was stronger than either Canada alone or Canada with a minimal British commitment. In short, Roosevelt was not prepared to be patient and wait for the United States to become any more powerful.

Second, only two months after McKinley's assassination, final agreement was reached on the Hay-Pauncefote Treaty. Once the canal issue was resolved, it obviously could no longer be used as leverage in the Alaska negotiations.[70] The Canadian government felt betrayed.[71] Canadian prime minister Wilfrid Laurier was compelled by circumstances to abandon any hard-line negotiating position and suggested instead immediate binding arbitration of the boundary dispute. Canada would then accept any settlement as long as it guaranteed it access to a port in the Yukon.

After some negotiation, the United States, Canada, and Great Britain agreed to a six-member arbitration panel. Washington insisted on the condition that the status quo would prevail if the arbitration panel deadlocked. The arbitration agreement was signed on January 23, 1903, and the U.S. Senate unanimously ratified the agreement on February 11.

The unanimous Senate vote was only made possible by Roosevelt's duplicity. The president secretly communicated to certain members of the Senate that he intended to violate the terms of the arbitration agreement. More specifically, the agreement called for impartial jurists to be appointed, three by Canada and three by the United States. But Roosevelt intended to appoint anyone but impartial jurists: Secretary of War Elihu Root and Senators George Jackson and Henry Cabot Lodge.[72] Both London and Ottawa were outraged by Roosevelt's nominations, but they were powerless to stop them unless they wanted to abrogate the entire agreement. Perhaps more worrisome to the British and the Canadians, the appointments signaled that Roosevelt would be unwilling to go along with an unfavorable arbitration result.[73] This intuition was accurate: in July 1903, Roosevelt wrote privately to Lodge that if arbitration generated an unfavorable ruling, then he would ask Congress for permission to settle the boundary dispute "on our own theory."[74] Arbitration began in London in September, and on October 20, British and U.S. representatives signed an agreement that was favorable to U.S. interests.[75] Canada abstained from the agreement, deeming it fundamentally unfair to Canadian interests.[76]

Again, London eventually acceded to a cooperative resolution of this dispute despite any long-term risks. London's time horizons were necessarily short and could not appreciate the long-term risks of conceding to the U.S. position on the boundary. The Alaskan boundary dispute was not a major threat to either Canadian or British security, but it also was not wholly insignificant. As Grenville notes, "Until 1900, the Alaskan boundary problem thus was the rock on which the development of good Anglo-American relations threatened to founder."[77] Campbell concludes, "Fisheries, fur seals, reciprocity—these were matters of undoubted significance; but demarcation of the boundary was a *sine qua non* of stable Anglo-American relations."[78] In the end, British short-term interests in garnering U.S. support for other battles trumped any concerns about long-term Canadian security and prosperity. Meanwhile, the United States was again not demonstrating much patience, but there was little reason to when opportunities for short-term gain presented themselves. With the final arbitration agreement, all the outstanding issues between the United States and Great Britain in the western hemisphere had been settled, and all of them had been settled in a way that favored the United States and its long-term interests.

Senator Lodge captured the importance of the boundary settlement for Anglo- U.S. relations: "If we had become involved in a war with England or in a serious clash on the boundary, not only would all the other questions have remain unsettled but the attitude of the United States toward England would have been of such a character to have embarrassed us most seriously when the Great War of 1914 broke out."[79] In the end, Great Britain sacrificed its relations with Canada to strengthen cooperative relations with the United States. In all three disputes in the western hemisphere at the turn of the century, British short-term interests led to a cooperative approach to the United States despite any risk posed by uncertain U.S. long-term intentions. As I will discuss in the concluding section of this chapter, though Britain's behavior was primarily motivated by short-term interests, London did have reason to be concerned by what the United States' behavior presaged about its long-term intentions. The now-or-later dilemma that London faced was alleviated because it found more to like in indications of long-term U.S. intentions. Before that, though, I turn to one more crisis outside the western hemisphere: the disposition of East Asia.

EAST ASIA: BRITISH BELIEFS ABOUT U.S. INTENTIONS

The British reaction to the U.S. acquisition of the Philippines at the end of the Spanish-American War provides a final illustration of London's response to the United States' rise. As in the western hemisphere, Britain could have resisted the growing presence of the United States, but it chose not to do so.

At the end of the nineteenth century, Britain had significant economic interests in East Asia, but London was not particularly interested in acquiring new colonies there (or elsewhere). The empire was stretched far enough, and Britain would be satisfied if it could sustain and expand its economic interests in the region without controlling additional territory.[80] China, in particular, held significant natural resources such as coal and represented a potentially lucrative market for British manufactured goods.[81] Given the importance of China to British economic interests, London was genuinely concerned by any threat to the unity of the Chinese state.[82]

In the 1890s, the primary threats to the integrity of China came from Germany and Russia. In 1896, German admiral Alfred von Tirpitz identified Jiaozhou as a promising site for a German naval base. A year later, the murder of German missionaries in China prompted the Germans to demand a ninety-nine-year lease for a base in Jiaozhou beginning in January 1898.[83]

The German lease at Jiaozhou instigated a European landgrab in China. Russia acquired Port Arthur and Dalian Bay. France then claimed territory around Guangzhou Bay. Partly in response to these various claims, Germany passed a new naval law in April 1898 that expanded the German navy. Thus, by 1898, Germany, Russia, and to a lesser extent France all posed threats to the unity of China and through that to British economic interests.

The Spanish-American War added the United States into the equation. When the war began in April, Admiral George Dewey, in command of the U.S. fleet in Asia, was compelled by neutral Britain to sail the U.S. fleet away from Hong Kong, where it had been docked.[84] The fleet steamed toward Manila, where on May 1 it destroyed the Spanish fleet in Manila Bay.[85] Following the arrival of reinforcements, Dewey took Manila itself on August 13 as the war was approaching its end.[86]

By the terms of the August armistice, Spain relinquished Cuba and Puerto Rico to the United States, and Washington was given an option to acquire the Philippines as well.[87] The United States had already anguished over whether or not to incorporate Hawaii, and the Philippines were both farther away and a more complex proposition than Hawaii.[88] Between August and the signing of the final peace treaty in December, U.S. leaders engaged in a contentious debate over whether to take possession of the Philippines.[89] In the end, the United States opted to pay $20 million to Spain for control over the archipelago, and in February 1899, the U.S. Senate approved the final peace treaty.

London accepted, even if it did not actively encourage, the growing U.S. presence in East Asia.[90] Even more tellingly, however, is that London was unwilling to accept the growing presence of any European power in East Asia. While Germany and Russia presented short-term threats to the British interests, London concluded that the United States was unlikely to be such a threat even over the long term.

For the British, unlike the other European great powers, the United States could be trusted to support open markets in China and across East Asia. Even before the Spanish-American War, British diplomats in Washington had attempted to discern U.S. attitudes toward China and open markets, and in response U.S. leaders had assured London of its intentions to open any territories it controlled to free trade.[91]

In July 1898, Britain made its views clear in a message to Hay, the U.S. ambassador in London. Hay was informed that Britain supported a prospective U.S. annexation of the Philippines, but if the United States opted not to acquire the islands, then Britain wanted an option to purchase the islands before any other European power. As Hay conveyed to Roosevelt, "I may add that the British Government prefer to have us retain the Philippine Islands, or failing that, insist on option in case of future sale."[92]

British expectations of U.S. behavior in Asia proved largely correct. In the immediate aftermath of the war, Hay was central to a debate between those who argued that the United States should continue to support an "open door" policy into a unified China and those who thought the United States should accept the inevitable division of China into spheres of influence.[93] On September 6, 1899, Hay issued his first Open Door note, which asked that states controlling any part of Asia keep their markets open to foreign trade.[94] Less than a year later, Hay's second Open Door note adopted an even more forceful position in favor of open trade and against spheres of influence.[95] Hay's commitment to open markets in China and the maintenance of the territorial integrity of China confirmed British expectations about long-term U.S. policy in China. In fact, through an agreement with Germany in October 1900, Britain itself arguably did more to close China to trade and instigate the division of China into spheres of influence than the United States ever did.[96]

As with the previous disputes reviewed in this chapter, the central point to conclude from developments in East Asia is that Britain, facing more immediate short-term threats from other European powers, welcomed U.S. expansion into East Asia even if it could not be certain about long-term U.S. intentions. On November 10, 1898, Salisbury declared, "No one can deny that [the United States'] appearance . . . is a grave and serious event which may not conduce to the interests of peace though I think that in any event it is likely to conduce to the interests of Great Britain."[97] London had to choose which threat to its interests to prioritize, and other European powers were of more concern to it. Had the United States reversed its position and advocated for spheres of influence with doors more closed to trade, London may have regretted the decision to welcome the expansion of the United States into East Asia.

By 1902, Britain's foreign secretary, Lord Lansdowne, opined that the British government "had every reason to believe that [the United States] desired the maintenance of the status quo in the Far East."[98] Thus the East Asia case confirms the same logic for British behavior as observed in the three western hemisphere cases. Faced with more immediate threats from European powers, London opted to manage its now-or-later dilemma by deferring until the future any reaction to a potential threat from the growing United States. Meanwhile, the United States acted opportunistically and somewhat impatiently, but Britain took solace in its beliefs that U.S. intentions were generally favorable to British interests.

Explaining Anglo-U.S. Cooperation

For London, a resolution of its now-or-later dilemma favored cooperation in the short term with the United States. Given the other threats that London faced and the potential costs of trying to prevent U.S. hegemony in the western hemisphere, the somewhat reluctant decision was made to cede British interests to U.S. control. Interestingly, in this case, U.S. behavior ought to have drawn attention to long-term U.S. intentions, but as I explain below, London was reassured that the United States had benign intentions over the long term. What had been true uncertainty about U.S. intentions and the threat posed by U.S. power to British power was transformed by indicators of intentions into manageable risk.

Meanwhile, the United States refrained from the strategy of biding its time that characterizes so many other rising powers in history. In this case, there seemed to be little incentive to do so. The only state that could stop the United States was Britain, but even Britain lacked much leverage with the United States, especially as leaders in Washington recognized the other threats that

Britain faced. Thus the United States chose to more opportunistically and unapologetically pursue its interests sooner rather than later regardless of what signals it might send about U.S. intentions. Moreover, domestic political pressure, as in the case of Cleveland and the Venezuela dispute, pushed for a more aggressive U.S. policy.

The evidence in this case confirms the importance of relative temporal threats. At the end of the nineteenth century, the most significant immediate threat to British interests was the rise of Germany on the European continent. In each crisis, London accepted a short-term accommodation despite any long-term risks of doing so. Short time horizons compelled London to accept the rise of the United States as it prepared to cope with the rise of Germany.[99] The United States did little to restrain itself, most likely because it recognized that Britain was powerless to stop U.S. claims. Contrary to the claims made by Charles A. Kupchan, there was no mutual accommodation leading to rapprochement. Instead, the British simply capitulated.[100]

What explains the pattern of British behavior in the four cases examined in this chapter? Why did London cede its interests to U.S. control despite the long-term risk that the United States would act in ways that would damage British interests? After all, the theoretical framework presented in chapter 2 would expect more competition when time horizons converge on a short-term focus.

Ultimately, it was the rise of alternative threats to British interests along with confidence in U.S. intentions that accounts for the shift to cooperative relations. One cannot simply dismiss British interests in these various disputes as insignificant. In a memorandum to the Foreign Office, a commissioner of the British Admiralty concluded, "To sum up the situation from a purely naval and strategical point of view, it appears to my Lords that the preponderance of advantage from the canal would be greatly on the side of the United States, and that . . . it is not really in the interests of Great Britain that it should be constructed."[101] Bourne writes that the Royal Navy viewed the canal, under U.S. control, as "absolutely antagonistic to Britain's naval interests."[102] And Aaron L. Friedberg cites a 1903 British army document lamenting, "The abandonment of Canada to the land forces of the United States and [the navy] would apparently leave our grain trade with the Dominion and South America at the mercy of American cruisers. Such a condition of affairs might result in our being compelled to sue for peace on humiliating terms."[103] Yet Britain conceded in each and every case.

My theoretical argument suggests that uncertainty about intentions can be a useful tool for rising powers. In this case, however, one can take the argument even a step further: Britain found itself viewing long-term intentions favorably despite improvements in U.S. capabilities and despite the assertive manner in which the United States pursued its interests in the crises reviewed in this chapter. The British did not assume the worst about U.S. intentions. Far from it. The simultaneous rise of social Darwinism and Anglo-Saxonism contributed to an optimistic British assessment of likely future U.S. intentions. This was not simply wishful thinking in the face of a realization that the United States was destined to be the more powerful country, though there likely was some of that. Instead, British leaders saw indicators of U.S. intentions that they believed were both positive and integral to U.S. identity. Rudyard Kipling famously invoked the "white man's burden" by offering congratulations "in the fact that the American Republic has now reverted to the hereditary policy of the Anglo-Saxon race."[104]

Not all accepted Anglo-Saxonism as a basis for British foreign policy. For example, Salisbury challenged Anglo-Saxon sentimentalism. "My doctrine is briefly this, that you cannot build up in any desirable form an influence or popularity among the governing classes of another country," Salisbury wrote to Henry Drummond Wolff in July 1899. "The benefits of today are forgotten tomorrow. The popularity of today disappears. . . . 'Influence' disappears; territory remains."[105] Put differently, friends and enemies, even those based on a shared identity, change, but interests remain and must be protected.

But Salisbury preferred to delegate the making of British foreign policy to other members of his cabinet. As a consequence, Colonial Secretary Joseph Chamberlain largely determined the nature of British policy toward the United States. Chamberlain made frequent trips to the United States, was married to an American woman, and generally felt a greater sense of attachment to the United States than Salisbury did.[106] As Stuart Anderson surmises, "Chamberlain believed that race feeling was one of the strongest sentiments binding nations together, and he hoped that eventually race feeling would draw the United States and Great Britain together in an Anglo-Saxon alliance."[107]

On May 13, 1898, Chamberlain delivered a speech in Birmingham, England, in which he advocated for an Anglo-U.S. alliance. In the speech, Chamberlain reviewed the various threats facing the British Empire around the globe, including distant threats to economic interests in Asia and more local threats in Europe from Germany and Russia. Urging the British government "to establish and to maintain bonds of permanent amity with our kinsman across the Atlantic," Chamberlain concluded, "They are a powerful and generous nation. They speak our language, they are bred of our race. . . . And I would go so far as to say that, terrible as war may be, even war itself would be cheaply purchased if in a great and noble cause the Stars and Stripes and the Union Jack should wave together over an Anglo-Saxon alliance."[108] Chamberlain's words alarmed other European powers—Germany, Spain, and Russia—that were suspicious of both Britain and the growing United States.[109]

In December of that same year, Chamberlain authored an article for the popular magazine *Scribner's* titled "Recent Developments of Policy in the United States and Their Relation to an Anglo-American Alliance."[110] In the article, Chamberlain welcomes the expanding influence of the United

States and concludes, "It can hardly be necessary to say that the British nation will cordially welcome the entrance of the United States into the field of colonial enterprise, so long and successfully occupied by themselves. . . . We shall find that our interests are identical and, while we shall prosecute them separately, we shall inevitably be drawn into closer union if they are threatened or endangered."

Though Salisbury remained unconvinced, he was in the minority.[111] As Anderson concludes, "By the 1890s, the Teutonic origins doctrine was the dominant historical viewpoint in Great Britain and the United States."[112] Arthur Balfour, at times leader of the House of Commons and a distinguished British diplomat, shared Chamberlain's vision as did Cecil Spring-Rice, a leading diplomat and friend of Theodore Roosevelt's.[113] In a speech in Manchester, Balfour declared, "The idea of war with the United States carries with it some of the unnatural horror of a civil war. . . . The time will come, the time must come, when someone, some statesman of authority . . . will lay down the doctrine that between English-speaking peoples war is impossible."[114] Political commentator Edward Dicey added, "The American republic has now reverted to the hereditary policy of the Anglo-Saxon race."[115] In short, shared identity contributed to confidence in long-term American intentions.[116]

The other attribute that Great Britain and the United States had in common was democracy. H. C. Allen writes, "Between the British and American nations . . . since the advent of democracy in both lands, and perhaps because of it, war has come to be little less than unthinkable."[117] Stephen R. Rock agrees, "War-weariness and fiscal constraints notwithstanding, the crucial factor in the Anglo-American accommodation appears to have been a continued appreciation of the ideological and cultural bonds between the two nations."[118] The combination of Anglo-Saxon identity and shared democratic institutions and ideology contributed to confidence that uncertainty about future U.S. intentions would be resolved in a manner favorable to British interests. Nor did this change as the United States grew more powerful. If anything, Britain came to welcome U.S. capabilities on its side.[119] Though U.S. behavior had perhaps been concerning, the composite picture of U.S. intentions that emerged was one that gave London confidence looking forward.

Put differently, Britain did not simply abandon its interests in the western hemisphere; it entrusted them to the United States. By 1903, Foreign Secretary Lansdowne declared, "The Monroe Doctrine has no enemies in this country that I know of. We welcome any increase of the influence of the United States of American upon the great Western Hemisphere."[120] The statement is quite the contrast from the initial British reaction to U.S. assertiveness in the Venezuela dispute less than a decade earlier. Events in the western hemisphere compelled London to look further into the future, but unlike in other cases, competition was not the result.

British behavior in Asia is perhaps even more telling. In the western hemisphere, geography is an important consideration: the crises in Venezuela, Central America, and Alaska were all local to the United States. It was somewhat natural for the British to cede in these crises to the local power. In Asia, none were local—Britain, the United States, or the other European great powers. While London ultimately supported the U.S. acquisition of the Philippines, it would not support the islands' acquisition by another European great power. Control of the Philippines would have long-term consequences. While this led to a cooperative approach with the United States, it generated more competitive instincts toward other European powers.

Beyond U.S. expansion simply being more acceptable than the European alternatives, London also came to see U.S. expansion as in its interests. As A. E. Campbell writes, "American expansion was assumed to be Anglo-Saxon expansion, and so could not be disadvantageous to Britain."[121] Along similar lines, Anderson concludes, "The assumed racial affinity of the two peoples accounted for much, if not most, of the sympathy Britons expressed for the American cause before and during the war with Spain, and for the spirited manner in which they greeted America's expansionist policy at the war's end."[122]

My argument is superior to accounts based on either buck-passing or engagement. Offensive realism expects states to assume the worst about intentions and react to capabilities, but Britain did neither. It felt it could trust the United States' intentions despite its rapidly growing capabilities. Nor did London seek to pass the buck, and even if it did, there were few other states that could conceivably have done so. Britain did not see the United States as a threat despite its significant military capabilities and expanding interests, but that only begs the question of why it saw the United States as less of a threat to its interests than others were given the acrimonious history of nineteenth-century Anglo-U.S. relations and the continuing British interests around the globe.

As for engagement, there is little evidence of either Britain or the United States seeking a sustainable international order. Nor is there evidence of Britain attempting to influence U.S. intentions through cooperation. London simply accepted the reality of a more assertive and powerful United States. The British position in all four of the cases examined in this chapter appears more like resignation than engagement. Cooperation was a product of beliefs about intentions, not an effort to shape U.S. intentions, as liberalism would have it.

Gelber describes the policy of Great Britain toward the rise of the United States as one of "friendly reinsurance."[123] Anglo-U.S. relations could have developed differently. Britain could have opted to adopt more competitive strategies with the United States, and even if circumstances compelled Britain to withdraw from the western hemisphere, it is striking that London went as far as it did in embracing U.S. assertiveness.

Importantly, this is one case of a power transition in which the relationship did not end in war but actually evolved into one of the strongest sustained friendships in international politics. Capabilities do not speak for themselves. Rather, states interpret those capabilities and make decisions about whether to address those capabilities now or later. In the case of Britain, other compelling threats led the British to procrastinate on addressing any potential threat from the United States. The argument presented in this chapter emphasizes the importance of beliefs about intentions but also about the temporal priorities that state leaders must establish.

Perhaps the British had no alternative but to cede to U.S. power and interests in the western hemisphere. While there is no doubt that growing U.S. power loomed large during this period, it is also the case that the British ultimately chose to respond to the more immediate challenges in South Africa and Europe than to the longer-time potential threat posed by the United States.[124] As long as the threat posed by the United States was uncertain, the British had to weigh the advantages and potential dangers of accepting increasing U.S. assertiveness in the western hemisphere. The question is why Britain prioritized potential threats in the manner that it did. To be clear, geography had much to do with the choices Britain made, and by the early twentieth century, the Anglo-German naval race was well under way.[125] But rather than attempt to use any bargaining leverage that might have been gained in the canal negotiations, Britain chose to cede to the U.S. position on both the canal and the boundary dispute. U.S. dominance over the western hemisphere might have posed a long-term threat, but it was not worth paying a heavy short-term cost to prevent further U.S. growth and the solidification of U.S. hegemony in the hemisphere.[126] When assertive U.S. behavior led London to focus on long-term U.S. intentions, Britain was more reassured than threatened by those intentions. "The British took pride in the achievements of the United States, in its growing strength and wealth and population, as one takes pride in the achievements of one's descendants, and gave the credit to the Anglo-Saxon stock which had first settled the country," Campbell writes.[127] Thinking about the long-term intentions of a powerful United States led to more, not less, cooperation.

The Resurgence of Interwar Germany

How great powers addressed a potential resurgent threat, interwar Germany, following war is the focus of this chapter. Even in this case, when one might expect great powers to be skeptical of a revisionist Germany, cooperation emerged and persisted between Germany and other European powers. Whereas the previous chapter illustrated a case in which an existing power had to weigh two different great power threats, this case is useful because there was only one emerging great power threat, yet states opted to procrastinate anyway.[1]

Despite immediate concerns about the uncertain intentions of interwar Germany, the other European great powers were willing to cooperate with Germany, especially in the 1920s and into the early 1930s. These other European powers stood to benefit economically from cooperation, while the short-term costs of competition would have been high. Meanwhile, the German leadership had a longer time horizon and, accordingly, attempted to maintain uncertainty about Germany's intentions. Uncertainty serves rising great powers well. As long as there was uncertainty, there was also space for cooperation. This interaction was conducive to a cooperative equilibrium that was only shattered when Adolf Hitler's behavior led to greater certainty about Germany's malign intentions.

I examine how three European countries—France, Great Britain, and the Soviet Union—formulated policy toward Germany in the period between the Treaties of Locarno in 1925 and Hitler's remilitarization of the Rhineland in 1936, when his malign intentions became more fully apparent.[2] While multipolarity complicated the relations between European great powers and Germany, I contend that the basic logic of my argument, illustrated dyadically in chapter 2, can explain the dynamics of this multipolar case as well. In particular, I focus on the middle to late 1920s, arguing that these powers were neither naïve about Germany's aims nor particularly hopeful of transforming German intentions through engagement. Instead, both international and domestic circumstances created imperatives for short-term cooperation despite any long-term risks.

Gustav Stresemann, who was briefly Germany's chancellor and then served as foreign minister, recognized the value in keeping other European powers focused on cooperative opportunities in the short term. Stresemann's ultimate ambitions remain unclear and debated, but it is conceivable that, like many leaders of resurgent great powers, he was biding his time until a more propitious moment arose to pursue Germany's revisionist aims. In the meantime, Germany would benefit from cooperation with other European powers that lightened the economic burden on Germany.

I begin by laying out the alternative arguments and their empirical expectations in this case. Then I establish the record of interaction between Germany and its neighbors in this period. Next I return to a consideration of which theoretical argument—my own argument, buck-passing, or engagement—best explains behavior during this period. Finally, I consider where the evidence in this chapter fits into the overall argument of the book.

Alternative Arguments

My argument emphasizes how the interaction of states' time horizons produces cooperation or competition. It further attributes shifts from cooperation to competition to shifts in the incentives for short-term cooperation and concern about the long term. In the case of interwar Germany, my argument expects that cooperation would occur as a result of Germany efforts to manipulate beliefs about its long-term intentions combined with short-term incentives to cooperate. A combination of domestic economic considerations and potential other threats in the system would drive the decision to procrastinate in dealing with the potential German threat. My argument also expects that changing beliefs about German intentions should subsequently produce changes in European strategies toward Germany by altering European time horizons.

One popular alternative argument for this case focuses on how Europe's great powers attempted to pass the buck for addressing the German threat.[3] Evidence supporting such buck-passing behavior would show that these states (a) recognized Germany as a future threat but (b) consciously decided that they would try to get another state to act to restrict German growth. Only when it was evident that buck-passing was going to fail should a more concerted effort at balancing be observed. Any shift in European strategies toward Germany should, in this argument, be a product of changing assessments of capabilities, not beliefs about intentions. I contend that while the behavior in this case appears to be consistent with buck-passing, it better resembles procrastination, as European leaders did not necessarily see Germany as a threat and, further, had no reason to expect that any other state would accept the buck being passed.

Others would see cooperation with Germany during this period as evidence of engagement. Declining powers adopt cooperative approaches in an attempt to push the intentions of a rising power in a more benign direction. Cooperation aimed at engagement should look qualitatively different than cooperation meant simply to capture short-term benefits. Such cooperation should be more institutionalized and focused on creating sustainable, long-term cooperative relations.

To preview, I argue that while Germany sought a more favorable environment for its long-term growth, other European powers faced both international and domestic incentives to focus heavily on short-term opportunities. True uncertainty about long-term German intentions only reinforced this instinct. Internationally, economic crisis compelled Europe's great powers to focus on the short term, and, domestically, economic upheaval left little room for states to pay short-term costs for a long-term reward. Until Hitler, Germany refrained from provocative behavior that might have compelled other European states to consider more the long-term implications of their policies. State leaders thought less about a future world in which Germany would return to being a great power peer and more about the short-term challenges they faced.

The buck-passing argument offers a less satisfactory account of European behavior. In the period studied in this chapter, the states of Europe failed to recognize a threat for which they could pass the buck, and they would have had little confidence that any other state would pick up that buck even if they did. The states of Europe did delay addressing the potential threat from Germany, but the motive was procrastination, not buck-passing.

Finally, liberalism fares better in this case than in others. While the states of Europe accepted that Germany was likely to be a revisionist state, some hoped that cooperation, including in international institutions, might moderate the means through which it sought that revision. What liberalism is less able to explain is any transition away from cooperation toward competition.[4]

In general, the novel contribution of this chapter is its focus on an earlier temporal period, unlike in most studies of the interwar years. The cooperation that emerged with Germany in the 1920s was not inevitable and took place despite reservations about Germany's future. Uncertainty created the space for cooperation rather than foreclosing it. The evidence presented in this chapter reinforces the argument that states' myopia often leads to cooperation that they later come to regret.

How Europe's great powers responded to the reemergence of Germany has obviously been the subject of a large number of historical studies. My argument disagrees with those that see the appeasement of Germany as hopeless naïveté. Given the incentives that the states of Europe faced, cooperation with Germany during this period was a sensible and rational strategy, even if it proved to be tragically mistaken. My argument finds more in common with that of Norrin M. Ripsman and Jack S. Levy, who contend that European great powers were "buying time" until an inevitable confrontation with Germany.[5] Where I diverge from Ripsman and Levy is in my focus on an earlier period in the interwar years when Europe's great powers were not yet resigned to an eventual conflict with a resurgent Germany.

Managing Germany in the Interwar Period

I organize this chapter around the grand strategies of three great powers during this period: Great Britain, France, and the Soviet Union. For each country, I identify the nature of the policy that it adopted toward Germany and factors that accounted for any variation in those policies. In particular, I focus on the now-or-later dilemmas that each confronted in the face of uncertain German intentions.

GREAT BRITAIN

The primary concern of British foreign policy immediately after World War I was preventing another major conflict in Europe.[6] World War I had imposed a terrible cost on Europe, while compelling a reluctant Britain to fight on the Continent. Throughout the 1920s, British leaders expected that Germany would have an interest in revising the postwar order, but they did not immediately assume the worst about long-term German intentions.[7] In fact, economic considerations led to shorter time horizons, while Germany offered reassuring signals of its long-term intentions.

That the Treaty of Versailles, ending World War I, disarmed Germany and forced it to pay sizable reparations has been much discussed and debated over the years.[8] Many British leaders believed that the settlement was unduly harsh and that German unhappiness was justified. These same leaders believed that French leaders were paranoid about a German threat that did not exist in a disarmed and devastated Germany.[9] And some were more concerned by French intentions than by German intentions. After all, France was a longtime and traditional rival of Britain. As Erik Goldstein observes, "France was Britain's centuries-old traditional rival, which now seemed to be attempting once again to exert its hegemony over Europe in the wake of Germany's defeat. . . . The British official mind remained very suspicious of French intentions."[10]

In the 1920s, Britain reverted to its traditional interests in a stable balance of power on the European continent that would not require British intervention.[11] James Headlam-Morley, historical adviser to the British Foreign Office, wrote in February 1925, "Our island is so close to the continent that we cannot afford to ignore what goes on there, and so we get the next fundamental requirement, that the opposite shores of the Channel and the North

Sea should never be brought under the control of a single great military and naval power."[12] Some leaders, including Foreign Secretary Austen Chamberlain, expressed skepticism at the possibility of keeping Germany down forever and considered ways that Germany might be peacefully reintegrated into the European balance of power.[13]

Not all were as unconcerned or inattentive to the potential long-term threat posed by Germany. In July 1925, Chamberlain wrote to Baron D'Abernon, the British ambassador to Germany, that Germany appeared no longer "in the role of far-seeing contributor to the general cause of peace, but rather in that of a somewhat unwilling participant, who acquiesces in a scheme, not because of its intrinsic merits, but merely in the hope that consent will enable him to drive a bargain in other directions."[14] German reluctance to join the League of Nations only led to increased concerns about future German intentions.[15]

By October, however, the tone of European diplomacy changed following agreement on the Treaties of Locarno, which had the effects of relieving short-term pressure and providing reassurance about German intentions.[16] The Locarno treaties consisted of arbitration conventions between Germany and four of its neighbors—France, Belgium, Poland, and Czechoslovakia.[17] Germany, France, and Belgium also joined in a treaty of mutual guarantee that committed each to peaceful means for resolving any disputes. Britain, France, Germany, Belgium, and Italy became guarantors by agreeing to enforce the demilitarization of the Rhineland, defend the existing borders between Germany, France, and Belgium, and assist any signatory whose interests under the treaties were violated. Finally, Germany committed to joining the League of Nations.[18] British leaders continued to recognize and even support Germany's desire to revise the Versailles settlement, and the Locarno agreements were taken as a signal of Weimar Germany's willingness to negotiate a revision of Versailles peacefully.

As German foreign minister, Stresemann understood the incentives to keep European powers focused on the short term rather than on the potential long-term threat posed by a resurgent Germany. In fact, the idea of a pact enforcing the demilitarization of the Rhineland—arguably, the centerpiece of the Locarno treaties—was originally the suggestion of Stresemann.[19] Stresemann had three motives. First, he hoped that the pact would prevent the consummation of an Anglo-French alliance that was rumored to be forming in late 1924 and that might inhibit Germany's attempts to regain its status as a great power. Second, he thought that the pact might convince France to evacuate the Ruhr valley, which it had occupied in 1923. Third, he saw the pact as the beginning of the process of revising Versailles. If Stresemann could offer indications that he was interested in peaceful change, then he might be able to convince others to alleviate the original Versailles demands that Germany deemed unfair and onerous. As Zara S. Steiner argues, the achievement of Germany's revisionist aims would be a matter of "time and persistence" after Locarno.[20] According to Jon Jacobson, author of the definitive history of the Locarno period, "Although Stresemann regarded French concern over military security as irrational, he was willing to give Paris written assurances against 'the nightmare of a future German attack,' as he called it."[21] Maintaining uncertainty, if not favorable views, about Germany's long-term intentions was very much in Stresemann's interests.

By maintaining this uncertainty, Stresemann encouraged his European interlocutors to resolve their now-or-later dilemmas in favor of short-term cooperation.[22] The sincerity of Stresemann's commitment to the peaceful pursuit of revisionism remains debated.[23] While it is impossible to know what Stresemann might eventually have done as Germany grew more powerful, he did argue in the late 1920s that "there was . . . no alternative to the policy of 'reasonable, peaceful understanding on the basis of equality' and it was this policy alone which had made it possible for [Germany] to put a serious case for the evacuation of the Rhineland."[24] Elsewhere, Jonathan Wright describes Stresemann's approach as one of a "practical politician who never took his eye off the real world of politics at home and abroad."[25]

In fact, the Locarno agreements had just the effect on British perceptions of Germany that Stresemann hoped they would. The cooperative "spirit of Locarno" defined European diplomacy until the 1930s. The famous British historian A. J. P. Taylor calls Locarno "the turning point of the years between the wars" and writes that "its signature ended the first world war; its repudiation eleven years later marked the prelude to the second."[26] Another historian, F. S. Northedge, concurs, "The Locarno accords are generally believed to have had psychological results in symbolizing the ending of the cold war between victor and vanquished in western Europe, marking, as Chamberlain said, the real dividing line between war and peace."[27] Even Winston Churchill told an audience in Montreal in 1929 that "the outlook for peace has never been better than for fifty years."[28] Cooperation benefited all sides, at least in the short term—Britain saw value in the restoration of the European balance of power and Germany could potentially gain a reprieve from the reparations that were impeding its recovery from war.

The Rhineland pact left Chamberlain optimistic about Stresemann's willingness to pursue revisionism peacefully. More importantly, it allowed London to focus on short-term opportunities for cooperation. The intersection of British short time horizons and German long time horizons was conducive to a cooperative relationship. The foreign secretary was now inclined to support Germany's interest in having foreign troops withdraw from the Rhineland and Ruhr valley. As British suspicions of France grew, Chamberlain saw himself increasingly as an honest broker in European diplomacy, working primarily to ensure that there would not be another catastrophe on the Continent.[29] Short-term cooperation, facilitated by Locarno, was in everybody's interest. Anne Orde captures Chamberlain's focus on the short term: "Chamberlain understood Stresemann's intentions on border revision to be limited, and believed they could be held off in the short to mid-term, after which they might not be dangerous."[30] In retrospect, we know how wrong Chamberlain was, but that does not negate the fact that cooperation was the prevailing approach to Germany in the mid-1920s.

Locarno did not resolve all the outstanding issues in European diplomacy. The timetable for the evacuation of foreign troops from the Rhineland was still unspecified, as was resolution of German disgruntlement over its reparations bill. France reluctantly began to withdraw its troops from the Rhineland in January 1926, but it did not complete that withdrawal until four years later and only after the issues surrounding German reparations had been settled.[31] The Young Plan for reparations relief was only finally completed in 1930.[32]

The Locarno era did not, then, reconstitute the Concert of Europe. It did, however, facilitate German entry into the League of Nations, the withdrawal of foreign troops from the Rhineland, and settlement of the contentious reparations issue. Britain, like the other European powers, faced a choice between strategies to deal with a resurgent Germany. A more cooperative strategy capitalized on opportunities for short-term cooperation despite any long-term risks posed by a Germany with undoubtedly revisionist intentions. A more competitive, long-term-oriented strategy would not have relented in the pressure put on Germany, but such a policy would have been costly in the short term, potentially contributing to instability. Stresemann, meanwhile, was only too happy to adopt a patient strategy that made his intentions appear benign and created the space for cooperation. The cooperative spirit of Locarno was seemingly in everybody's interests.

In June 1929, a new Labor government with Arthur Henderson as foreign secretary came to power in Britain. British Labor sought to arbitrate between the revisionist desires of the German government and the security needs of its longtime rival, but sometimes ally, France. Henderson held that it was primarily France that was behaving both obstinately and unreasonably, and he was more interested in furthering cooperative relations with Germany despite any risks. Relieving pressure on Germany might lead to a more cooperative Germany that was willing to pursue its revisionist goals peacefully. Thus Henderson's top priority was the withdrawal of the remaining British troops from the Rhineland.[33] On August 19, 1929, Henderson announced that Britain would unilaterally withdraw its troops regardless of whether France also withdrew or whether a final reparations agreement had been reached. By the middle of December, the last British troops had evacuated.[34]

The end of the Locarno era began with the September 1930 German Reichstag elections and the proposal for an Austro-German customs union in March 1931.[35] The election of 107 candidates from the National Socialist Party precipitated concern about the rise of fascist ideology in Germany.

Even more than the election and the ideology it represented, though, it was the actions of the German government under Nazi rule that raised concerns about long-term German intentions.

Although many British leaders found Hitler and his ideology to be repulsive, many of those same leaders also believed the internal politics of Germany could be separated from its foreign policy.[36] Nazi anti-Semitism was a concern, though anti-Semitism was hardly unheard of in Britain at the time.[37] Moreover, when it came to ideology, just as many British leaders were more concerned about bolshevism in the Soviet Union as they were about Nazism in Germany.[38]

Put simply, until the 1930s, British leaders left uncertainty about Germany's long-term intentions unresolved, and this facilitated the choice to cooperate in the short term and, if necessary, balance later.[39] This was not a naïve strategy, but simply reflected their read on the balance between short-term opportunities and long-term risks. In the now-or-later dilemma of the time, the choice was to defer any more competitive actions until later.

The economic devastation of the Great Depression compelled Western leaders to focus primarily on short-term interests. In some sense, then, it was pushing against an open door for Britain to accept German claims that any rearmament was motivated simply by a desire to reclaim Germany's place as a sovereign nation. In September 1932, German general Kurt von Schleicher told a newspaper reporter, "I can only assure you that Germany will in any case—yes, in any case—carry out such measures as are necessary to her national defense. We cannot submit any longer to being treated as a second-class power."[40] Importantly and famously, not all were persuaded by German proclamations of defensive motivations. Churchill argued in Parliament, "When I read what is going on in Germany . . . I cannot help rejoicing that the Germans have not got the heavy cannon, the thousands of military airplanes and the tanks of various sizes for which they have been pressing in order that their status may be equal to that of other countries."[41]

German behavior, not ideology, ultimately was to resolve the uncertainty about German intentions and push London toward a different resolution of its now-or-later dilemma. Much of this pattern of behavior is familiar to students of the period, but it is worth reviewing. The pace of German rearmament accelerated from the moment the Nazi Party took power. In October 1933, Germany withdrew from the disarmament conference in Geneva and then from the League of Nations. In doing so, Hitler argued that it was unreasonable for Germany to remain disarmed if the rest of Europe was not committed to disarming itself. Still, British reactions remained mixed. A Foreign Office memorandum lamented, "The failure of the Disarmament Conference would have incalculable consequences for Europe and the League."[42] Others, however, continued to sympathize with Germany's desire to reclaim its status as a European great power and viewed the German demand on disarmament to be reasonable.[43] As remarkable as it seems in retrospect, uncertainty remained, and British leaders were reluctant to pay the costs of assuming the worst about German intentions.

Hitler recognized that uncertainty about his intentions would be politically useful to him, so, like Stresemann, he tried hard to keep others from worrying about long-term German intentions. The more other European leaders focused on the short term, the less they would be willing to expend to curtail Germany's rebirth as a great power. In May 1933, Hitler told the Reichstag, "Germany has only one desire, to be able to preserve her independence and defend her frontiers. . . . Germany is prepared to agree to any solemn pact of non-aggression because she does not think of attacking but only of acquiring security."[44] These reassurances fit well with a British desire to focus on more immediate economic issues rather than expending resources on preventing the resurgence of Germany. As Edward W. Bennett writes, "In the British government, however, the reporting of German violations was discouraged in the mid-twenties, in the interests of reconciliation, and in the early thirties virtually no one wished to sound the alarm on Germany, even if he had disturbing information."[45] To be clear, Hitler's proclamations had decreasing credibility in the face of aggressive German rearmament, but the pressures to defer competitive actions until later remained.

Germany's provocative behavior only accelerated. In January 1935, the population of the Saar region voted overwhelmingly to join Germany.[46] Then, in the course of a week in the middle of March, Hitler announced plans to rebuild the German air force and resume conscription in the German military. In response, the leaders of Britain, France, and Italy met in April at Stresa—forming the so-called Stresa Front—to express their concern, but ultimately they did little more than avow their continued support for the principles of Locarno and the independence of Austria.[47]

Hitler responded with conciliation. On May 1, he volunteered to sign on to an agreement limiting the development of the German air force. And on May 21, Hitler pleaded innocent: "What then could I wish more than peace and tranquility? But if it is said that this is merely the desire of the leaders, I can reply that if only the leaders and rulers desire peace, then nations themselves will never wish for war. . . . Germany needs peace and desires peace."[48] While now openly rebuilding the German military and having withdrawn from every international institution that bound German growth, Hitler sought repeatedly to reassure other European states about his intentions. That he did so should not be surprising, but the question is, why did anybody believe him?

In fact, Britain continued to pursue more cooperative strategies toward Germany even as it increasingly anticipated that eventual conflict was likely. Such behavior is difficult to explain for any argument that expects states to assume the worst about intentions and respond to capabilities alone. In June 1935, Britain joined Germany in a naval agreement that allowed Germany to build a navy up to 35 percent the size of the British surface navy.

The agreement also left open the possibility of Germany building even greater forces at a future date.[49] Both France and Italy were dismayed by the agreement, and the Stresa Front, which initially presaged cooperation against a resurgent German threat, collapsed as a result.

The British decision to sign the naval agreement, despite the emerging pattern of German rearmament, was a product of two factors. First, not all British leaders were yet fully convinced of Hitler's malign intentions. For example, Foreign Secretary John Simon believed that Hitler was genuinely concerned about a threat from the Soviet Union, that Hitler's intentions toward western Europe were not necessarily malign, and that, if possible, Hitler should be encouraged to pursue his revisionist aims in central Europe. Moreover, arms control, like the naval agreement, was likely to be more effective at limiting German growth than a diplomatic effort like the Stresa Front would be.[50]

Other Conservatives found things to like in Nazi Germany. National Socialism may have been fascist, but at least it was not Bolshevik.[51] Moreover, Hitler's behavior could be understood simply as an earnest desire to reclaim Germany's place as a sovereign power in Europe. Finally, for some, the Nazi regime represented a return to traditional middle-class German values. If the Nazis could address Germany's unemployment problem, then Germany would be more prosperous and therefore stable.[52]

Second, the short-term costs of more aggressive behavior toward Germany were likely to be prohibitive and pushed in the direction of cooperation now and balancing later. With the lingering geopolitical instability in Europe, Britain's difficulties in managing its declining empire, and the economic crisis brought on by the Great Depression, London could not countenance the costs of attempting to inhibit Germany's rise, especially if other European powers also were more inclined to focus on short-term benefits rather than long-term costs. Moreover, with the Japanese invasion of Manchuria, British leaders increasingly had to weigh the management of threats on both the Continent and in East Asia.[53]

The Anglo-German naval agreement began the unraveling of the Versailles and Locarno systems. After the naval agreement, both France and Italy doubted Britain's commitment to European stability. When Italy invaded Ethiopia in October 1935, tension over how to respond only further divided France and Britain.[54] Disunity among France, Britain, and Italy created space for Hitler to achieve his goal of reestablishing German power in the center of Europe.[55] With all of Germany's neighbors focused on the short term, it made it difficult for any to focus on the long term.

In March 1936, Hitler seized on this disunity and took the opportunity to remilitarize the Rhineland. While Britain lacked the will effectively to respond to the German provocation, the French defenses, centered on the Maginot Line, were incapable of generating a significant military response. At the same time, Hitler recognized that Germany did not have the indigenous capacity to sustain Germany's military growth.[56] Even after he moved into the Rhineland, Hitler continued to try to reassure, telling a British journalist, George Ward Price, that he still intended to live up to his commitments.[57] But, as expected, the crises in Ethiopia and the Rhineland had the eventual effect of elongating European time horizons, leading to the first serious considerations of how to respond to an increasingly assertive Germany.

In short, by 1936—even before the period typically associated with "appeasement"—Hitler had managed to rearm and remilitarize the Rhineland without any substantial European effort to stop him. European leaders now recognized that Germany's successful move into the Rhineland served to secure its western border and allow Hitler to turn eastward.[58] While all of the European powers, including Britain, had recognized Germany's revisionist aims, none were willing to pay any short-term price to prevent German resurgence. Moreover, as Ripsman and Levy have persuasively argued, European leaders were inclined to postpone any response to Germany, as they anticipated that they would be able to muster a more capable response several years down the road.[59]

Britain employed various litmus tests throughout this period to discern German intentions, but even when the German response was unsatisfying, the British response was muted. Uncertainty provided the cover for British leaders to avoid the costs of aggressive balancing. Éva H. Haraszti summarizes the approach of British statesman Anthony Eden: "The very task of the British should be to try to impose 'a superstructure of mutual assistance above a general non-aggression pact,' so if Germany should decline to participate, her intentions would become clear to the whole world."[60] The Anglo-German naval agreement played a similar role. Its practical significance was limited, but its value lay as an indicator of German intentions.[61] Had Hitler not joined in these agreements, British leaders may have become more concerned with long-term German intentions. As is, the agreements represented a low-cost way for Hitler to keep British leaders focused on opportunities for short-term cooperation.

Both Stresemann and Hitler, meanwhile, attempted to reduce any concern that might arise about long-term German intentions. Broken Locarno commitments were met each time by reassurances of Germany's benign intentions. Consider the statement of British leader Stanley Baldwin in 1934: "We don't know what Germany really intends. We do know and have long known that France is pacific. . . . We cannot say that about Germany."[62] The combination of Germany's uncertain long-term aims and Britain's short-term needs made cooperation a sustainable equilibrium. To be clear, London certainly had its suspicions about German intentions, but enough uncertainty remained to justify a somewhat, if decreasingly, cooperative approach.

Had the British opted to deal with Germany immediately, they would have behaved differently during this period. For example, in August 1919, Britain adopted the Ten Year Rule for military planning. The rule authorized the British military to make plans under the assumption that there would not be another major war in Europe for at least ten years.[63] The Ten Year Rule persisted through the 1920s, even as rumors of potential German rearmament surfaced as early as December 1926.[64] Only in 1932 did Britain abandon the Ten Year Rule and begin, albeit haltingly, the process of preparing for a possible war with Germany.[65] British leaders clearly recognized the threat that a reborn German air force could pose to the British Isles, yet there was little effort to respond to Hitler's decision to redevelop the air force.[66]

If London was thinking more about the need to balance against Germany more immediately, it might also have paid more notice to Hitler's writings, which expressed long-term ambitions, not immediate priorities. In *Mein Kampf*, Hitler expresses clearly his racist, anti-Semitic ideology and the logic for German expansion. Some British leaders read Hitler carefully, whereas others dismissed his writing as fantasy.[67] While the British were focused on strategies that might create short-term benefits, they were less likely to fixate on the German leader's long-term, often bizarre ramblings written before he had taken power.

Finally, had Britain been more interested in addressing the potential long-term threat posed by Germany, it would have pursued a different diplomatic strategy. Britain might have been more cautious in embracing the "spirit of Locarno," which offered short-term relief from the tension of the 1920s but at the long-term risk of Germany's reemergence as a revisionist great power. Rather than allow the Stresa Front to collapse over the Anglo-German naval agreement, London might have prioritized diplomatic relations with France and Italy. In short, British behavior resembles procrastination more than anything else. Despite the recognition that Germany harbored revisionist intentions and despite evident reason to worry about the potential military capabilities of a rearmed Germany, there was little desire to pay a short-term cost for any long-term aim.[68] While the benefits of cooperation in the 1930s were relatively small, the costs of aggressive competition could have been substantial. It was the interaction of long-term German time horizons and short-term British time horizons that allowed sustained cooperation throughout much of the interwar period.

FRANCE

If any country had reason to be fearful of Germany both in the short and long term, it was France.[69] France had been decisively defeated in the Franco-Prussian War, and it had also endured World War I. Of all the European great powers, then, it is perhaps most surprising that even France cooperated with Germany in the interwar period.[70] After all, in 1924, the French foreign minister Édouard Herriot predicted, "On the day that Germany finds herself strong enough to refuse to pay us she would inevitably bring about a new war."[71] Or as Arnold Wolfers writes, "France was obsessed by the fear of a new war with Germany."[72] All of this makes the record of French coop-eration with Germany in the interwar period particularly worthy of atten-tion. In this case, it was not the presence of other threats or uncertainty about German intentions but rather the short-term benefits and costs of a more competitive approach that facilitated the French decision to procrastinate. Again, the interaction of time horizons generated a cooperative outcome.

The Locarno agreements produced a mixed reaction in France. On the one hand, the guarantees offered by Locarno excluded both Poland and Czecho-slovakia, with which France had cultivated relations.[73] These relationships were important to France, as the two smaller eastern powers could threaten to open a second front for Germany should it ever act aggressively in the west toward France. On the other hand, Locarno did offer valuable guaran-tees of France's own eastern border, and it made Britain a guarantor of the European order.

Though the actual content of the Locarno treaties was a mixed bag for France, the "spirit of Locarno" was welcomed in Paris. In the context of France's now-or-later dilemma, Locarno provided a reason to postpone any more aggressive (and costly) efforts to curtail German growth. The influen-tial leader of the French Socialists, Léon Blum, suggested, "No French leader, not even [Raymond] Poincaré, could now go back upon the Locarno policy."[74] When Germany formally entered the League of Nations in September 1926, Foreign Minister Aristide Briand proclaimed, "Away with rifles, machine guns, and cannon! Make way for conciliation, arbitration, and peace."[75] The German decision to join the league kept France and others focused on the short term while doing little to limit Germany's potential future growth.

Shortly after Germany entered into the league, Briand and Stresemann met at Thoiry on September 17.[76] The two ministers discussed a German proposal by which Germany would pay its reparations early in exchange for France ceding the Saar to Germany and evacuating its troops from the Rhineland. France, like Britain, saw valuable short-term benefits in the form of repara-tions and relief from the occupation of the Rhineland even though the deal carried long-term risks. The interest of France in the Thoiry proposal was motivated primarily by two factors. First, the French franc was under great pressure, making early payment of reparations attractive. Second, while the Locarno accords had initiated cooperative relations, there was hope that Thoiry could extend that cooperation going forward, leading to a more com-prehensive solution to Franco-German discord.[77]

By November 1926, negotiations between France and Germany stalled. France's economic woes abated—relieving the short-term pressure for a deal—and the implementation details of a reparations-for-evacuation swap became difficult to arrange. Additionally, the French military strongly op-posed any withdrawal from the Rhineland.[78] Marshal Ferdinand Foch contended, "By abandoning the Rhine we will give Germany the ability to dominate and subjugate central Europe—beginning with Austria. . . . There can be no question of France withdrawing from the Rhineland before the expiration of fifteen years . . . evacuation will mean a national disaster coming on the heels of the financial crisis. Security, foreign policy, reparations will all collapse with it."[79]

While the Thoiry bargain did not come to fruition, Briand continued to envision institutionalized cooperation that could bring lasting peace to Europe. At the broadest level, the Kellogg-Briand Pact of 1928 outlawed war as a method for resolving international disputes.[80] Then, in May 1930, Briand offered a plan for a European union that would include various institutions, a system of arbitration, security guarantees for all of Europe, and a common market.[81] Briand was under no illusions about either Germany's enormous potential power or its revisionist aims, but he accepted signals from Stresemann that Germany would be interested in a cooperative route for Germany to return to its status as a European great power.

Unlike many others, Briand appears to have been more oriented toward a sustainable long-term European order rather than pragmatic short-term benefits. As Wolfers writes, Briand believed that "to appease and satisfy the new democratic Germany required only that the Rightist policy of force, humiliation, and threats be replaced by a spirit of friendly co-operation and negotiation."[82] "It would be insane," argued Briand, "to insist on eternal containment of a nation of sixty million people."[83] Over the long term, Germany's return to great power status was inevitable, and Briand was willing to make short-term sacrifices if doing so could prevent more conflict as Germany rose.

As recounted above, Versailles and Locarno began to unravel in the early 1930s as the Nazis took power in Germany and issued ominous signals of their intentions, including the Austro-German customs union and then the withdrawal from the disarmament convention as well as the League of Nations. France was left with a dilemma. It could continue to pursue disarmament, but German signals suggested that this was unwise. Or it could accept the inevitability of German rearmament, but that course was likely to be costly and dangerous.[84]

Ultimately, the French acknowledged dangerous German intentions, yet the response was still relatively timid. There are three primary explanations for the weak French response. First, many French leaders saw Hitler as simply a continuation of, not a departure from, the theme of German revisionism that had persisted since Versailles.[85] Second, while Hitler's revisionism appeared more virulent than his predecessors', some French leaders believed this would backfire for Germany. The French Radical politician Édouard Daladier suggested that Hitler's aggression would make it easier for France to generate a coalition against Germany.[86] Third, even if Hitler's ideology and behavior were concerning, many French leaders predicted that Hitler would not last long. André Tardieu, a hawkish French minister, rejected a disarmament agreement in April 1934: "You are wasting your time, the agreement which you proposed will not be concluded . . . Hitler will not last long. . . . An agreement . . . would only strengthen him."[87] At least initially, then, French leaders found reason to be dismissive of the threat posed by Hitler.[88]

French policy toward Germany only began to shift in the spring of 1934, even though German rearmament had begun at least three years earlier. In March 1934, Hitler demanded that Germany be allowed an army of three hundred thousand troops and that France be limited to an army of the same size. Paris rejected Hitler's proposal. On April 17, French foreign minister Louis Barthou announced that France would start to build up its military in earnest in response to Germany's rearmament.[89] Barthou wrote to Ronald Campbell, the British ambassador in Paris, "Even before seeking to discuss whether an agreement can be reached on a system of guarantees effective enough to enable the signing of a convention which would legalize Germany's substantial rearmament, France must place in the forefront of her preoccupations the conditions of her own security, which she sees as including that of other interested powers."[90] Though domestic political and economic factors inhibited the rapid buildup of the French military until 1936, a shift was finally evident in French foreign policy.

Provocative German behavior led to even greater certainty about German intentions, and, as a consequence, France shifted its now-or-later resolution in the direction of more concern about the long term and thus more competitive strategies in the short term. The French strategy had three main components. First, Paris remained committed to finding a cooperative, multilateral solution to Europe's problems, even if it did not include Germany. Following Germany's resumption of conscription, France was the driving force behind the Stresa Front, which brought together France, Britain, and Italy in opposition to revising Versailles.[91]

Second, France sought bilateral agreements that would bolster its position in Europe. Foreign Minister Pierre Laval approached Britain about strengthening its commitment to the Continent but had little success. In January 1935, Laval met in Rome with Benito Mussolini. They joined in the Rome Agreements, which called for negotiating a non-aggression pact for Danubian countries, committed both signatories to act together in the event of unilateral German rearmament or a threat to Austria, and settled some of the outstanding African colonial issues between the two states.[92]

On May 2 of the same year, France and the Soviet Union agreed on a limited mutual assistance pact, which committed each to assist if the other was the target of German aggression.[93] France sought the pact to prevent Hitler from potentially co-opting Soviet resources for German expansion, while Moscow gained the possibility of assistance should Germany signal interest in expanding eastward.[94]

Third, France increased its own arms, but domestic political and economic difficulties slowed the pace of rearmament until 1936. From 1931 to 1935, French military spending remained relatively constant, between 4.1 percent and 4.7 percent of French gross national product. During that same period, German military spending increased from 1 percent to 8 percent.[95]

More specifically, French military development was limited by a combination of domestic and economic factors.[96] The short-term costs of addressing the long-term threat posed by Germany were prohibitive, especially if other European states were not going to participate. This was not French buck-passing, at least if France was acting rationally: the French could not have expected anybody else to pick up the buck of balancing against Germany. Domestically, despite Hitler's ominous rhetoric and threatening behavior, a strong pacifist sentiment still pervaded French public opinion. As late as 1933, the French army had 240,000 more men than the German army, so French pacifists could not understand the need for further French military development.[97] Moreover, rapid French rearmament would undermine efforts to develop cooperative international institutions. Economically, whereas most of Europe had struggled through the Great Depression in the early 1930s, France was hit by it a bit later.[98] The case for significantly increasing military expenditures in the midst of an economic crisis was tough to make. France's economic problems contributed to constant domestic political turmoil, making it difficult for any leader to undertake a bold rearmament campaign. Domestic and economic pressures had the effect of shortening France's time horizons even as international pressures were compelling the French to look further into the future.

On February 27, 1936, the French Parliament ratified the Franco-Soviet pact that had been negotiated nine months earlier. The next month, Hitler used the pact and the claim that it violated the Locarno agreements as a pretext to remilitarize the Rhineland.[99] To France, the lack of any concerted European response to the German aggression signaled the death of Versailles, Locarno, and all that they stood for in European diplomacy. Germany was now in position to threaten France as well as the smaller states of central and eastern Europe.

French leaders, like British leaders, were influenced by various litmus tests of German intentions. These tests helped France to resolve its uncertainty about German intentions. Under Stresemann, Germany's willingness to abide by the Locarno treaties and inclination to participate in the disarmament conference were both taken as reassuring signals of Germany's intention to peacefully pursue revisions of Versailles. Playing a long game, Stresemann understood that any early provocation would likely make it harder for Germany over the long term, even if it offered some short-term reward. This approach meshed well with the needs of European states that were reluctant to pay any short-term costs for confronting Germany. German withdrawal from both the disarmament conference and the League of Nations did not signal any specific intention, but it did elongate France's time horizons, as the French worried more about future German intentions and eventually pursued more competitive strategies as a result.

What is surprising, then, about this case is the extent to which even France, with its history of conflict with Germany, engaged in cooperation with Germany or at least abstained from any aggressive effort to balance against it. As France resolved its own now-or-later dilemma, the most important consideration was the short-term cost of trying to address the long-term German threat as well as uncertainty about how Germany would pursue its revisionist goals. Given such an unacceptable cost, Paris opted for a cautious, but cooperative, approach to Berlin. Consider Jacobson's observation: "It was not until late in the 1930's that the threat of a German military offensive ceased to be potential and became actual and immediate. What France had to fear was not present German military capability [in the late 1920s] but her potential power and future intentions."[100] But to do anything about those intentions in the late 1920s would have required (a) either accurately discerning those intentions or making assumptions about them and (b) paying a substantial cost at a time when France faced domestic division and continuous economic problems. Stresemann and other leaders acted in ways that facilitated mutually beneficial cooperation until Hitler's provocative behavior served to draw attention to long-term German intentions and make the need for more aggressive counterbalancing evident. Meanwhile, French leaders like Briand hoped for an institutionalized solution to Europe's troubles, so they welcomed indications of German receptiveness to such approaches.

THE SOVIET UNION

During the interwar period, Soviet relations with Germany fluctuated from furtive military cooperation in the 1920s to antagonism in the mid-1930s to secret cooperation immediately prior to the outbreak of World War II.[101] Throughout this period, domestic upheaval in the Soviet Union contributed to resolving its now-or-later dilemma in ways that led the Soviets to favor cooperation with Germany over competition. The Soviets had few friends and sought to avoid any short-term costs that would have been incurred by confronting Germany. Given their own domestic challenges, the Soviets were preoccupied with the short term, giving little thought to a world in which a resurgent Germany would be a competitor.

The peace ending World War I was beneficial neither to Germany nor to what was to become the Soviet Union. Germany had been disarmed and ordered to pay extraordinary reparations. Russia, in the midst of the Bolshevik revolution, was excluded from the victor's peace that the Western powers formulated.[102] The two powers found friendship in their estrangement. During the Genoa economic conference in April 1922, German and Soviet representatives concluded the Treaty of Rapallo, which helped alleviate their sense of diplomatic isolation.[103] Beyond any psychological effect, the treaty facilitated the exchange of German manufactured goods, which the Soviet Union needed to build its industrializing economy, and for Russian raw materials, which Germany needed to feed its industry and rebuild its economy in the aftermath of war.[104] The short-term benefits of cooperating with a resurgent power exceeded concerns about long-term German intentions.[105]

Rapallo laid the foundation for significant German-Soviet cooperation throughout the 1920s.[106] In the summer of 1923, Germany, despite its own economic difficulties, agreed to loan M50 million to Moscow to help build industrial plants. In exchange, the Soviets offered secret military cooperation, including a school for training pilots, a training ground for tanks on Soviet territory, and cooperation in the development of poison gas. Versailles forbade Germany from such military activities, making Soviet cooperation invaluable. Moscow benefited from observing German training exercises as well as from the marks that Germany provided in exchange. Short-term, mutually beneficial cooperation was a stable equilibrium despite any long-term risks of such cooperation.[107]

Soviet-German relations were not without their problems. The revolutionary Soviets under Joseph Stalin believed in fomenting world revolution among the proletariat, including in heavily industrialized Germany. Germany's leadership insisted that Russia stop supporting communist groups in Germany.[108] Both sides also faced domestic opposition to cooperating with the other. For some Soviet leaders, cooperation with any capitalist bourgeois state was abhorrent, no matter the specific short-term, instrumental benefits that might be gained from cooperation with Germany.[109] On the German side, some leaders were concerned by the influence that training with Soviet Communists might have on the development of the German military.

Moscow also feared that Germany would reach a rapprochement with the West, leaving the Soviet Union isolated. The Locarno agreements only amplified these concerns, as Soviet leaders worried that Germany would now direct its revisionism eastward. Going even further, many Soviets believed that Locarno had been designed precisely for this reason: the Soviet Union was conspicuously not invited to Locarno so that German revisionism could then be redirected to the east.[110] In an effort to allay Soviet fears, in April 1926, Germany and the Soviet Union agreed to the Treaty of Berlin, which bound each side to remain neutral if the other were attacked. For Germany, the treaty allowed for the continuation of military training in Soviet territory and also signaled to the West that Germany would look to form cooperative relationships beyond Locarno. For the Soviet Union, the treaty was valuable reassurance that Locarno did not imply Germany's abandonment of the Soviet Union in favor of rapprochement with the West.[111]

German-Soviet cooperation persisted through the remainder of the 1920s. Despite occasional crises between the two sides—such as the Shakhty show trial of 1928 in which three German citizens working in the Soviet Union were accused of sabotage—both the Germans and the Soviets benefited from short-term cooperation that took priority over any long-term risks introduced by such cooperation.[112] Moscow was also increasingly concerned with a potential threat from Japan, which only added to the benefits of cooperation with Germany.

Germany sought to continue this cooperation by, in part, keeping its ultimate intentions well hidden. As with Germany's relations with both Britain and France, Germany's relationship with the Soviet Union was recast by the decision to withdraw from the disarmament negotiations and then the League of Nations. Once Hitler publicly announced his intention to rearm, the need for German military training in the Soviet Union was obviated. Now fearful that nothing stood between it and a rearmed Germany, Moscow became an advocate of a collective security solution to international threats. Opportunities for short-term benefit were abandoned in favor of more long-term solutions to the threat now recognized from Germany. In other words, Moscow settled on a different resolution of its now-or-later dilemma.

Soviet views of National Socialism, fascism, and the rise of Hitler were mixed. On the one hand, Stalin did not necessarily consider fascism to be an impediment to fruitful relations between the Soviet Union and Germany. Stalin had managed to maintain cordial relations with fascist Italy after the rise of Mussolini, so similar relations might be possible with Hitler's Germany. "We are far from feeling elated about the fascist regime in Germany," observed Stalin, "but what counts here is not fascism, if only because fascism in Italy, for example, has not prevented the USSR from establishing excellent relations with that country."[113] Stalin also believed that a German dictatorship under Hitler would be more predictable than Western liberal democracies.[114]

On the other hand, Hitler's views of communism were concerning to Soviet leadership. In Mein Kampf, Hitler expresses his contempt for communism and envisions an expansionist German military campaign directed eastward against the Soviet Union.[115] As in Britain and France, however, officials in the Soviet Union differed in their assessments of the importance and credibility of Mein Kampf. Prominent Soviet diplomat Karl Radek employed Hitler's writings to bolster his contention that Hitler's Germany posed a threat to Soviet security.[116] But the chief of the Soviet General Staff, Aleksandr I. Egorov, dismissed Mein Kampf: "Hitler wrote that in the bitterness of his [Landsberg] prison cell. We do not therefore take this seriously!"[117] While fascism and Hitler's writings may have driven some Soviet leaders to think more seriously about long-term Soviet intentions, they did not persuade all.

Hitler's provocative behavior, however, did have the anticipated effect of altering Moscow's approach to Germany. Soviet time horizons shifted forward to considering the implications of a more powerful Germany for Soviet security. Importantly, though, it was information about Germany's intentions, not its capabilities, that led to this shift. In February 1933, the German Communist Party (Kommunistische Partei Deutschlands, or KPD) was prohibited from holding open-air demonstrations and the Nazi police ransacked the party's headquarters. Hitler then blamed the KPD for the February 27 Reichstag fire and used it as yet another excuse to intensify his persecution of German Communists. The German press was replete with virulent attacks on both the Soviet Union, specifically, and communism, in general. As was his way, though, Hitler tried to assuage any concerns raised by his behavior. On May 5, 1933, Hitler ratified the Berlin protocol that extended the Berlin neutrality agreement of 1926.[118]

The behavior of the Nazi regime and police toward German Communists raised some initial concerns that were then amplified by ominous changes in foreign policy.[119] The official Soviet newspaper *Izvestiya* reflected on the German decision to leave the League of Nations: "Germany's exit from the League of Nations is, for the supporters of peace, an alarming warning of the need to be on guard."[120] Then, in June 1933, German economics minister Alfred Hugenberg submitted a provocative note to the World Economic Conference calling for the creation of additional German living space, presumably in the east toward the Soviet Union.[121]

Soviet alarm grew even further with the signing of the German-Polish non-aggression pact on January 26, 1934. Hitler had hoped that the pact would be another reassuring sign of his benign intentions. By cooperating with Poland—so often the target of aggression—Hitler hoped he could convince others that he did not intend to attack toward the east. According to Donald Cameron Watt, "For Hitler, the naval agreement, together with the German-Polish non-aggression pact of 1934, was to be the much-invoked proof of his will for peace and of his ability to keep his word, proof employed most notably whenever these two qualities were, or were likely to be, called into question."[122] Hitler, like Stresemann, tried his best, at a minimum, to hide his intentions and, at a maximum, to represent those intentions as peaceful and benign.

Moscow worried, however, that the non-aggression pact was possibly a signal that Poland would simply acquiesce to German aggression, leaving the Soviet Union vulnerable. Edward Hallett Carr concludes, "What this meant in practice was that Hitler was prepared to sacrifice the German population of Danzig and the German minority in Poland for the sake of a political alliance with Poland. The fatal blow had been struck at the perennially sensitive point of German-Soviet friendship. The policy of Rapallo, the diplomacy of the Weimar republic, had been finally abandoned."[123] Short-term pragmatic cooperation was lapsing, to be replaced by longer-term fear and antagonism.[124]

Following the German-Polish pact, Moscow devised a series of litmus tests through which to evaluate long-term German intentions in eastern Europe. On March 28, 1934, Soviet foreign affairs minister Maxim Litvinov offered Germany a bilateral agreement that would guarantee the independence of the Baltic states. When Germany rejected this agreement, Moscow took it as yet another indicator of malign long-term German intentions.[125] The Soviets then proposed an agreement whereby Germany and the Soviet Union would renounce threatening each other's territory and commit to noninterference in each other's domestic affairs.[126] Again, Hitler rejected this agreement, leading to ever more doubt about the credibility of Hitler's rhetoric of benign intentions.

Still, some Soviet leaders held out hope that Hitler's regime would be short-lived and, with its departure, would come an improvement in relations with Germany. Optimists hoped that the German army, with which the Soviet military maintained good relations, might gain control over Germany. These hopes were, however, illusory. When Hitler supported the attempted overthrow of the Austrian government and the assassination of Austrian chancellor Engelbert Dollfuss on July 25, 1934, it was taken as an indication that Hitler's control was, if anything, strengthening.[127]

The attempted coup in Austria, the German refusal to guarantee the integrity of the Baltic states, and the continuing persecution of German Communists led to the Soviet decision to accede to the League of Nations.[128] German provocations had extended Soviet time horizons, and the decision to join the League of Nations is indicative of a more forward-looking Soviet grand strategy. Prior to the summer of 1934, Soviet decision makers had steadfastly opposed entry into the league.[129] The origins of Soviet-German collaboration in the 1920s lay in a mutual discontent with the Treaty of Versailles. While Germany viewed the treaty as unfair, Soviet Communists took the treaty as reflecting the abhorrent nature of Western capitalism. But as the Soviets became more concerned by German long-term intentions, collective security became more attractive. If Germany had gained the acquiescence of Poland and could threaten the Baltics with impunity, then the Soviets could find themselves isolated in a battle against a rearmed Nazi Germany. On September 18, 1934, the Soviet Union joined the League of Nations to prevent its own isolation. From an early harsh critic of Versailles, the Soviet Union was to become a later ardent supporter of the league.

Other moves followed in an effort to bolster Soviet security and reflected a shift to more competitive strategies toward Germany. On December 5, after two months of difficult negotiations, France and the Soviet Union pledged not to join in any agreement with Germany without the approval of the other. Moscow's hope was to contain potential German expansionist efforts by augmenting its entry into the League of Nations with a more focused bilateral agreement with France. As remote as a Franco-German agreement might have seemed, Stalin continued to fear being isolated from Europe and left to confront a resurgent Germany on his own.[130]

At the same time, it is worth noting that Stalin still had not completely abandoned attempts to achieve cooperation with Germany. As noted above, the resumption of German conscription in March 1935 prompted the leaders of France, Italy, and Britain to meet at Stresa, but Stalin was again not invited.

The Soviet Union continued to worry about being abandoned by the rest of Europe and left to face Germany on its own. As a consequence, Moscow then turned again to the possibility of cooperation with Germany. On April 9, a Soviet-German credit agreement was signed, granting the Soviets a credit line of RM200 million.[131]

This economic cooperation, however, could not forestall yet more ominous signs in eastern Europe. Most significantly, attempts to conclude an "Eastern Locarno" guaranteeing the security of eastern European countries failed in the spring of 1935. Negotiations over an Eastern Locarno pact had intermittently taken place throughout the 1930s, but it was German (and, after the German-Polish agreement, Polish) opposition that ultimately made any agreement impossible. In the end, Hitler simply had little desire to guarantee the security of eastern Europe.[132]

With the Eastern Locarno idea having failed, the Soviet Union concluded its own mutual assistance agreements with France and Czechoslovakia in May 1935.[133] Prior to May, France had been reluctant to enter into a formal mutual assistance pact with the Soviet Union out of concern that it would violate both the spirit and the letter of the Locarno agreements. Paris moved on from these concerns as it became more concerned by indications of German long-term intentions.

Even after the conclusion of the Franco-Soviet and Czech-Soviet pacts, Stalin continued to pursue a rapprochement with Germany. Stalin did not completely trust France, and he trusted Great Britain even less.[134] Ongoing discussions with Germany were sensible in case France attempted to reach its own rapprochement with Germany. The continued negotiations also reflected divisions among Stalin's advisers. Litvinov advocated for collective security and thought Soviet security concerns had been well addressed by the pact with France. Limited economic cooperation might be possible with Germany, but a political agreement was unlikely with Germany given Hitler's revisionist aspirations in eastern Europe.[135] David Kandelaki, the Soviet trade representative in Berlin from 1935 until 1937, advocated for a more cooperative approach toward Germany. Increased economic cooperation could facilitate political reconciliation.[136] During the summer of 1935, Kandelaki engaged in negotiations for an economic agreement with German economics minister Hjalmar Schacht. Eventually, a statement of common economic interests emerged, but little concrete was produced and certainly nothing with larger political implications.[137]

At the same time, Litvinov proposed a Soviet-German non-aggression pact to the German ambassador in Moscow, Friedrich Werner von der Schulenburg. Coming on the heels of the Franco-Soviet pact, Litvinov viewed the German reaction as an important indicator of long-term German intentions. When Hitler rejected the pact, Litvinov employed the rejection as leverage in Moscow to convince other Soviet leaders that cooperation with Hitler's Germany was untenable. According to Jonathan Haslam, Germany's refusal of the proposed pact "was revealing," as "Litvinov evidently hoped that Berlin's rejection of the offer would confirm to his supervisors that the Germans were still of aggressive intent."[138]

Germany's rejection of the pact focused Soviet leaders on alternative ways of securing Soviet interests in the face of uncertain, but increasingly concerning, long-term German intentions. None of these signals of German intentions were necessarily costly—other interpretations of their meaning were possible—but as a whole they formed a composite image that played a pivotal role in convincing the Soviet Union of Germany's malign intentions. Taken together, they had the effect of shifting Soviet time horizons toward the future. To be clear, the substantial growth in German capabilities was, of course, also worrisome to European powers, but it was the marriage of those capabilities to increasing indications of malign future intentions that led eventually to the shift in European strategies.

In sum, Soviet policy by the end of 1935 was somewhat Janus-faced, but it had evolved to favor more competitive strategies over cooperation. As indicators of German long-term intentions turned more concerning, time horizons converged in a way to make cooperation less likely. The sincerity of Stalin's engagement with Germany continued to be a source of debate, with some seeing genuine interest in cooperation and others seeing an attempt to protect the Soviet Union against French defection.[139] Either way, the core of Soviet security policy was collective security under the League of Nations combined with mutual assistance pacts with France and Czechoslovakia.

The final breaking point in relations was reached in early 1936. On January 11, Soviet premier Vyacheslav Molotov delivered a belligerent anti-German speech. In response, in late January, Hitler prohibited any further arms deals with the Soviet Union. Finally, Moscow suspended any further negotiations with Germany following the remilitarization of the Rhineland, a move that Hitler justified as a response to ratification of the Franco-Soviet pact.[140] An *Izvestiya* editorial explained, "The Soviet Union, which has been against every attempt to deny self-determination to the German people . . . declares itself opposed to Germany's breach of the Locarno treaty, against a breach that will only enhance the danger of war."[141] Previously, Moscow had been weighing the intensity of the German threat against a potential threat from Japan, but now the Soviet Union turned its attention fully to Germany.[142]

Even still, Germany and the Soviet Union signed another credit agreement for an additional RM200 million in April 1936, only a month after the remilitarization. Soviet hedging continued, but by the end of the summer, Soviet-German relations had reached a low point. First, in July, the Spanish Civil War began, with Germany and the Soviet Union supporting opposite sides. From Moscow's perspective, Germany's support of Franco's fascist movement could have left the Soviet's closest partner, France, surrounded by fascist states in Spain, Italy, and Germany.[143] Second, in August, Stalin's show trials began in Moscow. The prosecutions of several Soviets accused of involvement in a Gestapo-Trotskyist conspiracy were replete with anti-Nazi messages. This, in turn, led to an intensification of anti-Soviet rhetoric in Germany, in particular at a rally in Nuremberg in September.[144] Third, in November, the Anti-Comintern Pact was signed between Germany and Japan, signaling cooperation between the two greatest and likeliest threats to Soviet security.[145]

By the end of 1936, then, German-Soviet relations had completely deteriorated. Although occasional efforts were made until 1939 to patch relations through economic cooperation, these efforts failed. Cooperation was not restored until the eve of World War II, when Stalin and Hitler reached their infamous non-aggression pact in August 1939. Only when Soviet leaders became convinced that France and Britain would not come to their aid were they compelled to reconsider cooperating with Hitler.[146]

Explaining Cooperation and Competition with Interwar Germany

This chapter has attempted to explain British, French, and Soviet strategy toward Germany in the interwar period. I have focused on the decade from the mid-1920s until the mid-1930s. Early in that period, all three powers pursued short-term-oriented cooperative strategies with Germany.[147] Later in that period, all three shifted toward more long-term-oriented competitive strategies. These strategies were not naïve appeasement but rather were strategies adopted based on how each state resolved its own now-or-later dilemmas with regard to an uncertain future German threat.

As expected by my argument, Germany worked to manipulate others' beliefs about its intentions. Uncertainty about how Germany would pursue revisionism created the space for cooperation between Germany and myopic European leaders. Early in the interwar period, Germany saw that cooperation could enable it to emerge from its economic predicament. This, however, was only likely to succeed if Germany could maintain uncertainty about its future intentions. Later in the interwar period, Hitler saw less value in retaining uncertainty about German intentions, and the imperative became stronger for Germany to grow in order to continue to feed its rearmament industry. As Germany did less to hide its intentions and as uncertainty became measurable risk, the cooperative equilibrium among Europe's great powers disintegrated.

Other European powers confronted now-or-later dilemmas in responding to the potential German threat. How states resolve such a dilemma depends on the benefits of cooperation, the need to attend to more pressing immediate threats, and assessments of the long-term intentions of a potential emerging threat. Moscow worried about the threats posed by both Japan and Germany. Cooperation with one or the other was necessary to avoid the possibility of a two-front war. Though the British were wary of French intentions in the 1920s, they did not see the need to devote substantial resources toward an emerging threat from France. Both of the other considerations, however, pushed European states in the direction of deferring competitive behavior until later. Uncertainty about the means by which Germany would pursue its revisionist goals gave leaders the opportunity to engage in beneficial short-term cooperation with Germany. In some cases, these benefits were economic, as with France and Great Britain. In other cases, the benefits were more security related, as with the Soviet Union.

Procrastination was the dominant strategy for Germany's interlocutors. As Adam B. Ulam says of Soviet strategy, "For the immediate and foreseeable future, the Soviet aims were not the punishment of aggressors or the preparation of a grand military alliance against them, but the noninvolvement of the Soviet Union in war."[148] German leaders like Stresemann and Hitler took advantage of the situation by doing all they could to discourage more long-term thinking. Michael I. Handel is worth quoting at length: "The preparatory stage of deception was intended to divert attention from his [Hitler's] actual goal and reassure potential opponents that he did not intend to do what they feared he might. The fait accompli was then followed by a flood of new assurances that since Germany desired peace, this was the last such act of its kind; in this manner, he allayed fears and set the stage for the next move."[149] Reassurance was accepted at face value because it allowed leaders to avoid paying heavy costs for balancing against Germany and attempting to prevent its reemergence as a great power. As Orde summarizes, "It is clear that there was over-optimism and a false estimate of German motives. Had the objectives for Stresemann's policy been more frankly faced, the rejoicings might have been more tempered and the expectations more realistic."[150]

Buck-passing provides a less compelling explanation for cooperation in this period in European history. Again, buck-passing requires that states recognize the threat but attempt to get somebody else to pay for dealing with that threat. European leaders, however, ought to have had no faith that anybody else was going to deal with the German threat. This was not buck-passing; it was procrastination.[151] Buck-passing also expects that such behavior will cease once the capabilities of a state are sufficiently threatening, but it was not German capabilities that brought an end to the cooperative approach to Germany.[152] Focusing on the year 1932 when Germany began to withdraw from various international institutions, Bennett argues that "Germans did not want war, and they had no significant military power; thus there was no need to think of trying to balance German military power."[153] Or as Taylor notes, "As late as 1934 Germany could not contemplate war against Poland, let alone against France."[154] And "Germany was little more prepared for a great war between 1933 and 1936 than she had been before Hitler came to power."[155]

Contrary to offensive realist expectations, European great powers did not assume the worst about German intentions. Even if one wants to argue that these states were simply buck-passing, they still should have been expected to balance internally, yet they refrained from rearmament for much of this period. Nor did states respond to German capabilities alone. Rather, they reached judgments about German intentions, relying on German reactions to a variety of litmus tests, that allowed for cooperation. As long as those intentions were uncertain, cooperation was possible, but it ceased to be so with increasingly ominous indications of Hitler's plans. To be clear, as the 1930s progressed, it became difficult to disentangle the effects of increasing German capabilities from the influence of increasingly ominous signals of German intentions. What is clear, however, is that European leaders did not simply assume the worst about German intentions; they inferred those intentions from German behavior.

Engagement can explain the effort by Europe's great powers to create international institutions to govern the postwar order. Even here, however, the evidence suggests that not many European leaders, save Briand, put much faith in the long-term ability of the League of Nations to govern the international system. They understood that Germany had revisionist intentions, and they only hoped that Berlin would pursue those intentions peacefully rather than aggressively.

What changed in the 1930s were the increasingly ominous indications of German intentions. Bennett argues, "A real problem lay in the difficulty of fathoming German long-range intentions, something particularly difficult when those intentions ran counter to both the expectations and the hopes of observers."[156] Taylor writes, "No one therefore need pride himself on his perspicacity in divining Hitler's intentions."[157] Few doubted German interests in revising the international system, but equally few wanted to pay any costs to prevent that revisionism. Rather than be reassuring, Hitler's behavior was provocative and raised questions about Germany's long-term intentions. One could argue that an account based simply on material threats could explain the shift from cooperation to competition, but such an account cannot explain the timing of the shift. If states assume the worst about intentions and capabilities, then Germany's neighbors should have taken steps to prevent Germany's resurgence much sooner than they did.

Take the example of France. When France did look to the future, its concerns were amplified by the history of relations between France and Germany. From the day World War I ended, in the back of every French leader's mind was the fear that Germany would one day seek through violence to reclaim its great power position in Europe. As Anthony Adamthwaite notes, "Geography imposed a simple, harsh logic on French thinking. The greatest single external threat was Germany and after two wars in living memory the French could not be other than firm in their insistence on security."[158] Yet France did not act this way. Short-term expedience—and the economic benefits it offered—took precedence over long-term solutions to sources of French insecurity. The short-term costs of more competitive strategies toward Germany were prohibitive. As in the Anglo-U.S. case discussed previously, as time horizons extend into the future, different indicators appear to become important in judging intentions: history and identity become more important than immediate behavioral signals.

In short, the interaction of German and other European time horizons produced cooperation early in the interwar period. While Germany looked toward the long term—and therefore refrained from provocative behavior—European powers were focused on short-term economic challenges. This interaction was conducive to cooperation. Only when doubt about long-term German intentions arose did relationships in Europe begin to shift.

That European powers would ultimately regret cooperating with interwar Germany does not negate the fact that such cooperation occurred. If anything, it makes it even more important to understand why rational states may nonetheless opt for cooperation that offers short-term rewards. My argument focusing on the effects of uncertainty about future intentions and temporal dynamics helps explain this surprising and, ultimately, regrettable behavior. In the next chapter, I examine the origins of the Cold War and the emergence of Soviet-U.S. rivalry. Here again, an ominous shadow was cast over international politics. As the United States started to think more long term, it also became more competitive in its approach to the Soviet Union.

CHAPTER 5

The Origins of the Cold War

This chapter examines the dynamics of emerging threats in an environment where other threats were absent. During World War II, the pressing threat of Nazi Germany and imperial Japan produced short time horizons and the mutual benefits of cooperation for the Allied powers. At the end of World War II, time horizons became elongated, and competition resulted. The United States was by any measure the most powerful country in the world after World War II. Given the small short-term rewards for cooperation, the absence of alternative threats, and growing concern about long-term Soviet intentions, the United States transitioned from the cooperation that characterized World War II to the competition that characterized the Cold War. As much as emerging bipolarity set the stage for the Cold War, it was U.S. beliefs about long-term Soviet intentions that explain the timing and emergence of the conflict. While the United States might have preferred to come home after the conclusion of World War II, growing concern about Soviet intentions made that impossible.[1] To be clear, U.S. behavior was not blameless in the origins of the conflict, but this chapter aims to provide a better understanding of how the United States came to regard the threat posed by an emerging postwar Soviet Union.

This chapter serves a different purpose than the other empirical chapters. It is not surprising that the United States and the Soviet Union found value in a marriage of convenience to defeat Hitler's Germany. What this case does allow for is a more careful examination of the role that beliefs about intentions, rather than simply capabilities, play in resolving uncertainty about the threat posed by a rising power. While there is no denying that the structural environment of bipolarity after World War II made Soviet-U.S. competition more likely, this chapter demonstrates that it was increasing evidence of Soviet intentions that was the driving force behind the evolution of U.S. strategy toward Moscow. The United States was not overly concerned by the immediate military threat that Moscow posed to Western Europe. In fact, Washington's inclination was to pull back and come home once the war had concluded. But ominous signals of Soviet intentions added to the weight of the evidence supporting a reasonable probability that the Soviets did, indeed, pose a threat. It was beliefs about intentions and the transformation of uncertainty into risk that generated the Cold War.

Aside from the inherent value in a better understanding of the origins of the Cold War, the case is also instructive for the contemporary Sino-U.S. case. If the international system transforms to Sino-U.S. bipolarity in the coming years, then the only modern case of bipolarity may provide useful lessons about how states respond to emerging threats in such contexts. I contend that the early Cold War emerged not simply out of relative power relationships between the United States and the Soviet Union, though they played a critical role, but rather from elongated time horizons on both sides and dwindling uncertainty about Soviet intentions.

The analysis in this chapter emphasizes the primacy of intentions in how states assess and address potential long-term threats and how those beliefs about intentions affect time horizons. Rather than simply assume the worst about Soviet intentions, the United States inferred malign intent from the pattern of Soviet behavior as World War II was ending. Those indicators transformed uncertainty about Soviet intentions into measurable risk to which a strategy could be directed. While different Soviet behavior may not have prevented the Cold War, the timing of emerging Soviet-U.S. tension is inexplicable without attention to temporal factors and evolving U.S. beliefs about Soviet intentions. If U.S. leaders were simply assuming the worst about soviet intentions, then the continuous U.S. efforts to test and discern those intentions would be puzzling. Once again, litmus tests were employed in an effort to discern and demonstrate Soviet intentions and ambitions.

I make three central arguments in this chapter. First, during World War II, the necessity of defeating the Axis powers left each side little choice but to postpone any competition until later. Relative temporality among threats matters, and Germany was clearly a more pressing threat. That said, President Franklin Roosevelt, in particular, was not resigned to an adversarial relationship with the Soviet Union after the war, and he attempted to build the foundation for a friendly relationship with Moscow. Such engagement, however, was based not on any particular hope that Soviet intentions could be made more benign but simply on the belief that a cooperative order could help manage any potential for conflict.

Second, the impetus for the Cold War was not simply fear of Soviet capabilities. At the time, U.S. leaders were concerned more with economic instability in Europe that could create a political opportunity for the Soviets than they were with any Soviet military threat. The Soviets were exhausted after World War II, and an invasion of Western Europe appeared infeasible.

Third, the Cold War grew out of U.S. concern about long-term Soviet intentions, but not because U.S. leaders simply assumed the worst about those intentions. The United States intensified its efforts to balance against the Soviet Union as uncertainty about Soviet intentions resolved itself. Wealthy and essentially secure after World War II, the United States was in the unusual position for a great power of being able to address a more long-term threat if it wished.

More specifically, the Cold War was precipitated by a series of crises that had the effect of drawing attention to long-term Soviet intentions. Concern about long-term intentions, in turn, led to more competitive short-term behavior. After World War II concluded, the United States was initially willing to cede a sphere of influence to the Soviet Union, but when Moscow overstepped the bounds of that sphere in Iran, Turkey, and Germany, the United States became more concerned.[2] In the absence of other threats and with increasingly ominous Soviet behavior, the United States opted to address the threat sooner rather than later.

These crises did not themselves represent "costly signals" of future Soviet intentions. A defensively oriented Soviet Union could have had interest in maintaining a presence in Iran or Turkey. However, these crises increased the perceived probability that the Soviet Union had long-term aggressive intentions. Each crisis added Keynesian "weight" to the argument that Soviet intentions were malign. Bipolarity alone helps explain the broad pattern of competition between the United States and the Soviet Union, but it cannot explain the timing of how that competition came to be.

Yet if the Soviet Union stood to benefit from cooperation with the United States (and it did, given its own devastation from World War II), why would it act in provocative ways that were likely to bring about more adversarial relations? Why was Moscow not more patient? Soviet long-term ambitions answer this question. The Soviet Union was less interested in short-term opportunities for economic gain that would have undermined both its ideology and its economic system and was more interested in establishing what it saw as the long-term basis for Soviet security. Stalin mostly eschewed efforts to influence others' beliefs about Soviet intentions because of what he saw as a nearly inevitable conflict with the West.

In the remainder of this chapter I present the alternative arguments that might be able to explain this case. Then I examine the historical transition from World War II cooperation to cold war competition, with particular attention to the crises that intensified the Cold War. Next I consider why the Soviet Union did not try to hide its long-term intentions in an effort to promote mutually beneficial short-term cooperation, as the other powers examined in this book did. I conclude the chapter by revisiting the alternative explanations and reviewing which one provides the most compelling explanation for this case. While there is little disputing that the United States perceived a great and growing threat from the Soviet Union, the critical question is in where that threat was rooted.

Alternative Arguments

The alternative arguments for this case need to account for the level of competition between the United States and the Soviet Union. Unlike in the previous cases examined in this book, cooperation between Washington and Moscow was fleeting, and explaining that cooperation is not as important as explaining why and how it ended. Offensive realists would maintain that while concerns about long-term Soviet intentions may have emerged over time, it was primarily Soviet capabilities that led the United States to a more competitive posture.[3] In this argument, a competitive relationship between the United States and the Soviet Union was made inevitable by the structural balance of power. In the absence of any other state that could conceivably catch the buck if it were passed, the United States pursued competitive strategies itself. Advocates of engagement would expect that existing powers might attempt to engage rising powers to shape their intentions, but they have a less satisfying account of why engagement sometimes fails and how states behave when those efforts at engagement fail, as they did in this case.

My own temporal theory expects that the transitions from cooperation to competition can be explained by the interaction of state time horizons. With the end of World War II, both the United States and the Soviet Union had long time horizons, which created an ominous shadow of the future and led to more competitive behavior in the short term.

More interestingly, though, this chapter explores whether the United States was simply responding to emerging Soviet capabilities or whether that response was affected in important ways by perceptions of Soviet intentions. Did the United States simply assume the worst about Soviet intentions as World War II was drawing to a close, or did it more carefully weigh the available evidence of Soviet intentions? Importantly, my argument is not to exonerate the United States for actions that it may have taken that contributed to the origins of the Cold War; rather, my focus is on how the United States perceived the emerging Soviet threat.[4]

The Cold War case is distinct from the other cases in this book in that it looks at a period of emerging bipolarity. Both the United States and the Soviet Union had longer time horizons in the bipolar system of the postwar period. Each recognized that they were the only two great powers. And each developed a fear of the other, but that fear had as much to do with the other's long-term intentions as with its capabilities.[5]

From World War II to the Cold War

The German invasion of the Soviet Union in June 1941, Operation Barbarossa, thrust the United States and the Soviet Union into the uncomfortable position of wartime allies.[6] Less than twenty-five years earlier, in the summer of

1918, approximately seven thousand U.S. troops had participated in an intervention in Russia aimed at thwarting the Bolshevik revolution.[7] For President Woodrow Wilson, the Bolshevik revolution was repugnant, representing a challenge to his own liberal democratic ideology. Even after the United States formally recognized the Soviet Union in 1933, ideological difference and repressive Soviet behavior, including the purges of the 1930s, prevented any significant warming of Soviet-U.S. relations.[8]

Despite this history of animosity, Franklin Roosevelt committed the United States to providing aid to the Soviets only two days after Barbarossa commenced.[9] By early October, the United States and Great Britain formally pledged in the Moscow Protocol to provide desperately needed supplies to the Soviet Union.[10] The choice of supporting the Soviet Union or surrendering to German hegemony over Europe was an easy one for both Washington and London.[11] A Soviet victory, Roosevelt wrote, would "mean the liberation of Europe from Nazi domination—and at the same time I do not think we need to fear any possibility of Russian domination."[12] War generates imperatives to delay dealing with long-term potential threats in the interest of addressing short-term actual threats, and little attention could be or would be paid to a potential long-term Soviet threat while the defeat of Germany was the sole priority.

For Roosevelt, maintaining cordial relations with the Soviet Union was important both for the Allied war effort and in anticipation of a postwar settlement.[13] Throughout the war, he remained optimistic that cooperation among the great powers including the Soviet Union would be possible after the war. More specifically, Roosevelt's vision for the postwar order had four components.[14] First, Roosevelt believed that Versailles had failed because it did not appropriately punish the aggressors. The harsh treatment of Germany had only encouraged German revanchism and eventually the rise of Hitler. Second, Roosevelt shared Wilson's liberal internationalist principles. He aimed to create a postwar system undergirded by institutions, supportive of national self-determination, and fostered by open economies. Third, in the president's view, the League of Nations had failed because of the absence of the United States, and he sought to rectify that in a new postwar collective security organization.

Fourth, and perhaps most importantly, Roosevelt envisioned "four policemen" managing the postwar world. Any collective security organization would be unsuccessful unless it was led by all the world's great powers—Great Britain, China, the Soviet Union, and the United States. The alliance formed to defeat Germany was unlikely to persist after Germany's defeat, but cooperation among the Allied powers would be necessary if the post–World War II international order was to be more peaceful than the order after World War I.[15] So Roosevelt did look beyond the war itself, and the wartime cooperation among the Allies encouraged him that the postwar order could be run cooperatively. Like Aristide Briand in the interwar period, he saw possibilities for cooperation in the postwar period. For Roosevelt, the best way to deal with potential postwar adversaries was to engage them and involve them in the construction of a peaceful postwar order.

As for his Soviet allies, Roosevelt did not simply assume the worst about their long-term intentions. Instead, uncertainty about Soviet intentions permitted the decision to procrastinate on addressing the potential threat from Moscow, at least until after the war. As Warren I. Cohen summarizes, "Soviet and American statesmen were still circling each other warily, mistrustful after a generation of enmity, which Hitler had forced them to shelve. But the Soviet Union and the United States had no vital interests in conflict, cooperation would be nearly as urgent after victory, and Roosevelt was confident that he and Stalin could find a way to sustain it."[16] In his 1944 Statue of the Union address, Roosevelt argued, "All our allies have learned by bitter experience that real development will not be possible if they are to be diverted from their purpose by repeated wars—or even threats of war. China and Russia are truly united with Britain and America in recognition of this essential fact: the best interests of each nation, large and small, demand that all freedom-loving nations shall join together in a just and durable system of peace."[17] If Soviet security concerns could be met and if, in exchange, the Soviets backed away from their ideological zeal, then Soviet-U.S. cooperation could prosper even after the war ended and the common threat had been defeated.

But the absence of other pressing threats to the United States along with more menacing indications of Soviet long-term intentions allowed a powerful and secure United States to begin to elongate its time horizons. Starting as early as 1943, U.S. and British leaders observed worrisome Soviet behavior, suggesting that postwar cooperation with Moscow might be more difficult than Roosevelt had hoped. Emboldened (yet exhausted) by their defeat of the Germans at Stalingrad in January, the Soviets began to make more demands on the direction that the war was taking as well as in any discussions about the postwar order. In April, Moscow broke off diplomatic relations with the Polish government, which had been exiled to London. In Washington and London, this was interpreted as an ominous signal of Soviet territorial ambitions in Poland. The long-awaited opening of a second front against Germany by the United States and Britain was predicated on a Soviet commitment not to seek further territory for itself in the Baltics or Eastern Europe. Any indications of Soviet interest in Poland could be viewed as a violation of this agreement. When the Allies informed Stalin in June that the cross-channel invasion had again been delayed until 1944, Moscow withdrew its ambassadors from Washington and London in yet another foreboding sign.[18]

The Allies met in Moscow in October 1943 and in Tehran the following month to begin to address issues critical to the postwar settlement. Success in these negotiations would indicate the possibility of postwar cooperation; failure would foreshadow trouble to come. In Moscow, the foreign ministers created the European Advisory Commission to address issues surrounding the surrender of enemy states.[19] At Tehran, Winston Churchill, Roosevelt, and Stalin focused on immediate wartime challenges, including planning for the Anglo-U.S. cross-channel invasion. The Allies also discussed the likely postwar occupation of German territory and lingering border issues between Poland and the Soviet Union. During a Christmas Eve fireside chat following the conferences, Roosevelt told the people of the United States, "I believe that we are going to get along very well with [Stalin] and the Russian people—very well indeed."[20] But the president's optimism was the result of putting off resolution of the most difficult postwar issues. Already, through his behavior in Poland and the Baltic region, Stalin was making little effort to hide his territorial objectives, but the primary focus on concluding the war successfully prevented these issues from being addressed at either Moscow or Tehran.[21]

On June 6, 1944, the Allied forces landed on the beaches of Normandy, finally delivering Stalin's long-awaited second front. The Continental invasion made the eventual defeat of the Third Reich almost certain. As a consequence, the focus of the Allies began to shift even further toward the postwar order. Roosevelt clung to his hopes for postwar cooperation, and Stalin reciprocated by indicating at least a willingness to cooperate as long as Soviet interests were recognized and protected. Here Stalin appears to have recognized the value of not drawing attention to any malign long-term intentions.[22] Stalin's efforts to demonstrate a cooperative spirit met a receptive audience, as U.S. leaders preferred cooperation to the far more costly alternative.

How did the Allies transition from this relative optimism of 1944 to the bitter enmity that would be entrenched by the middle of 1946? Roosevelt was not naïve about the realities of power in the international system, nor was he blind to ominous Soviet behavior in Eastern Europe. But his remaining hopes for robust postwar cooperation with Moscow would soon evaporate as Washington and London became more concerned with long-term Soviet intentions. The convergence of U.S. and Soviet time horizons on the long-term future created conditions conducive to competition.

INITIAL INDICATORS OF SOVIET INTENTIONS: THE POLISH QUESTION AND PREPARATIONS FOR PEACE

Events in Central and Eastern Europe, in particular Poland, provided early clues about the likely nature of postwar relations.[23] Throughout the war, the official Polish government had operated in exile in London, awaiting the end of the war and reclamation of Polish sovereignty.[24] Soviet military successes in early 1944 prompted the exiled government to declare its desire to return to power. Stalin, however, planned to retain parts of Poland as Soviet territory and described the exiled Polish government as "incorrigible."[25]

Sensing this developing acrimony and worried about the consequences for broader postwar cooperation, Churchill and Roosevelt intervened. The British prime minister implored the exiled government to slow down its plans to return to power and asked Stalin to avoid turning Poland into a divisive issue among the Allies. Churchill immediately rebuffed Stalin's suggestion to create an alternative government in Poland: "The creation in Warsaw of another Polish government different from the one we have recognized up to the present, together with disturbances in Poland would raise issues in Great Britain and the United States detrimental to that close accord between the Three Great Powers upon which the future of the world depends."[26] For Churchill, Soviet attempts to undermine the legitimacy of the exiled Polish government raised questions about long-term Soviet intentions in Poland and beyond.[27]

In July, Moscow took the unwelcome step of recognizing the Polish Committee on National Liberation based in Lublin. Known as the Lublin Committee, it was a communist, pro-Soviet group, and Moscow's endorsement was taken by many Poles as an indication of Soviet plans to establish a sphere of influence in Poland. Once Soviet troops crossed the Curzon Line in late July, Churchill asked Stalin to meet with the leader of the exiled government, Prime Minister Stanislaus Mikolajczyk. Stalin and Mikolajczyk did eventually meet from August 3 to August 9, generating some optimism that a cooperative solution to Poland's future could be found.[28]

That optimism quickly evaporated, however, with the onset of the Warsaw uprising in August.[29] As Soviet troops approached Warsaw, the underground Polish resistance, which supported the exiled government, rose up in an effort to expedite Poland's liberation from Germany. Stalin refused to aid the uprising even after a German counteroffensive reestablished control over Warsaw. Roosevelt and Churchill implored Stalin to aid the Poles, but to no avail.[30] By the time the uprising ended in early October, approximately 250,000 Poles—a quarter of the population of Warsaw—had been killed. The lack of Soviet assistance to the pro-London Poles indicated again to many that the Soviets were intent on claiming a sphere of influence in Poland.

In early September, W. Averell Harriman, the U.S. ambassador to the Soviet Union, summarized the signals that Moscow had been sending: "[U.S.] relations with the Soviet Union have taken a startling turn evident during the last two months. They have held up our requests with complete indifference to our interests and have shown an unwillingness even to discuss pressing problems." Harriman continued, "What frightens me is that when a country begins to extend its influence by strong arm methods beyond its borders under the guise of security it is difficult to see how a line can be drawn. If the policy is accepted that the Soviet Union has a right to penetrate her immediate neighbors . . . penetration of the next immediate neighbors becomes at a certain time equally logical." In short, Harriman stated, "Unless we take issue with the present policy there is every indication the Soviet Union will become a world bully wherever our interests are involved."[31] The alarming behavior present in Poland served to draw attention to uncertain long-term Soviet intentions.[32]

As expected, the elongation of U.S. time horizons led to the consideration of more competitive strategies. Harriman proposed "a firm but friendly *quid pro quo* attitude" toward Moscow.[33] The Russians should be forced to justify any requests for aid that did not appear to contribute directly to the war effort, and the United States should be wary of providing any aid for the postwar reconstruction of the Soviet Union until Stalin offered more reassuring signals of his postwar intentions.

Growing concern about long-term Soviet intentions also precipitated a change in the tone of Anglo-U.S. relations. In mid-September, Roosevelt and Churchill met in Quebec. Recent Soviet behavior led to a particular focus on postwar issues. In addition to discussions over the disposition of Germany, Churchill, in particular, advocated a tougher stand against Soviet aggression. The two leaders agreed to cooperate in the development of the atomic bomb, excluding the Soviet Union.[34] Concern about Soviet intentions revealed by Soviet behavior, not any change in Soviet capabilities, prompted a move toward a more competitive strategy.[35]

Roosevelt, however, was still not prepared to abandon his hopes for postwar cooperation. He sought to hedge his bets by protecting U.S. interests from a potential Soviet threat but also leaving open the possibility of postwar cooperation. Simultaneous to Harriman's warning about Soviet behavior, representatives of the United States, Great Britain, and the Soviet Union met at Dumbarton Oaks in Washington to discuss the prospects for a postwar cooperative security organization. Such an organization remained the centerpiece of Roosevelt's postwar vision, and meeting at Dumbarton Oaks, he hoped to overcome Soviet intransigence on the design of the institution.[36]

At the end of September, Churchill decided to try again by requesting a meeting with Stalin. As he wrote to Stalin, "On the agreement of our nations . . . stands the hopes of the world."[37] Roosevelt endorsed a meeting between his two allies, though he also feared that Churchill might accede to unacceptable agreements with Stalin. Roosevelt, himself, would not attend the meeting due to the impending U.S. elections, so he sent Harriman instead.[38]

In their first meeting in Moscow on October 9, Churchill and Stalin agreed on a spheres-of-influence agreement for the Balkans. The Soviet Union would retain 90 percent "dominance" in Romania and 75 percent in Bulgaria. Great Britain would be 90 percent dominant in Greece, while control of Yugoslavia and Hungary would be split evenly.[39] Roosevelt endorsed the agreement: "I am most pleased to know that you are reaching a meeting of your two minds as to international policies in which, because of our present and future common efforts to prevent international wars, we are all interested."[40] His realist inclinations accepted the need to divide the world among the great powers, while his more idealist hopes welcomed the cooperative spirit that produced the agreement. The end result was to draw lines around spheres of influence in Europe. Respect for these lines would reflect more modest Soviet ambitions, whereas transgressing these lines would be yet further indication of aggressive Soviet intentions.

Even at this late date in the war, then, there was hope that postwar relations might be managed cooperatively. Churchill wrote to Stalin that the Moscow meeting had shown that "there are not matters that cannot be adjusted between us when we meet in frank and intimate discussion."[41] Stalin added in a letter to Roosevelt: "The talks made it plain that we can without difficulty coordinate our policies on all important issues and that even if we cannot ensure immediate solution to this or that problem, such as the Polish question, we have, nevertheless, more favorable prospects in this respect as well."[42] Even as leaders in both Moscow and Washington began to contemplate the postwar order, cooperation between the great powers seemingly remained possible.

But the optimism generated by the Moscow meeting was fleeting. By late December, the Soviet Union announced that it recognized the Lublin Committee as the official Polish government. In response, Roosevelt told his secretary of war, Henry L. Stimson, "Stalin had taken Britain's desire to have a *cordon sanitaire* of friendly nations around it in past years as an excuse now for Russia's intention to have Czechoslovakia, Poland, and other nations whom it could control around it."[43] Roosevelt's advisers suggested withholding any further economic assistance to the Soviets, and Stimson reiterated his recommendation that the United States not share any information about its atomic weapons program with Moscow.

By the end of 1944, Soviet behavior in Poland and Eastern Europe, more generally, had exacerbated concern about long-term Soviet intentions.[44] As the end of the war began to come into sight, the absence of other threats allowed the United States to focus on the long-term indicators. Any signals of benign intentions, such as cooperation at the Moscow summit, were offset by more ominous signals of malign intent. By December, only 44 percent of the U.S. public still trusted its ostensible ally, the lowest figure since the Moscow conference the previous year.[45] The United States moved haltingly toward a more competitive strategy, including Harriman's call for a quid pro quo strategy, but Roosevelt remained hopeful that a cooperative approach to postwar issues was still possible.

YALTA: COOPERATION AMID UNCERTAINTY

The final wartime summit with Churchill, Roosevelt, and Stalin convened in Yalta on February 4–11, 1945.[46] The conference began with a discussion of military issues in the still ongoing war, but the meeting then focused on five pressing postwar issues. These issues all reflected how U.S. time horizons were elongating to consider the potential long-term threat posed by the Soviet Union and its uncertain intentions.

First, both Washington and London were troubled by the Soviet recognition of the Lublin Committee as the legitimate Polish government. Second, in addition to Poland, the postwar fate of other Eastern European countries, such as Hungary and Romania, was unresolved. Third, with an end to the war with Germany appearing imminent, the Allies needed to agree on Germany's postwar disposition. Fourth, Roosevelt remained hopeful that a cooperative institution would undergird the postwar order, but many details of that institution remained undetermined. Fifth, once the war with Germany was concluded, the Allies needed a strategy for similarly bringing the war with Japan to a close and for how to manage Japan after the war.

The central consideration at Yalta quickly became the first two issues— the fate of Poland and, more generally, Eastern Europe. Roosevelt acknowledged the centrality of Poland to Soviet security concerns, but he was unwilling to cede Poland entirely to the Soviets for fear of the domestic political repercussions of abandoning Poland. Instead, Roosevelt suggested that the foundation for cooperative Soviet-U.S. relations would be stronger if Moscow supported a democratic Poland.[47] Stalin was not convinced. In Stalin's view, Poland was "not only a question of honor for Russia, but one of life or death."[48]

In the negotiations, Stalin intimated that he would consider a reconfiguration of the Polish government in exchange for territorial concessions to the Soviet Union on the eastern border of Poland. The proposal was unacceptable to Roosevelt and Churchill, but they also did not want the Polish issue to prevent progress at Yalta in other areas. Final agreement on the borders of Poland was deferred until a postwar peace conference, but Stalin was willing to accede to a vague agreement that the Polish government would be democratic.

On the more general disposition of Eastern Europe, Roosevelt sought Churchill's and Stalin's agreement to the Declaration on Liberated Europe.[49] This declaration would become the foundation of a litmus test of long-term Soviet intentions. The declaration committed the Allies to supporting democracy in postwar Europe. The agreement also reaffirmed the 1941 Atlantic Charter that had endorsed the wider spread of democracy.[50] For Roosevelt, the agreement buoyed his hope that the Soviet Union and Great Britain were not pursuing postwar empires. For Churchill, the declaration was acceptable since it omitted any mention of the British Empire as an antidemocratic system. For Stalin, the agreement worked because it continued to call for the destruction of Nazism and fascism without requiring anything specific of Moscow. Stalin could appear cooperative without actually doing much of anything.

Importantly, though, while Stalin saw the declaration as not requiring much, Roosevelt viewed it differently. Specifically, he connected the declaration with the situation in Poland.[51] The first test of the declaration would be whether Stalin would agree to allow democratic elections in Poland. Roosevelt continued to acknowledge that the Soviets were likely to retain a postwar sphere of influence in Eastern Europe, but he hoped that Stalin would allow democracy within that sphere. Notably, if Roosevelt was simply assuming the worst about Soviet intentions, there would seem little reason to test those intentions in this manner.

With regard to Germany, the Yalta discussions focused primarily on possible reparations.[52] Secretary of State Edward R. Stettinius wrote, "We were most anxious to avoid the disastrous experience of reparations after World War I."[53] Stalin proposed $20 billion in German reparations, half of which would go to the Soviet Union.[54] Having paid the greatest price in World War II and desperately in need of funds to finance their own recovery, the Soviets insisted that they were entitled to an unprecedented level of reparations. Roosevelt, however, believed that the reparations imposed on Germany after World War I had played a significant role in the origins of World War II, and he was determined to avoid repeating that mistake. Roosevelt advocated instead for a "first charge" principle, which would have allowed Germany to pay for any necessary imports before being charged any reparations.[55] The principle would have enabled Germany to rebuild (to the benefit of the U.S. economy, which would provide many exports to Germany), but such a policy was unacceptable to Stalin, forcing the Allies to postpone further consideration of the reparations issues.

On the final issue, the war in the Pacific, Stalin demanded certain territorial concessions in exchange for a Soviet commitment to enter the war.[56] While Roosevelt was aware at the time of the likely availability of the atomic weapon to use against Japan, the Soviet Union could still play a useful role in defeating Japanese forces in Manchuria and disrupting vital Japanese trade. In a secret agreement reached at Yalta, Stalin pledged that the Soviet Union would enter the war against Japan within three months of Germany's surrender. In exchange, the Soviet Union would receive the postwar reward of the territory it had lost during the Russo-Japanese War. Stalin also committed to seeking a pact of friendship with the Chinese nationalist Kuomintang government.[57]

U.S. leaders were encouraged by the results achieved at Yalta. According to presidential adviser Harry Hopkins, "We really believed in our hearts that this was the dawn of the new day we had all been praying for. The Russians had proved that they could be reasonable and farseeing and there wasn't any doubt in the minds of the President or any of us that we could live with them and get along with them peacefully for as long into the future as any of us could imagine."[58] Uncertainty about Soviet intentions together with the continuing short-term benefits of cooperation combined to sustain cooperation.

Still, the United States was not fully relieved by the results of Yalta, and uncertainty led to considerable hedging. Privately, Roosevelt had reservations about Yalta. As he began to think more about the future and uncertain Soviet intentions, he became wary of cooperation with Moscow. Stalin had not conceded on any of the most difficult issues, and Roosevelt recognized that he would be powerless to halt any future Soviet aggression in Eastern Europe. Publicly, however, Roosevelt expressed optimism about the Yalta agreements. Addressing Congress on March 1, the president pleaded for congressional support for the Yalta accords and declared the death of traditional power politics.[59] Admitting any doubt about Yalta could have undermined Roosevelt's ultimate goal of creating the United Nations to manage postwar relations.[60]

In March, Soviet behavior in Poland and Romania confirmed Roosevelt's concerns about Yalta. In Romania, Stalin insisted that the Romanian king appoint a communist government.[61] Such an insistence appeared to be in direct violation of the Declaration on Liberated Europe. The Soviet leader, however, viewed the behavior as consistent with the sphere of influence granted by Churchill in Moscow in October 1944.

Even more troubling than developments in Romania was the government Stalin attempted to establish in Poland. The Soviets refused to allow more than three pro-Western representatives into the new eighteen-member Polish government. Soviet adherence to the Declaration on Liberated Europe in Romania and Poland remained an important litmus test of long-term Soviet intentions.[62] Provocative Soviet behavior would reduce uncertainty about Soviet intentions, making cooperation between the Allies more difficult to sustain.

On April 12, 1945, Roosevelt died and was succeeded by Harry S. Truman. Truman was more skeptical of the prospects for cooperation with Moscow than Roosevelt had been. Shortly after taking office, Truman told Stettinius, "We must stand up to the Russians. We have been too easy with them."[63] The new president was most troubled by apparent Soviet violations of the Yalta agreement to allow democracy in Eastern Europe. On April 23, Truman met in Washington with Soviet foreign minister Vyacheslav Molotov, who was en route to San Francisco for the United Nations planning conference. To Molotov's surprise, Truman greeted him with a sharp reprimand for Soviet behavior in Poland. The president demanded that the Lublin government be removed and replaced with a more representative government. "I have never been talked to like that in my life," an astonished Molotov replied to Truman. To which Truman answered, "Carry out your agreements and you won't get talked to like that."[64]

Throughout the spring, Washington pressed Moscow to abide by the Yalta accords. The United States attempted to prevent the Lublin government from representing Poland at the San Francisco conference, and as soon as the war in Europe ended on May 9, the United States immediately suspended all lend-lease aid to the Soviets.[65] And when communist Yugoslavia under

Josip Broz Tito attempted to annex Trieste, the United States resisted for fear that Tito's aggression was being encouraged by Moscow.

THE SHIFT TO THE LONG TERM: THE WAR COMES TO AN END

With the conclusion of the war against Germany, the most pressing issues confronting the Allies were the ensuing division of Europe and concomitant troop withdrawals. The short-term benefits of cooperation evaporated, leaving the United States and its allies to reconsider whether to confront the Soviet Union now or later. While Soviet-U.S. relations appeared to be in a downward spiral, Truman still retained some hope that great power cooperation could be salvaged. If nothing else, short-term cooperation would be necessary for the defeat of Japan.

The challenge before the United States and Great Britain was how to reconcile the granting of a Soviet sphere of influence with the desire for democracy. It would be difficult, if not impossible, for the United States to dictate the type of political regimes that would take hold within the Soviet sphere. Truman sent Hopkins, a longtime adviser to Roosevelt, to Moscow in late May to discuss possible areas of Soviet-U.S. cooperation. The United States eventually accepted a compromise on Poland that only modestly altered the Lublin government, while the Soviet Union agreed, in exchange, to certain provisions of the nascent United Nations.[66] Together with the standing Soviet commitment to assist in ending the war with Japan, the agreements reached during Hopkins's mission appeared again to provide some hope for postwar cooperation. Such cooperation gave both the United States and the Soviet Union time to consolidate their postwar positions.

The Soviet sphere of influence continued to take shape in June when Truman moved ahead with the withdrawal of U.S. troops from Eastern Europe. The United States could not expect Soviet cooperation if the United States did not live up to its end of the sphere-of-influences bargain.[67] On July 1, U.S. and British troops withdrew from the area between eastern Germany and the Soviet border, creating space for the Soviets to consolidate their control.

Two weeks later, the final Allied wartime conference opened in Potsdam.[68] The main accomplishment of the Potsdam conference was the creation of the Council of Foreign Ministers, which was to meet periodically to negotiate various postwar issues. Further progress was also made on the territorial boundaries of Poland as well as the Soviet zone in eastern Germany. Truman's approach at Potsdam was shaped by news of the successful test of the atomic weapon in the New Mexico desert. With the atomic bomb now in hand, the need for Soviet cooperation concluding the war in the Pacific diminished. If the short-term benefits of cooperation continued to shrink as concern about Soviet long-term intentions grew, then competition would become more likely. In fact, the goal arguably became to keep the Soviets out of the war in order to prevent any postwar Soviet territorial claims.[69]

Shortly after the end of the war in the Pacific in early September, the first meeting of the Council of Foreign Ministers convened in London. The foreign ministers of the United States, the Soviet Union, Great Britain, France, and China met with the primary purpose of devising peace treaties for Finland, Hungary, Romania, and Bulgaria.[70] With the war now over, the United States was less willing to tolerate Soviet violations of the Declaration on Liberated Europe. U.S. leaders were hopeful that economic carrots combined with the stick of the atomic weapon would provide the United States with leverage in negotiations with Moscow.[71] But absent any other immediate threats, U.S. resolution of its now-or-later dilemma continued to shift, with an increasing focus on the long-term threat posed by the Soviet Union.

The Soviets, however, seemed unimpressed, as they continued to insist that Washington accept Soviet-sponsored governments in Romania and Bulgaria. Molotov upped the ante, declaring that Moscow would not accept Western proposals for the disposition of Italy's postwar future until the West accepted Soviet arrangements in Eastern Europe. Moreover, Molotov suggested that an Allied Control Council with representatives from the United States, the Soviet Union, Great Britain, and China be created to oversee the postwar occupation of Japan. This last proposal was especially unattractive to Washington, which had resolved to exclude the Soviet Union from any say in the future of Japan.

Allied relations had reached a new low point when the London conference adjourned in early October.[72] The disappearance of the short-term imperative for cooperation during the war was replaced by long-term concern. Accordingly, the United States was increasingly resolved to deal with the likely threat posed by the Soviet Union now rather than later. Secretary of State James Byrnes concluded that Moscow was intent on violating all the commitments it had made at Yalta and Potsdam, and neither the atomic weapon nor U.S. financial strength would be able to prevent that.

Still, Byrnes had not abandoned hope, nor was he convinced that the Soviets would necessarily be expansionist. Instead, he adopted a policy of attempting to reassure Soviet leaders by publicly declaring that the United States would not intervene in any country bordering on the Soviet Union or "join any groups in those countries in hostile intrigue against the Soviet Union."[73] Byrnes combined this carrot with the stick of withholding any reconstruction aid to the Soviet Union until the Soviets abided by their Yalta obligations in Eastern Europe.

Other opinion within Washington was split on how to approach the Soviet Union in the wake of the London conference.[74] Conservative congressional Republicans and a faction of the State Department saw the London conference as signaling the end of potential cooperation with Stalin. Moscow was determined to spread its influence throughout the world, and the Soviets would only be deterred by the adoption of hard-line diplomacy backed by military force.

Alternatively, a group of diplomats, including Cloyce K. Huston, Charles Bohlen, and Geroid Robinson, saw a glimmer of hope for cooperation. The United States could still protect its interests through a strategy of compromise. For this group, both the United States and the Soviet Union had an interest in peaceful negotiation.

Truman was unsure. In an October 27 Navy Day speech in front of a large crowd in New York City, he pledged that the United States would never recognize any government that was not representative of its people.[75] The United States would also maintain a strong military to protect democracy around the world. At the same time, while he recognized that the end of the war had removed the primary impetus for cooperation, he also still believed that the United Nations could facilitate a more peaceful postwar order. Byrnes himself began to question whether he had adopted too hard of a line in London, and he discouraged Truman from adopting the aggressive stance he took in the Navy Day speech.[76]

What ensued was a wave of analyses of future Soviet intentions that belie the notion that the United States simply assumed the worst about Soviet intentions. In the absence of immediate short-term threats and with a commanding economy, the United States was free to focus on the longer term. In particular, Bohlen and Robinson completed a report in early December that presented a detailed analysis of likely future Soviet intentions. Far from making assumptions about Soviet intentions, the report investigated the implications of different conceivable Soviet intentions.

The report offered two alternative strategies for the United States. The first was a more cooperative strategy that could go as far as sharing atomic weapons technology with Moscow. Alternatively, according to the second, the United States could adopt a more competitive strategy that prepared for aggressive Soviet behavior. The decision of which policy to adopt would depend on an assessment of Soviet intentions, not simply its capabilities. Bohlen and Robinson advocated for the more cooperative approach: "It is by no means certain that Soviet intentions are set irrevocably in the pattern of expansion facilitated by revolution."[77]

Robert L. Messer writes, "The December 1945 Bohlen-Robinson study represented the considered opinion of the department's preeminent Soviet affairs specialists."[78] The report is significant for two reasons. First, it demonstrates that as late as the fall of 1945 there was *still* indecision in Washington over policy toward Moscow, and that indecision was largely a product of the remaining uncertainty about Soviet intentions.[79] Second, the analysis in the report reveals how U.S. thinking about the Soviet Union was stretching out over a longer time horizon. The report relied on both Soviet revolutionary ideology and Soviet behavior to infer Soviet intentions.

Byrnes's behavior in late fall 1945 suggests that perhaps he was persuaded by the more cooperative alternative. In late November, he requested another meeting of the foreign ministers of the United States, Great Britain, and the

Soviet Union with the primary goal being the final resolution of the Romanian and Bulgarian peace treaties. Byrnes held two cards that he hoped would persuade the Soviets to compromise: he might offer to negotiate over Japan and he might offer to create a United Nations agency to oversee the development of atomic weapons.

Byrnes and Stalin met in Moscow on December 23. The United States agreed to recognize the governments of Poland and Romania if the Soviets would undertake relatively modest reforms. The United States also offered to create the Allied Control Council for Japan as the Soviet Union had requested at London, even though the United States fully intended for that to be a token institution. All in all, the United States had conceded more to the Soviets at Moscow than vice versa, though the overall results were unimpressive.[80]

By the end of 1945, then, cooperation was producing only limited results and signs of potentially ominous Soviet long-term intentions were emerging. With the end of the war, the short-term imperative to cooperate had disappeared, and the United States was now free to think about longer-term threats, including those posed by uncertain future Soviet intentions. The interaction of long Soviet and U.S. time horizons was likely to lead to more competition rather than cooperation.

ASSESSING SOVIET INTENTIONS: THE LOGIC OF LITMUS TESTS

On his return from the largely uneventful Moscow meeting, Byrnes was greeted by an angry Truman.[81] Truman increasingly felt pressure from congressional Republicans, who would not countenance any further cooperation with Moscow without meaningful Soviet concessions. The president felt that Byrnes had granted too much to the Soviets without receiving any concrete commitment to democratic elections in Eastern Europe. Truman was also upset that Byrnes had withheld a more pessimistic appraisal of Soviet intentions that State Department analyst Mark Ethridge had prepared.[82]

On January 5, 1946, Truman summoned Byrnes to the White House to reprimand him. "Until Russia is faced with an iron fist and strong language," Truman argued, "only one language do they understand—'how many divisions have you?' . . . I'm tired of babying the Soviets."[83] Looking forward, Truman ordered Byrnes to stop compromising with Moscow until the Soviets' behavior improved.

The evidence of malign long-term Soviet intentions was only to grow in 1946. Stalin delivered a provocative speech on February 9.[84] Stalin praised the combined efforts of the Allies in defeating fascism. He went on, however, to suggest that World War II had been a unique event and that future wars would be the result of an inevitable clash between capitalism and communism. *Time* magazine observed that the speech was "the most warlike pronouncement uttered by any top-rank statesman since V-J Day," while

Justice William O. Douglas of the Supreme Court suggested that Stalin's speech was a "declaration of World War III."[85]

Adding to the provocative speech was even more provocative behavior. On February 16, twenty-two people were arrested in Ottawa on charges of trying to steal information about atomic weapons to give to the Soviet Union.[86] In China, Stalin had promised that Soviet troops would evacuate Manchuria by February 1, but they failed to do so, with Stalin pushing Chiang Kai-shek to allow joint Soviet control over Manchurian mines. But the most provocative behavior occurred in Iran, Turkey, and Germany. As Marc Trachtenberg argues, "The Cold War did not develop out of the quarrel over Eastern Europe. It was the dispute over Iran and Turkey that instead played the key role in triggering the conflict."[87] If the United States was simply assuming the worst about intentions, then such crises should have been epiphenomenal. In fact, they played a critical role in transforming U.S. policy toward the Soviet Union. Concern about Soviet intentions reinforced longer U.S. time horizons and thus a more competitive strategic relationship with Moscow.

Iran British and Soviet troops had jointly occupied Iran in August 1941. Their goal was to prevent Germany from capturing Iranian oil fields and from cutting off supply routes to the Soviet Union.[88] Soviet troops occupied the north, while British troops were located in the south. A treaty of alliance was signed by Iran, the Soviet Union, and Great Britain in January 1942. In March 1942, the United States extended lend-lease assistance to Iran, and thirty thousand U.S. troops were deployed in Iran to ensure the distribution of that aid, provide for Iranian security, and transport supplies to the Soviet Union.[89] The treaty of alliance allowed the Soviet Union and Great Britain to retain their troops in Iran but mandated that both countries evacuate within six months of an armistice agreement ending the war with Germany.[90]

Over the course of 1943, both Tehran and Washington became increasingly anxious about the prospects for Soviet withdrawal once the war concluded.[91] On December 1, as part of the Tehran conference, the United States, Great Britain, and the Soviet Union agreed to the Tehran Declaration, affirming that they were "at one with the Government of Iran in their desire for the maintenance of the independence, sovereignty and territorial integrity of Iran."[92] The Tehran Declaration complemented the 1942 alliance treaty, but importantly, it also committed the United States to maintaining the territorial integrity of Iran.

The scramble for control in Iran accelerated over the following year. In October, Stalin demanded a Soviet oil concession, and the next month, the Soviets instigated political change in northern Iran that brought to power the more pro-Soviet Tudeh Party.[93] By the end of the year, the United States and the United Kingdom were worried about both the interests of their oil companies and the political fate of Iran even as Stalin was determined to protect the southern Soviet border.[94]

At the Yalta conference, the Iranian government pressured the United States to ensure that the Soviet Union would withdraw its troops once the war ended. Churchill and Roosevelt pushed for an even earlier withdrawal, but the Soviets avoided the discussion. Molotov saw little reason to withdraw Soviet troops earlier when at least some elements within Iran had been inclined to cooperate with the Soviet Union. Both sides quickly realized that nothing regarding Iran would be resolved at Yalta.[95]

Soviet behavior in Iran when World War II ended would provide yet another valuable test of Soviet intentions. As a U.S. briefing book prepared for the Yalta conference surmised, "Iran is considered a testing ground for United States, United Kingdom, and USSR cooperation and for the principles of Dumbarton Oaks."[96] If Moscow met its obligation and withdrew within six months, then that would be an encouraging sign. If the Soviets did not meet their commitment and continued to meddle in Iranian domestic politics, then both Washington and London would have reason to be concerned. Soviet behavior in Iran was not necessarily a credible indication of anything about long-term Soviet intentions—genuine concerns about security could have motivated the same behavior—but it had the effect of drawing attention to long-term Soviet intentions. The United States and Britain had accepted a Soviet sphere of influence in Eastern Europe, but they could not countenance expansion beyond that.

As soon as the war ended, the Iranian government requested that any foreign occupation troops leave as required by the Tehran Declaration. Britain was prepared to withdraw its troops but would not do so until the Soviet Union withdrew its forces. Meanwhile, Moscow argued that it should be permitted to keep its troops in Iran until the end of the war with Japan. Iran appealed to the United States for assistance, but Washington demurred for fear of unnecessarily antagonizing either Britain or the Soviet Union.[97] At the September Conference of Foreign Ministers in London, the Soviets pledged to abide by what they viewed as their commitment to withdraw their troops from Iran by March 2, 1946, six months after the defeat of Japan.

Loy Henderson, director of the Office of Near Eastern and African Affairs in the U.S. State Department, observed that the Iran situation was "a test of the ability of the permanent members of the Security Council to cooperate with each other on a basis of respect for the sovereignty of smaller members of the United Nations."[98] Henderson advised that the United States be amenable to some Soviet oil rights in Iran as long as Moscow was willing to recognize the sovereign independence of the Tehran government.

At the December foreign ministers meeting in Moscow, Stalin insisted that the Soviets must maintain troops in northern Iran because the central Iranian government was hostile to Soviet interests. To bolster his case, Stalin cited an obsolete 1921 treaty between Russia and Iran that had granted Russia the right to intervene in northern Iran in cases of instability.[99] The

United States attempted to establish a tripartite commission to manage the Iran situation, but those efforts were rebuffed, and 1945 ended with the Soviet Union essentially recognizing a separate government in northern Iran.

As 1946 began, the U.S. position on Iran began to harden. Washington had tried to accommodate Soviet interests at Yalta, Potsdam, London, and Moscow over the course of 1945, but ominous signs of Soviet intentions continued to appear. In a New Year's Day column, *Washington Post* commentator Barnet Nover focused on the significance of the Iran issue. For Nover, Iran was a "touchstone of the good faith and mutual forbearance of the Big Three in their dealings with weak and smaller powers." Soviet behavior in Iran would "throw light on Russian ambitions in the Middle East." And "should Russia retain her present foothold in Iran, the presumption will be hard to avoid that she will sooner or later go further."[100] Provocative Soviet behavior in Iran was a valuable indicator of broader Soviet intentions. Rather than simply assume the worst about Soviet intentions, the United States was still gauging Soviet behavior as an indicator of those intentions.

By January 1, all U.S. troops had withdrawn from Iran, and Britain was committed to withdrawing its troops by the six-month deadline of March 2. The remaining question was whether the Soviets would withdraw their troops or simply attempt to annex northern Iran. Inflammatory Soviet press reports inciting opposition to the central Iranian government exacerbated U.S. and British concerns.[101]

The situation deteriorated further in February. On top of Stalin's provocative February 9 speech, negotiations in Moscow between the Iranian prime minister, Ahmad Qavam, and Molotov ended unsuccessfully. The Soviets insisted on oil concessions as well as political autonomy in northern Iran, both of which were unacceptable to the Tehran government.[102]

George F. Kennan issued his "long telegram" on February 22. Kennan famously expressed his concern over both Soviet current behavior and long-term intentions. He attributed Moscow's behavior to the need for Soviet leaders to legitimate their domestic rule. Kennan mentions Iran specifically, and his views are worth quoting at length: "Whenever it is considered timely and promising, efforts will be made to advance official limits of Soviet power. For the moment, these efforts are restricted to certain neighboring points conceived of as being of immediate strategic necessity, such as Northern Iran, Turkey, possibly Bornholm. However, other points may at any time come into question, if and as Soviet political power is extended to new areas. Thus, a 'friendly' Persian government might be asked to grant Russia a port on the Persian Gulf."[103] Kennan's recommendations to contain possible Soviet expansion became the basis for U.S. grand strategy during the Cold War.[104]

Less than a week after Kennan's telegram arrived, Byrnes delivered a speech to the Overseas Press Club in which he insisted that the nascent United Nations charter must be defended and endorsed. He asserted that the United States would not respond passively to any use of force or threatened force that would violate the charter.[105] The stage was set for a crisis in Iran.

On March 2, the Soviet Union announced that it would withdraw most of its troops from northern Iran, but some units would remain behind until the region was stable. The United States protested vigorously, and Robert Rossow, the U.S. vice-consul in Tabriz, alerted Washington of increased Soviet troop activity in Iran.[106] On the same day as Rossow's warning, March 5, Churchill delivered his famous "iron curtain" speech in Fulton, Missouri, in which he argued that Soviet expansionism could only be repelled if met with military force.[107] Byrnes made clear the U.S. response: "Now we'll have to give it to them with both barrels."[108]

Apprehension over Soviet behavior and what it foretold for Soviet intentions was evident in the media. A *New York Times* editorial in the midst of the crisis asked two questions, "What does Russia want?" and "Where does the search for security end and where does expansion begin?"[109] Walter Lippmann, who up until March had held out hope for a cooperative resolution in the Middle East, argued that the point had only now been reached where failure was more likely than success in resolving the Iran crisis.[110]

Finally, with the threat growing of more active involvement of the United States and the United Nations, the Soviet Union and Iran reached an agreement on March 25.[111] The Soviet Union would withdraw all of its forces within six weeks, barring any "unforeseen circumstances." In return, Iran agreed to joint oil exploration with the Soviets. U.S. leaders supported this resolution, as they could claim that it was the combined threat of the involvement of the United States and the United Nations that had compelled Moscow to capitulate.[112] To bolster the credibility of the United Nations, Washington insisted that the agreement be approved by the Security Council. On March 29, the Security Council did so and requested a progress report on April 3.[113]

The Iran crisis ended on May 20, when the Tehran government reported that the last of the Soviet troops had left northern Iran. The Soviets continued to assert their influence on Iranian domestic politics through their support for the communist Tudeh Party, but the international crisis had passed. As a consequence of the crisis, U.S. time horizons extended into the future to consider the long-term implications of a Soviet rise and thus drove the United States to more competitive strategies in the short term. Importantly, Soviet behavior in Iran was not necessarily a credible indication of long-term Soviet plans for expansion. After all, Moscow saw the border with Iran as vital to its core national security. But the critical effect of the crisis was to draw attention to the long-term threat that Soviet intentions, combined with Soviet capabilities, posed.

Turkey Iran was but one of a few crises that raised concerns about Soviet intentions and helped instigate the Cold War. These crises were inherently important, but they also held larger significance as indicators of long-term Soviet intentions. As the United States became more concerned about those intentions, it became more focused on taking actions to address the long-term Soviet threat.

In March 1945, Stalin renounced the Treaty of Friendship that Turkey and the Soviet Union had signed in 1925. Then, at Potsdam, the Soviets demanded revision of the Montreux Convention governing passage through the Dardanelles. Moscow wanted freedom to pass through the straits and also wanted a naval base in the straits in order to secure Soviet interests.[114]

U.S. leaders were open to a revision of the Montreux Convention, but they were wary of granting too much control to the Soviets. A U.S. Army report explained their objections: "Neither the United States nor the British Empire can by the greatest stretch of the imagination be accused of expansionist or aggressive ambitions. . . . Russia, however, has not as yet proven that she is entirely without expansionistic aims." The report continued with concern about future Soviet intentions: "Russia must be sorely tempted to combine her strength with her ideology to expand her influence over the earth."[115]

Eventually, Truman proposed international control over the straits, but Stalin was not interested.[116] Truman reported bluntly, "I had proposed the internationalization of all the principal waterways. Stalin did not want this. What Stalin wanted was control of the Black Sea straits and the Danube. The Russians were planning world conquest."[117] Yet Soviet behavior through the remainder of 1945 and into 1946 was restrained. In October 1945, Harriman reported that "the U.S.S.R. has remained remarkably inactive with regard to Turkey."[118]

Decision making in Washington at this time was complicated by competing and contradictory assessments of Soviet intentions in Turkey. In late 1945, U.S. Army intelligence indicated that the Soviets were withdrawing their forces from eastern and southeastern regions of Europe, but other reports warned that the Soviets were massing large numbers of troops in Bulgaria in preparation for an attack on Turkey.[119] A report of the Joint Intelligence Staff of the Joint Chiefs of Staff concluded that there was considerable reason to be concerned about Soviet ambitions in Turkey: "In light of all known factors one must draw the conclusion that the aggressive Soviet policy in respect to Turkey is based not on a concept of defense, but of expansion, or that, if basically defensive, the projected Soviet security zone will embrace wider areas to which a subservient and truncated Turkey will constitute a stepping zone."[120] The report expressed direct concern about Turkey and also about what Soviet behavior in Turkey might indicate about broader Soviet intentions.

Concern continued to grow in early 1946. The U.S. ambassador to Turkey, Edwin C. Wilson, sent a report to Washington of ominous Soviet troop movements around Turkey. In abbreviated language, he suggested that the Soviet objective in Turkey was "to break present Turkish government, install 'friendly' government, resulting in closing Turkish gap in Soviet security belt from Baltic to Black Sea, giving USSR physical control of Straits and putting end to Western influence in Turkey. In short, domination of Turkey."[121] Truman resolved to protect Turkey from Soviet aggression, and, symbolically, he ordered the battleship U.S.S. *Missouri* into the straits.[122]

In an April 4 meeting with U.S. ambassador Walter Bedell Smith, Stalin reiterated that the Soviet Union did not harbor aggressive intentions toward Turkey. While the Soviets did desire a base in the Dardanelles and unfettered access to the straits, these demands were motivated by security not aggression. But Stalin's reassurances failed to convince, and the U.S. military spent much of the summer of 1946 preparing war plans to respond to Soviet aggression in Turkey.[123]

On August 7, Moscow again formally demanded a revision of the Montreux Convention.[124] The request precipitated an international crisis that would consume the world's attention for the following two months.[125] As in Iran, U.S. officials viewed events in Turkey and the straits as having wider implications for long-term Soviet intentions. As Melvyn P. Leffler reports, "U.S. policymakers agreed that Soviet proposals were a ploy to secure bases in Turkey, take it over, and then gain control of Greece, the Middle East, and the Eastern Mediterranean. Once having sealed off these areas from the Western world, the Soviets would maneuver to achieve their goals in China and India."[126] Moscow could have its sphere of influence in Eastern Europe, but that was it. Henderson, of the U.S. State Department, suggested that the Soviet Union was maneuvering in Turkey so that its "power and influence can sweep unimpeded across Turkey and through the Dardanelles in the Mediterranean, and across Iran and through the Persian Gulf into the Pacific Ocean." Further, "the Russians, once in possession of the new position conceded to them . . . would undoubtedly begin preparations for further attacks upon such barriers . . . as might remain."[127] In another major policy brief prepared for the secretary of state, Henderson added, "The establishment by the Soviet Union of bases in the Dardanelles or the introduction of Soviet armed forces into Turkey on some other pretext would, in the natural course of events, result in Greece and the whole Near and Middle East, including the Eastern Mediterranean, falling under Soviet control and in those areas being cut off from the western world."[128]

The scare in Turkey ultimately passed quietly without conflict as all sides settled into their postwar positions. The Soviets abandoned efforts to revise the Montreux Convention, and Turkey moved slowly but surely toward the West. But the crisis had the expected effect of drawing attention to Soviet intentions in Turkey and also around the world and into the future. As Daniel Yergin concludes about the Turkish episode, "Interpretations and assessments from this point on derived from the axiomatic construct that the Soviet Union was not a Great Power operating within the international system but rather a world revolutionary state bent on overturning that system."[129]

Again, the United States did not simply assume the worst about Soviet intentions but rather inferred those intentions from ominous Soviet behavior. In the absence of other threats, the United States was free to consider long-term threats, and indications of the Soviet Union's malign intentions only led to dire assessments of the long-term Soviet threat. While the demonstrated capabilities of the Soviet Union undoubtedly led to concern, it was events like the crisis in Turkey that focused attention on the long-term threat that it might pose to Western interests.[130]

Germany While developments in Iran and Turkey were peripheral to U.S. interests, the dispute over the postwar settlement of Germany raised doubts about Soviet intentions at the core of U.S. interests in Europe. The Paris Peace Conference opened in April 1946 with the goal of resolving remaining postwar issues including economic and political arrangements for Germany. Apprehensive over uncertain Soviet intentions, Byrnes resolved to use Germany as a test of Soviet intentions.

Specifically, the test took the form of a proposal for a treaty among the United States, the Soviet Union, Great Britain, and France that would demilitarize Germany for twenty-five years.[131] Byrnes explained to Molotov that in the United States many were uncertain about long-term Soviet intentions. If the Soviets would agree to the demilitarization, then U.S. concerns about Soviet goals would be alleviated. If, however, Moscow rejected the proposal, then concerns would persist.[132] Byrnes told Molotov, "There were many people in the United States who were unable to understand the exact aim of the Soviet Union—whether it was a search for security or expansionism. . . . Such a treaty as had been proposed . . . would effectively take care of the question of security."[133] Republican senator Arthur H. Vandenberg added, "If and when Molotov refuses this offer, he will confess that he wants expansion and not 'security.' . . . Then moral conscience all around the globe can face and assess the realities—and prepare for the consequences."[134]

In early July, Molotov rejected Byrnes's proposal. Byrnes and British foreign secretary Ernest Bevin interpreted the rejection as a ploy to win Germans over to communism by ostensibly supporting a unified, normal Germany rather than a divided and disarmed Germany.[135] Ironically, then, the Soviet refusal led the United States and Britain to accept the inevitability of a divided Germany, and their attention turned to how best to manage the divided occupation of Germany, including the creation of "Bizonia"—a fusion of the U.S. and British zones of occupation.[136]

THE HARDENING OF THE COLD WAR

By the summer of 1946, then, Soviet behavior beyond its acknowledged sphere of influence in Eastern Europe had provoked both immediate concerns about how to resolve the situation in the short term and long-term concerns about what these crises foretold about Soviet intentions. In Europe, the division of Germany was becoming a reality, and Soviet-inspired communist movements in Greece, Italy, and France were of increasing concern.[137] In the Middle East, concerns about Iran and Turkey persisted, while in East Asia there was continuing uncertainty regarding Soviet intentions in Japan, Korea, and China.

On July 12, Truman instructed presidential counsel Clark Clifford and his aide George Elsey to prepare a report on Soviet compliance with international agreements.[138] With an understanding of how the Soviets had behaved thus far, Truman thought he would be able to make better policy going forward.[139] The document produced, the Clifford-Elsey report, was perhaps the most systematic attempt to evaluate Soviet capabilities and intentions since the end of the war. As Leffler summarizes, "The Clifford-Elsey Report was the first comprehensive interdepartmental effort to assess Soviet intentions and capabilities, analyze the Kremlin's motivations, evaluate Russian behavior, and prescribe American behavior."[140] Even at this late date, far from assuming the worst about Soviet intentions, the United States continued actively to investigate what those intentions might be.

The report, submitted to the president in September, concluded that the Soviet Union was an ideologically driven communist state bent on world domination. "The Kremlin acknowledges no limit to the eventual power of the Soviet Union, but it is practical enough to be concerned with the actual position of the U.S.S.R. today," Clifford and Elsey wrote. "The key to an understanding of current Soviet foreign policy, in summary, is the realization that Soviet leaders adhere to the Marxian theory of ultimate destruction of capitalist states by communist states, while at the same time they strive to postpone the inevitable conflict in order to strengthen and prepare the Soviet Union for its clash with western democracies."[141] The increasingly powerful and ideological Soviet Union had long time horizons, and premature conflict would not be in its interests.

More specifically, the report detailed Soviet violations of the Atlantic Charter as well as agreements reached at the Tehran, Yalta, and Potsdam conferences and the Council of Foreign Ministers meetings. Clifford and Elsey focused, in particular, on the Soviet Union's threatening ambitions with regard to Germany and warned of the day when the Soviets' capabilities would enable them to pursue their intentions. Intentions, not capabilities, were the lead concern about the Soviet Union. The solution was for the United States to improve substantially its military capabilities and presence around the globe: "The language of military power is the only language which disciples of power politics understand. The United States must use that language in order that Soviet leaders will realize that our government is determined to uphold the interests of its citizens and the rights of small nations."[142] The Soviets' threatening intentions were inherent to the Soviet domestic political system, and military power was the only response that would influence Soviet behavior.

The report was a political document that employed evidence selectively to advance its argument. Notably, the report failed to address some of the more encouraging signs of Soviet intentions or account for U.S. actions that might have provoked Moscow's behavior. The Soviets had abided by the occupation agreement in Korea, accepted the presence of U.S. forces in Manchuria, and allowed elections in Czechoslovakia and Hungary. The Soviets also appeared to be withdrawing their forces from areas of potential conflict in the Middle East and northern Europe.[143] The report also accelerated the time frame in which Soviet capabilities were likely to become a threat to U.S. interests. U.S. Army intelligence estimated that it would be as much as fifteen years until the Soviet military was rebuilt and prepared for another major war, yet the Clifford-Elsey report suggested that the threat was more urgent.[144]

All that said, the Clifford-Elsey report served an essential function. As Leffler summarizes, "The Clifford-Elsey report simplified international realities, distorted Soviet behavior, and probably misread Soviet motivations and intentions. But the authors were no fools. They wanted to parry their domestic critics and insure against worst-case scenarios."[145] The report bolstered support for a more aggressive strategy toward Moscow on the basis not of Soviet capabilities but of concern about Soviet long-term intentions. The Soviets were years away from having a rebuilt military, but that long-term threat was worth addressing now.[146] By drawing attention to the long-term threat, the report made action in the present more likely.

During World War II, the pragmatic need for cooperation led to a myopic focus on the short term. Dealing with any emergent threat from the Soviet Union was necessarily deferred until later. Little thought was given to the long-term consequences of cooperation with the Soviet Union. Once the war was over, however, and as Soviet behavior beyond its Eastern European sphere of influence became more aggressive and provocative, U.S. time horizons shifted toward the future. Soviet capabilities were remarkably weakened by the destruction of World War II, yet concern about the Soviets only grew. The United States became more willing to pay a short-term cost to address the long-term threat posed by the Soviet Union.

As an illustration of the evolving U.S. policy toward the Soviet Union, consider the record of economic cooperation. The last U.S. lend-lease shipment to Russia arrived on September 2, 1945, the same day that Japan surrendered.[147] Even after the war was over, the Soviets requested a postwar loan to aid in reconstruction.[148] Washington was willing to consider the request, but given increasing concern about long-term Soviet intentions, the loan would be conditional on Soviet behavior in Iran and on other sources of potential conflict.[149]

Unsurprisingly, Stalin was not willing to meet all of the U.S. conditions, and as Soviet-U.S. relations continued to deteriorate in the summer and fall of 1946, the prospects for any U.S. financial assistance to the Soviet Union evaporated. As George C. Herring summarizes, "Thus, by the end of September 1946, the Truman administration had reoriented its foreign aid policy, abandoning any further pretense of treating all nations on an equal basis and concentrating its program on those outside the Soviet sphere."[150] In the course of a little over a year, the United States had gone from providing extensive lend-lease assistance to the Soviet Union to being unwilling to offer any assistance in postwar reconstruction. The path toward the grand strategy of containment that would dominate the Cold War was now clear.

Explaining Cooperation and Competition with the Soviet Union

The transition from cooperation to competition in the postwar period was a product of lengthening U.S. time horizons and troubling indications of Soviet intentions. My argument expects that whether great powers cooperate or compete is a product of the interaction of state time horizons. Immediate threats make it more difficult for a state to trade off short-term opportunities for mutually beneficial cooperation in exchange for potential long-term benefits. When immediate threats are absent, states are more inclined to look toward the long term. In this case, the short-term pragmatic need for cooperation in World War II trumped any possible long-term concerns about the Soviet Union. In this context, it is perhaps not surprising that Roosevelt also contemplated postwar cooperation arrangements, such as the four policemen concept. The United States provided financial and material assistance to Stalin with seemingly little concern for the long-term consequences of that cooperation.[151]

Stalin, meanwhile, indicated an interest in cooperation at Tehran, Yalta, and Potsdam, which prevented the emergence of any longer-terms concerns. As Vojtech Mastny writes, "Stalin made the attainment of his preferred postwar order dependent less on the vagaries of war than on the emergence after its conclusion of a congenial international environment. He tried to accomplish what he wanted with rather than against his powerful western allies, whose support, or at least acquiescence, he deemed indispensable for achieving the kind of security he craved."[152] The best way to achieve this was, at least at first, to maintain his allies' focus on the short term rather than on uncertainty surrounding his long-term intentions. As Vladislav Zubok and Constantine Pleshakov observe, "Stalin ardently believed in the inevitability of a postwar economic crisis of the capitalist economy and of clashes within the capitalist camp that would provide him with a lot of space for geopolitical maneuvering in Europe and Asia—all within the framework of general cooperation with capitalist countries."[153] The Soviets could continue to benefit from cooperation while awaiting the self-destruction of the capitalist order.[154]

At the same time, however, Stalin could not accomplish his goals for the Soviet Union without further expansion, and the end of World War II provided the opportunity to act on those goals. As I argued in chapter 2, rising great powers are sometimes pushed toward aggressive action even if that behavior removes uncertainty about their intentions. Again, Zubok and Pleshakov write, "In 1945, euphoric from military victory, [Stalin] again ascribed a special mission to the Russians: to be a world power, second to none."[155] Stalin saw the end of World War II as the opportunity to act now to advance Soviet interests rather than continuing to try to manipulate Western beliefs about his intentions. Molotov, explaining his view on the origins of the Cold War, states, "All this simply happened because we were advancing. They [the Western powers], of course, hardened against us, and we had to firm up what we had conquered. . . . Everywhere it was necessary to make order, suppress the capitalist ways. That's what the 'Cold War' was about."[156] Once cooperation with the West and the achievement of Soviet aims became incompatible, the overlapping preferences for cooperation disappeared. Stalin faced little incentive to try to mislead others about Soviet intentions.

Still, once the war ended, Washington did not immediately resign itself to a more competitive strategy, nor did the balance of material capabilities lead ineluctably to competition. But concerns did begin to emerge. A series of crises in Iran, Turkey, and Germany brought attention to long-term Soviet intentions and made competition more likely. The Clifford-Elsey report, written in the summer of 1946, expressed the emerging longer-term concerns of U.S. decision makers driven by Soviet behavior in these crises.

While Soviet ideology certainly contributed to the long-term concern about Soviet intentions, it was not determinative. As John Lewis Gaddis writes, "Truman harbored a healthy skepticism toward all totalitarian states: ideology, he thought, whether communist or fascist, was simply an excuse for dictatorial rule. But, like Roosevelt, he did not see totalitarianism in itself as precluding normal relations."[157] Ideological difference was a relative constant, but it did not prevent cooperation with the Soviets when the war made it a pragmatic necessity.[158]

Soviet behavior was most critical to the shift in the United States' resolution of its now-or-later dilemma. As Leffler observes, "The Kremlin's policies in Eastern Europe and the Balkans, however, could serve as a clue to Soviet intentions elsewhere. . . . If they abrogated their commitments, they would fail the litmus tests of their intentions and prove their nefarious ambitions."[159] If the United States was simply assuming the worst about Soviet intentions, then these litmus tests would be unnecessary. Importantly, these litmus tests did not produce truly costly signals of Soviet intentions, but together they created a composite picture of likely Soviet ambitions. For example, even U.S. policymakers recognized that Poland was of strategic importance to the Soviet Union, yet they still drew conclusions about long-term expansionist Soviet intentions from Moscow's support for the Lublin government.[160] Again, U.S. concern about long-term Soviet intentions grew as Soviet short-term behavior became more provocative.

Employing litmus tests for intentions is, however, tricky and may produce misleading results. For example, Stalin's rejection of the Byrnes proposal to demilitarize Germany for twenty-five years may have been driven by his own sense of insecurity. Zubok and Pleshakov write, "He wanted a new Germany to become his ally, and until then he was prepared to keep the Soviet zone of occupation permanently, while doing everything to neutralize the threat that the revanchist forces in West Germany could pose to the U.S.S.R."[161] Even if litmus tests do not provide credible indicators of a state's intentions—intentions can always change and there may be multiple explanations for any behavior—they can have a significant framing effect. They allow states to update their probabilistic beliefs about another state's intentions. Views of intentions are not all-or-nothing but rather are calibrated in a probabilistic manner based on available information about intentions.

Buck-passing explains cooperation as an attempt by great powers to get somebody else to pay the bill for balancing against a great power. In this case, however, there was no other power to which the United States could pass the buck. Moreover, while buck-passing might be able to explain the absence of balancing during a certain period, it is less capable of accounting for the presence of cooperation that potentially strengthens another state. Buck-passing would also predict that states move away from passing the buck when the material threat posed by another state becomes great enough that states realize that they must adopt a more competitive strategy. Offensive realists also expect states to assume the worst about others' intentions, so the decision to balance is dictated by material capabilities. In this case, the evidence suggests that it was not just capabilities but rather capabilities together with concern about long-term Soviet intentions that led to the adoption of more competitive strategies. U.S. concern about the Soviet threat was rooted not in uncertainty but in increasing certainty about malign intentions.

Material power certainly provided the foundation for U.S. concern about the Soviet Union, and bipolarity focused U.S. attention on the Soviet Union, but the balance of capabilities cannot explain the timing of shifts in U.S. strategy. By the end of World War II, the United States contained more than half of the world's manufacturing capacity and was the world's largest exporter of goods and services.[162] The Soviet Union had lost over twenty million people during the war, and its gross national product at the end of the war was one-third that of the United States.[163] The Soviet military machine remained daunting at war's end: 175 army divisions, supported by twenty-five thousand tanks and nineteen thousand aircraft.[164] But even this significant military capacity was in danger of falling behind the development of the U.S. military, including the U.S. monopoly on the atomic weapon.[165] What came to concern the United States as its time horizons extended was the combination of likely future Soviet capabilities and intentions. As Kennan remarked in 1947, "Remember that . . . as things stand today, it is not Russian military power which is threatening to us, it is Russian political power."[166] Finally, there is good reason to question whether U.S. and Soviet leaders had an accurate understanding of each other's capabilities. As William C. Wohlforth writes, "People on the ground in 1946, however, had no idea what the precise configuration of power would look like."[167] A precise understanding was unnecessary for U.S. leaders to recognize that a threat was present, but the key point remains that capabilities alone have a difficult time explaining the shift from a willingness to explore opportunities for cooperation with Moscow to the more competitive strategies of the Cold War.

Finally, engagement explains cooperation as an effort by a great power to moderate the intentions of another great power. Roosevelt did sincerely attempt to create a stable international order in which the growing Soviet Union would be enmeshed, so there is evidence to support attempts at engagement. Tellingly, though, Roosevelt's efforts did not succeed, and it was Soviet behavior, indicative of long-term intentions, that led the United States to shift to more competitive strategies. Engagement theory offers a less compelling account of when and why states abandon efforts at cooperation and shift to more competitive strategies.

The United States did not pass the buck on the Soviet threat; it procrastinated, as the other great powers in this book did. States put off dealing with threats in the short term because it is expensive to do so or because they face other more pressing threats, and they only address long-term threats when they are wealthy and secure in the short term, as the United States was beginning in 1946. Our understanding of the evolution of Soviet-U.S. relations is enriched by the addition of temporal dynamics and appreciation of the role of beliefs about intentions in threat perception. Beliefs about intentions, more than assessments of capabilities, account for the transformation of uncertainty about the future into measurable and manageable risk.

Part of the reason to study this case is that it is the only available modern case of emerging bipolarity. It is useful to consider whether the lessons from this case might be applicable to potentially emerging Sino-U.S. bipolarity. In the next, and concluding, chapter, I consider this question.

Conclusion and the Contemporary Rise of China

Almost a century and a half ago, in an 1870 essay titled "Wanted, a States-man!," the American preacher and author James Freeman Clarke surmised, "A politician . . . is a man who thinks of the next election; while the statesman thinks of the next generation."[1] "Statesmen" have typically been viewed with admiration. They have foresight; they anticipate future threats, and they have the patience to pay short-term costs to enjoy future rewards. By compari-son, "politicians" are dismissed as brash, impulsive, and myopic. But how often do leaders act like politicians and how often as statesmen? How do the time horizons of political leaders affect international politics?

This book has explored these questions in the context of how states and their leaders respond to emerging threats in international relations. This concluding chapter has three tasks. First, I review the key elements of the argument and the evidence presented to evaluate it against alternatives. Second, I discuss the theoretical implications of the argument, including beyond the realm of security affairs. Third, I conclude with a discussion of how the argument may help explain the evolution of Sino-U.S. relations in the coming years.

Reviewing the Argument

Why do existing great powers sometimes cooperate with emerging threats, and why do they sometimes adopt more competitive strategies? Coopera-tion may be puzzling, as existing powers presumably have good reasons to fear the uncertain intentions of a potential emerging threat. I argue that co-operative or competitive outcomes are the product of the interaction of state time horizons.

Choosing which strategy to pursue toward a rising power poses what I call a now-or-later dilemma for an existing power. State leaders must decide whether to expend resources in the short term to respond to a nascent threat or defer addressing that threat until later, when the threat may either have fizzled or grown far more menacing. Short-term cooperation is attractive both to existing powers, which may view cooperation as a way of delaying their own decline, and to rising powers, which can use cooperation to fuel their growth.

The resolution of such now-or-later dilemmas is critically affected by both the short-term benefits of cooperation and the presence for an existing power of more immediate threats that must take priority over an uncertain long-term threat. In the absence of a more immediate threat, existing powers are more likely to choose to address a long-term threat than to defer until later. When an immediate threat is present, it only increases the probability that an existing power will cooperate with a long-term potential threat.

When an existing power's strategies shift from more cooperative to more competitive strategies, it is likely to be a product of changing beliefs about intentions as much as assessments of capabilities. Capabilities alone are indeterminate of behavior. Existing powers do not simply assume the worst about a rising power's intentions (whatever doing so would actually imply). Instead, they assess and adapt to changing assessments of a rising power's intentions. States view each other's intentions probabilistically, not absolutely, and these calculations leave the space for cooperation between states that would otherwise be unexpected. Alarming information about an emerging threat's long-term intentions leads to more competitive strategies in the short term.

As a consequence, rising powers attempt to manipulate the beliefs that an existing power holds about their intentions. To the extent that they succeed in persuading an existing power that they have benign intentions or they at least maintain uncertainty about those intentions, mutually beneficially cooperation becomes more likely.

Aside from explaining the empirical puzzle of variation in relations between existing and emerging powers, the argument draws attention to two novel theoretical considerations. First, it introduces more explicitly a temporal dimension to international politics. Threats are not just a product of capabilities and intentions. They also have a temporal component: When is the threat going to emerge, and when do states confront that threat? Moreover, the effect of temporality on international politics varies. As I have argued, the shadow of the future often looms ominously over great power politics.

Second, the argument offers a different and more compelling account of the role of uncertainty about intentions in great power politics. Contrary to offensive realist assumptions, states do not just assume the worst about other states' intentions. They might be better off if they did in some normative sense, but there are good logical reasons for them not to, and the evidence suggests that they do not. Instead, existing powers wait to resolve uncertainty about intentions before acting, and emerging powers, therefore, view uncertainty about their intentions as a political tool they can manipulate to their advantage. By combining temporality with a more sophisticated understanding of the role of uncertainty in international relations, this argument presents a more compelling account of how existing powers and emerging potential threats to those powers interact.

In the previous chapters, I have evaluated this argument against two primary alternative arguments. Offensive realism expects existing powers to assume the worst about the intentions of an emerging potential threat. Competitive behavior should covary with capabilities, and cooperation is the result of states attempting to pass the buck of balancing to other states. Liberalism expects that existing, but potentially declining, great powers will attempt to engage rising powers in an effort to institutionalize an international order that will protect their interests once they have declined. Cooperation with an emerging potential threat is an attempt to lock it into a stable, constitutional order.

To adjudicate among those alternative arguments, I have presented evidence from four cases of emerging potential threats to existing great powers. On the basis of that evidence, I reach four conclusions.

First, the addition of temporal considerations provides a richer understanding of how states respond to emerging potential threats. States must weigh whether to respond now or later to such threats, and cooperation is directly the result of strategic decisions by existing and emerging powers to defer more aggressive balancing behavior until later, if it proves necessary.

Second, uncertainty about the future intentions of a potential emerging threat is a critical variable, not a constant. That is, states may be more or less uncertain about those intentions, and when they are more uncertain, they often opt to wait until some of that uncertainty is resolved before acting. Over time and as the "weight" of the evidence accumulates, uncertainty becomes risk that can be incorporated into prudent strategic responses to a rising great power. In other words, state leaders prefer to procrastinate. For emerging powers, that provides an incentive to attempt to manipulate the degree of uncertainty about their intentions. Contrary to existing arguments, uncertainty creates the space for cooperation rather than making such cooperation impossible.

Third, largely because of its misunderstanding about both the meaning of uncertainty and the ways that states resolve uncertainty about long-term intentions, offensive realism provides an unsatisfying account of how states react to emerging potential threats. Indicators of intentions, more than indicators of capabilities, have led states to shift the strategies that they pursue toward emerging potential threats. One might make the normative argument that existing powers *ought* to assume the worst about the intentions of a rising threat, but, empirically, the argument fails.

Fourth, liberalism recognizes the attempts that existing powers might make to shape the interests and intentions of emerging powers, but it misidentifies the immediate, opportunistic motives that drive most cooperation. Creating a shadow of the future may not engender cooperation when it comes to great power politics. Cooperation with emerging potential threats has tended to be for the purposes of short-term economic benefit, not long-term political institutionalization of international politics. Liberalism also makes an unwarranted assumption about the foresight of great powers. G. John Ikenberry claims that dominant powers are willing to bind themselves in the short term because they believe that the long-term benefits will warrant any short-term costs. In truth, however, great powers may have doubts about either forgoing short-term benefits or accepting the willingness of rising powers to adhere to the institutional order once they are more powerful. Finally, liberalism suffers from an inability to explain when and why states abandon efforts at cooperation.

Theoretical Implications

The argument in this book has implications for at least three major research agendas in international relations.

POWER TRANSITIONS

The most prominent literature on how states respond to emerging threats is the power transition literature.[2] In situations in which a rising power is on a trajectory to overtake a declining power, the declining power has a range of strategies available to it, including preventive war. But power transition theorists have not presented convincing arguments for why states choose certain strategies over others. Why do some states pursue preventive war and others seek accommodation? Moreover, while this literature is particularly attentive to that dangerous moment when the rising power surpasses the declining power, it has not paid as much attention to earlier formative moments in the relationship. If the rise of a power is reasonably predictable, then should we not see declining powers acting sooner in response to that rise? This book improves on the power transition literature by considering the broader life cycle of interaction between rising and declining powers. In a sense, it explains why power transitions even happen. That is, why states do not attempt earlier to forestall the rise of a potential threat.

Another approach to power transition that does think explicitly in terms of this longer relationship is power cycles theory.[3] This literature emphasizes the recurrent cycles of relative power relationships in international relations. It argues that one can explain developments in international politics simply by mapping the trajectories of different states' capabilities. One shortcoming of this literature, however, is that it treats objective measures of capabilities as unproblematic, as if state leaders have a correct grasp of both their own and others' material capabilities. Yet the historical record suggests that leaders regularly misjudge material power relationships.[4] In addition, power cycles theory is, by design, apolitical. It offers a spare, parsimonious theoretical account that claims that developments in international relations follow the ebb and flow of material capabilities, but the logic encounters difficulty when political developments do not shadow changes in material capabilities. In contrast, I contend that perceptions of material capabilities and beliefs about how those capabilities might be used are formed through a political process.

In sum, the existing power transition literature has had two unfortunate tendencies that this book corrects. First, it moves away from a purely material understanding of power transitions. It emphasizes how beliefs about the future intentions of rising great powers are important and how temporal considerations shape the ways that states view threats. Second, the book does more to account for variation in responses to rising great powers. States do not view all rising great powers equally, and the strategies they adopt to contend with such rising powers vary significantly.

THREAT PERCEPTION

This book also speaks to a larger debate over how states perceive threats. Offensive realists, like John J. Mearsheimer, contend that threats are a product of capabilities. Future intentions are unknowable, so states must assume the worst about those intentions and base strategies on capabilities alone.[5] Defensive realists, by contrast, argue that states assess threats based on more than just capabilities. For example, Stephen M. Walt has argued that threats are a product of material capabilities plus perceived intentions, offensive capabilities, and geography. For Walt, his "balance of threat" theory can better explain alliance behavior over time, including the choice of Western European states to ally with the United States rather than the Soviet Union after World War II.[6] Notably, however, Walt avoids assessing the relative importance of these different elements of threats or the ways that they might interact.

My argument differs from both of these well-known approaches. In particular, my argument pays attention to temporal factors that these others ignore. Time is less an alternative variable than it is an additional dimension along which strategic choices vary. Great powers may be concerned about the future intentions of other great powers, but that does not mean that they assume the worst about those intentions.[7] Assuming the worst implies paying a heavy cost in the present out of concern for the future, but how often are state leaders willing to pay this price? The critical issue is not just what capabilities and intentions another state possesses, but *when* it has those capabilities and intentions and whether states should act on that potential threat now or later.[8]

Realists have long been concerned with uncertainty about intentions in the future and the time inconsistency problem raised by state intentions.[9] Even if a state commits now to doing something in the future, it can decide differently once that future arrives. Stephen G. Brooks identifies time horizons as one of the key distinctions between "possibilistic" and "probabilistic" realism.[10] While possibilistic realism expects that states act out of the simple possibility of something happening in the future, probabilistic realism argues that states act after assessing the probability of that same thing happening.

But Brooks's distinction only highlights what is a muddled concept in realist theory. Brooks identifies Kenneth N. Waltz's neorealism as possibilistic with the implication that states must have short time horizons except in a forgiving security environment. Yet Waltz himself challenges this characterization, arguing that it is precisely concern about the long-term future that generates competition in the short term.[11] Mearsheimer's argument is even more possibilistic than Waltz, yet Mearsheimer claims that rational states have long time horizons: "States pay attention not only to the immediate consequences of their actions, but the long-term effects as well."[12] That state actions in the short term are motivated by long-term implications explains the realist fixation on relative gains and losses. Finally, Brooks characterizes probabilistic realists, like Robert Gilpin, as more mindful of the willingness of political leaders to pay short-term costs for long-term gain. Preventive war, one of the central predictions of power transition theory, implies that states may accept the short-term costs of war to prevent the emergence of a long-term threat, yet the factors that lead politicians to choose costly action now over deferring until later have not been theorized by Gilpin or any of his theoretical successors. This book has sought to clarify thinking about the role of different time horizons in the conduct of national security strategy.

Finally, in the context of threat perception, the book offers a new take on the role of uncertainty in international politics. Brian C. Rathbun delineates four common understandings of uncertainty in international politics: realist, rationalist, constructivist, and cognitive.[13] My argument borrows from all of these to develop a more accurate understanding of the way in which uncertainty affects state behavior. I argue that uncertainty can open the space for cooperation rather than leading to worst-case assumptions about a state's intentions. Uncertainty is a variable, and it can be manipulated for political purposes by both existing powers and emerging potential threats.[14] To be clear, the argument of this book implies not that material capabilities are irrelevant, just that they are insufficient to explain variation in state behavior. As a state becomes more capable, other states become less willing to take a risk on the uncertain intentions of that rising power, but they continue to assess those intentions rather than simply assuming the worst about them.

At a broader level, the book contributes to discussions of time as a social phenomenon. Time is a much-studied concept in the social sciences.[15] In sociology and historical institutionalism, the theoretical focus has tended to be on time as a process.[16] That is, one cannot understand social behavior without understanding the temporal sequence in which events take place.[17] Scholars have focused on notions such as turning points—temporal moments that shift events in a new direction. Relatedly, the popular historical institutionalist concept of path dependence has an ineluctable temporal dimension to it, as events inexorably move forward in time.[18] Other studies have focused on the experience of time. Technology shifts the way in which humans experience time, seemingly speeding up or slowing down how humans go through life.[19] Finally, some in the social sciences have borrowed the concept of "punctuated equilibrium" from the study of evolution and applied it to the social sciences.[20]

Time horizons have received less attention in this literature. This book makes a contribution by thinking explicitly about how time horizons influence one area of social life, international relations, but it is not difficult to imagine applications of these theoretical concepts to other areas.[21]

Policy Implications: The Rise of China

The argument of this book also has significant policy implications. As the world's most powerful country, the United States must consider how to respond to emerging threats to its interests. Does the United States want to pay the costs now of addressing a potential threat, or does it opt to defer dealing with that threat until later, when it may be much more expensive to do so? Political leaders are often lauded for being forward-looking, but in my argument the implications of such foresight may be more competition and conflict rather than cooperation. Perhaps the most interesting case to consider is the rise of China, though one might also consider the resurgence of Russia or even non-state actors such as the Islamic State in Iraq and Syria (ISIS).

U.S. behavior toward China over the past few decades is an example of the basic puzzle driving this book.[22] If the United States is fearful of an emerging, potentially threatening China, then why has it been abetting its rise? Nothing is certain about the contemporary rise of China, and there are questions to be asked about the ability of China to sustain its growth and to deal with the mounting domestic challenges that it faces. Nor is it preordained that the United States and China will become rivals, let alone enemies.[23] But the historical track record suggests that the rise of great powers has led to some of the most dramatic—and deadly—events in human history.[24]

Offensive realists like Mearsheimer have argued that the United States should not enrich a future potential rival and that as a rational actor it will not do so.[25] But yet it has. For decades, the United States has maintained a large trade deficit with China. While this economic exchange has undoubtedly been valuable to the United States, it has also fueled the growth of the Chinese economy, which only now is transitioning to more of a domestic consumption–led economy. In addition, the United States has cooperated in bringing China into a wide range of international institutions and thereby presumably advanced China's standing in the international system.[26] To be clear, the U.S. approach to China has not been entirely cooperative. The U.S. military has consistently been preparing itself for the possibility that it will someday have a confrontation with China, but the question is why U.S. strategy toward China has been as cooperative as it has been despite the potential threat that China poses to U.S. interests and despite considerable uncertainty about China's long-term intentions.[27]

The short-term benefits to the United States of cooperating with China have been substantial. The U.S. economy has benefited from the ability to import manufactured goods from China, and U.S. industry has taken advantage of the ability to manufacture goods less expensively in China.[28] The political costs of limiting this economic exchange could be substantial for any U.S. president. The more substantial the short-term benefits from cooperation, the more likely existing powers are to adopt cooperative strategies toward an emerging potential threat, like China. But still, that cannot explain why U.S. efforts to prepare for a Chinese threat to its interests have been less than some might expect.

The pattern of Sino-U.S. relations can be understood with the argument made in this book. Washington faces a continuing dilemma with regard to how and when to address the potential threat posed by China. This is a difficult calculation. The costs of more aggressive competitive strategies toward China could be significant, including the opportunity costs of economic exchange. To pay this price out of concern for a potential long-term threat from China may be politically unpalatable to U.S. political leaders. Moreover, such behavior may only incite Chinese nationalists, who will become increasingly certain that the United States is seeking to encircle it.[29] If, however, the United States waits too long to act to constrain China, then it may find its options limited if uncertainty about Chinese intentions turns into more confident beliefs that Chinese interests are contrary to U.S. interests. Act now and the short-term costs will be significant. Act later and the long-term costs may be even greater.

Resolution of this now-or-later dilemma has ebbed and flowed with the presence of other, more pressing threats to the United States. In the immediate aftermath of the Cold War, with no other apparent threats on the horizon, much attention was paid to the rise of China and its implications. Not many remember that one of the few foreign policy issues to be debated in the 2000 U.S. presidential campaign was how to formulate policy toward China. The United States was more inclined to address the potential threat sooner rather than later. That all changed after September 11, 2001, when the United States and China found common cause in fighting Islamic extremism.[30] With the rise of an alternative, more immediate threat to its interests, Washington was increasingly inclined to address the potential threat from China later. Now that the United States has withdrawn most of its troops from Iraq and is attempting to conclude its large-scale efforts in Afghanistan, the question is whether the United States will shift attention again toward a still emerging China that nonetheless poses a longer-term threat to U.S. interests. Developments such as the Air-Sea Battle strategic doctrine and "rebalancing" to Asia suggest that the United States has become increasingly concerned with the rise of China and with indications of Chinese intentions.[31] In the absence of alternative threats, existing powers are more inclined to address potential threats now rather than later.

In turn, the future direction of U.S. strategy toward China is as likely to be influenced by U.S. perceptions of future intentions as it is by developments in Chinese capabilities. While the United States has certainly been wary of China's intentions, uncertainty remains about just how aggressive those intentions are and in what direction any aggression may be pointed. The U.S. reaction to this uncertainty has been to hedge its bets. On the one hand, the U.S. military has been preparing for the possibility of confrontation with China. On the other hand, the United States continues to engage and cooperate with China. This strategy has been motivated both by an effort to capture short-term rewards and by the hope that China's intentions might be shaped in a direction that is not threatening to U.S. interests. Uncertainty about Chinese intentions has allowed cooperation to continue rather than leading to worst-case assumptions that presumably would foreclose cooperation. Truly assuming the worst about Chinese intentions would lead to prohibitively costly behavior for the United States.

The importance of beliefs about intentions has presented incentives to China to attempt to manipulate U.S. beliefs about its intentions. By deferring any potential aggression until the future, China has forgone any immediate advantages from resources it might capture, but it also perhaps gives itself a greater chance of succeeding in the future when it is more capable. Of course, opting to defer will only be successful if China can continue to maintain useful uncertainty about its intentions. Maintaining uncertainty about its intentions has been critical to China precisely because it has allowed the continuation of cooperation that offers substantial short-term benefits. China's economy has been substantially export-driven in the absence of a lucrative domestic market. If one presumes that China is aware that uncertainty about its intentions allows the continuation of this cooperation, then it behooves Beijing to avoid any behavior that might bring an end to this uncertainty. Deng Xiaoping understood that being patient and maintaining uncertainty about intentions can be of real value for a rising great power. As I mentioned in the book's introduction, in his famous "24-character policy," he called on China to "hide our capacities and bide our time."[32] Even as Chinese material capabilities increased, it would not, in Deng's view, be advantageous for China to assert itself immediately, thereby drawing attention to itself and its growth.

Given that, the puzzle arises as to why China has been acting more assertively.[33] In a string of disputes with Japan as well as various nations in Southeast Asia, China appears to be motivated less by the pure acquisition of territory or resources and more by a political desire to assert its influence across Asia.[34] In particular, much Chinese behavior may be well characterized as "reactive assertiveness," in which China responds to the provocative behavior of others. Were various Japanese or Southeast Asian claims to territory to go unchallenged, then China presumably would forfeit various status and prestige claims. The result is that China has been pulled into various crises that have consequently served as litmus tests of China's intentions. Whether China's interlocutors in these crises intended it or not, the result of these crises has been to resolve the uncertainty about China's intentions in a worrisome direction, making cooperation less likely. As Thomas J. Christensen writes, "Beijing—with a few important exceptions—has been reacting, however abrasively, to unwelcome and unforeseen events that have often been initiated by others."[35]

Increasingly vocal nationalist voices in China have also been pushing for a more assertive Chinese foreign policy, despite the concern about long-term Chinese intentions such behavior is likely to create.[36] Jessica Chen Weiss has written persuasively on the potentially dangerous role that nationalism plays in Chinese foreign policy: "A prudent Chinese leadership should also balance the long-term risks of stoking Chinese nationalism against the short-term gains of diplomatic pressure."[37] In sum, on both determinants of rising power patience—the value of uncertainty and the imperative for aggressive action—China's behavior has, until recently, generally leaned in the direction of more patience, favoring a later, rather than now, resolution of its dilemma. China has little to gain and much to lose by resolving uncertainty about its intentions in a negative direction. China's various territorial crises have compelled it to act aggressively in ways that are perhaps more revealing of its intentions than it would have preferred.

In the end, my argument helps explain why strategies of "reassurance" adopted by rising powers often succeed despite other states' uncertainty about the rising states' future intentions.[38] The analysis implies that the popular contemporary parlor game of tracking Chinese capabilities relative to the United States may be misplaced. While attention to the relative capabilities of China and the United States is warranted, those capabilities are unlikely to be wholly determinative of the Sino-U.S. relationship going forward. The nature of Sino-U.S. relations is not simply going to be determined by whether or not a new bipolarity replaces the unipolarity of the post–Cold War world. The intersection of the two states' time horizons will significantly frame their interaction. It is up to the United States and China to manage that potential transition in ways that could be more or less peaceful.

This understanding of Sino-U.S. relations offers two important contributions. First, it grasps an essential temporal dimension to the relationship. The question is not just whether the United States views China as a potential threat, but when it views that threat coming to fruition and how best to manage relations in the short term to achieve long-term aims. Second, it offers a novel understanding of the role of uncertainty about intentions. Uncertainty can be a useful political tool for both existing powers and rising powers. For existing powers, it makes beneficial short-term cooperation both palatable and explicable. Assuming the worst about an emerging threat's intentions is both exorbitantly expensive and likely to create a self-fulfilling prophecy. States are not naïve about the danger posed by an emerging threat, but they hedge their bets, weighing the short- and long-term implications of the policies they might adopt. For emerging threats, uncertainty becomes a political tool that, as long as they are patient, enables them to continue to benefit from cooperation whether their ultimate intentions are benign, malign, or unknown even to them. It is, therefore, not surprising that Beijing has adopted a strategy of maintaining uncertainty about its intentions when that uncertainty is useful to the United States as well.

Prescriptively, what might this analysis suggest for U.S. foreign policy toward emerging threats, including China? First, Washington ought to be cognizant of the incentives that others have to mislead about their intentions. While short-term cooperation is likely to be attractive for a variety of domestic political and economic reasons, the long-term costs may be significant. Second, Washington needs to continue to work on the challenge of multitasking. A superpower like the United States will face numerous simultaneous short- and long-term threats. Balancing the United States' reactions to these different threats is a profound challenge, but the United States must resist the urge to simply play "whack-a-mole" with the most immediate threat. Finally, if intentions and not just capabilities are what determine the direction of foreign policy, then the United States ought to invest even more resources in developing tools to discern intentions as accurately as possible.

Future Research

The primary theoretical goal of this book has been to draw attention to the previously understudied temporal dimensions of international politics.

Temporal considerations, including time horizons, are implicit in a number of theoretical approaches to international politics, but explicit attention to these factors has been less common. Moving forward, there remains much work to be done both theoretically and empirically.

Theoretically, future research ought to investigate the causes of variation in time horizons. That is, why do some political leaders value the future more than others do? Why are some more inclined to make intertemporal trade-offs than others are? I have identified specific factors that affect the resolution of now-or-later dilemmas when states are confronted with emerging threats, but these factors might be expected to vary by issue area. For example, a state might face a now-or-later dilemma related to trade with another state, but the pressures to act now or defer until later are likely to be different.

Future theoretical work also ought to examine more closely how states assess the intentions of others. For example, is it possible that states rely on seemingly less dynamic indicators of intentions, like identity or regime type, for assessing long-term intentions and rely more on behavioral indicators for assessing short-term intentions? How important are the personal impressions of leaders as opposed to other potential indicators?[39] Acknowledging the significance of beliefs about intentions is an important first step, but also necessary is theoretical work that helps us understand the roots of beliefs about intentions.

Empirically, future research ought to investigate precisely how temporal considerations affect the decisions that state leaders make in a wider array of issue areas. My contention is that studies of international relations have literally been missing a dimension, but this claim can only be confirmed by careful study across different areas. A preliminary list of useful empirical issue areas would include international trade and financial agreements, transfer of sensitive technology, and international environmental agreements. Prima facie evidence suggests how temporality has affected decision making in these areas, but careful research is necessary to confirm that.

By incorporating temporal considerations into our theories and our empirics, the study of international relations will become richer. Decision making is not static, and it does not take place only at one moment in time. Instead, leaders must make decisions that weigh short-term pressures versus long-term considerations. Such trade-offs involve complicated calculations regarding the certainty of the short term versus the relative uncertainty of the long term. Uncertainty does not ineluctably lead to competition but rather can often lead to cooperation that states may later regret. That, in many ways, may be the true tragedy of international politics.

Notes

Introduction

1. On the "socialization" of China, see Alastair I. Johnston, *Social States: China in International Institutions, 1980–2000* (Princeton, N.J.: Princeton University Press, 2008).

2. On the disputes in the South China Sea, see Bill Hayton, *The South China Sea: The Struggle for Power in Asia* (New Haven, Conn.: Yale University Press, 2014).

3. Thucydides, *History of the Peloponnesian War*, trans. Rex Warner, Penguin Classics (New York: Penguin, 1954), 83–84; emphasis added.

4. Niccolò Machiavelli, *The Prince: A New Translation, Backgrounds, Interpretations*, trans. and ed. Robert M. Adams (New York: W. W. Norton, 1977), 8.

5. François Barbé-Marbois, *The History of Louisiana: Particularly of the Cession of That Colony to the United States of America*, ed. E. Wilson Lyon (Baton Rouge: Louisiana State University Press, 1977 [1830]), 276, quoted in Chad E. Nelson, " 'My Foresight Does Not Embrace Such Remote Fears': Time Horizons and the Response to the Rise of the United States," unpublished manuscript, September 2016.

6. For a discussion of this guidance, sometimes referred to as the "24-character policy," see M. Taylor Fravel, *Strong Borders, Secure Nation: Cooperation and Conflict in China's Territorial Disputes* (Princeton, N.J.: Princeton University Press, 2008), 134–35; Dingding Chen and Jianwei Wang, "Lying Low No More? China's New Thinking on the Tao Guang Yang Hui Strategy," *China: An International Journal* 9, no. 2 (2011): 195–216.

7. Ting Shi and David Tweed, "Xi Outlines 'Big Country Diplomacy' Chinese Foreign Policy," Bloomberg, December 1, 2014, http://www.bloomberg.com/news/2014-12-01/xi-says-china-will-keep-pushing-to-alter-asia-security-landscape.html.

8. Barack Obama, "National Security Strategy of the United States," February 2015, https://www.whitehouse.gov/sites/default/files/docs/2015_national_security_strategy.pdf.

9. The "special peril of defection" may account for shorter time horizons in security than in economic affairs. See Charles Lipson, "International Cooperation in Security and Economic Affairs," *World Politics* 37 (1984): 14. For an experimental approach to time horizons, see Dustin H. Tingley, "The Dark Side of the Future: An Experimental Test of Commitment Problems in Bargaining," *International Studies Quarterly* 55, no. 2 (2011): 521–44. Tingley's study is derived from James D. Fearon, "Bargaining, Enforcement, and International Cooperation," *International Organization* 52, no. 2 (1998): 269–305. On time horizons and international bargaining, see Glenn H.

Snyder and Paul Diesing, *Conflict among Nations: Bargaining, Decision Making, and System Structure in International Crises* (Princeton, N.J.: Princeton University Press, 1977), 77–79.

10. On the general effects of time horizons on international cooperation, see J. Samuel Barkin, "Time Horizons and Multilateral Enforcement in International Cooperation," *International Studies Quarterly* 48, no. 2 (2004): 363–82.

11. On preventive war, see Douglas Lemke, "Investigating the Preventive Motive for War," *International Interactions* 29, no. 4 (2003): 273–92; Jack S. Levy, "Declining Power and the Preventive Motivation for War," *World Politics* 40 (1987): 82–107; Randall L. Schweller, "Domestic Structure and Preventive War: Are Democracies More Pacific?," *World Politics* 44 (1992): 235–69.

12. Jonathan Mercer, *Reputation and International Politics* (Ithaca, N.Y.: Cornell University Press, 1996); Daryl G. Press, *Calculating Credibility: How Leaders Assess Military Threats* (Ithaca, N.Y.: Cornell University Press, 2005). Mediators may also behave differently depending on their interest in developing a reputation. See Andrew H. Kydd, "When Can Mediators Build Trust?," *American Political Science Review* 100, no. 3 (2006): 459–60. Reputation may also be consequential for how states address separatist disputes. See Barbara F. Walter, *Reputation and Civil War: Why Separatist Conflicts Are So Violent* (Cambridge: Cambridge University Press, 2009).

13. Martha Finnemore, "Legitimacy, Hypocrisy, and the Social Structure of Unipolarity," *World Politics* 61, no. 1 (2009): 74.

14. Matthew Kroenig, *Exporting the Bomb: Technology Transfer and the Spread of Nuclear Weapons* (Ithaca, N.Y.: Cornell University Press, 2010).

15. Sarah E. Kreps, *Coalitions of Convenience: United States Military Interventions after the Cold War* (New York: Oxford University Press, 2010).

16. John B. Goodman, "The Politics of Central Bank Independence," *Comparative Politics* 23, no. 3 (1991): 329–49; Kathleen R. McNamara, "Rational Fictions: Central Bank Independence and the Social Logic of Delegation," *West European Politics* 25, no. 1 (2002): 47.

17. Daniel J. Blake, "Thinking Ahead: Government Time Horizons and the Legalization of International Investment Agreements," *International Organization* 67, no. 4 (2013): 797–827; Daniel Yuichi Kono and Gabriella R. Montinola, "Foreign Aid, Time Horizons, and Trade Policy," *Comparative Political Studies* 48, no. 6 (2015): 788–819; Chungshik Moon, "Foreign Direct Investment, Commitment Institutions, and Time Horizon: How Some Autocrats Do Better than Others," *International Studies Quarterly* 59, no. 2 (2015): 344–56.

18. Beth A. Simmons, *Mobilizing for Human Rights: International Law in Domestic Politics* (New York: Cambridge University Press, 2009), 79–80.

19. David C. Barker and David H. Bearce, "End-Times Theology, the Shadow of the Future, and Public Resistance to Addressing Global Climate Change," *Political Research Quarterly* 66, no. 2 (2013): 267–79; Hal E. Hershfield, H. Min Bang, and Elke U. Weber, "National Differences in Environmental Concern and Performance Are Predicted by Country Age," *Psychological Science* 25, no. 1 (2014): 152–60.

20. For a theoretical argument that variation in time horizons represents an important source of uncertainty in a signaling context, see Kyle Haynes, "A Question of Costliness: Time Horizons and Interstate Signaling," unpublished manuscript, September 2016. For an argument examining the long-term consequences of crisis diplomacy, see Robert F. Trager, "Long-Term Consequences of Aggressive Diplomacy: European Relations after Austrian Crimean War Threats," *Security Studies* 21, no. 2 (2012): 232–65.

21. For an interesting empirical discussion, see Jack S. Levy and Joseph R. Gochal, "Democracy and Preventative War: Israel and the 1956 Sinai Campaign," *Security Studies* 11 (2001): 1–49.

22. Randall L. Schweller, "Managing the Rise of Great Powers: History and Theory," in *Engaging China: The Management of an Emerging Power*, ed. Alastair I. Johnston and Robert S. Ross (New York: Routledge, 1999), 1–31.

23. Robert Gilpin, *War and Change in World Politics* (New York: Cambridge University Press, 1981).

24. Ibid., 191.

25. See, e.g., Moon, "Foreign Direct Investment."

26. For a similar attempt, albeit more limited, see Barry Buzan and Michael Cox, "China and the US: Comparable Cases of 'Peaceful Rise'?," *Chinese Journal of International Politics* 6, no. 2 (2013): 109–32. For a comparison between China and Bismarck's Germany, see Avery Goldstein, "An Emerging China's Emerging Grand Strategy: A Neo-Bismarckian Turn?," in *International Relations Theory and the Asia-Pacific*, ed. G. John Ikenberry and Michael Mastanduno (New York: Columbia University Press, 2003), 57–106.

27. Data from U.S. Census Bureau: https://www.census.gov/foreign-trade/balance/c5700.html.

28. On the responsible stakeholder approach, see the comments of U.S. deputy secretary of state Robert Zoellick, "Whither China? From Membership to Responsibility?," September 21, 2005, https://www.disam.dsca.mil/Pubs/Indexes/Vol%2028_2/Zoellick.pdf.

29. On the military side, this concern for China is manifest in the "Air-Sea Battle" strategic concept. See U.S. Department of Defense, Air-Sea Battle Office, "Air-Sea Battle: Service Collaboration to Address Anti-Access and Area Denial Challenges" (Washington, D.C.: Department of Defense, May 2013), http://archive.defense.gov/pubs/ASB-ConceptImplementation-Summary-May-2013.pdf.

30. Bettina Wassener, "For China, a Shift from Exports to Consumption," *New York Times*, January 20, 2014, http://www.nytimes.com/2014/01/21/business/international/for-china-a-shift-from-exports-to-consumption.html.

31. Thomas J. Christensen, *The China Challenge: Shaping the Choices of a Rising Power* (New York: W. W. Norton, 2015), 118.

32. On Japan, e.g., see Greg Austin, "Is Japan Becoming a Threat to Peace?," *Diplomat*, July 31, 2015, http://thediplomat.com/2015/07/is-japan-becoming-a-threat-to-peace.

1. Time Horizons and International Politics

1. The literature on responses to threats in the context of crises is more substantial. Notable examples include James D. Fearon, "Signaling Foreign Policy Interests: Tying Hands versus Sinking Costs," *Journal of Conflict Resolution* 41, no. 1 (1997): 68–90; Branislav L. Slantchev, "Feigning Weakness," *International Organization* 64, no. 3 (2010): 357–88; Robert F. Trager, "Diplomatic Calculus in Anarchy: How Communication Matters," *American Political Science Review* 104, no. 2 (2010): 347–68.

2. For an exception that does address the role of time explicitly, see Norrin M. Ripsman, Jeffrey W. Taliaferro, and Steven E. Lobell, *Neoclassical Realist Theory of International Politics* (New York: Oxford University Press, 2016).

3. For studies of temporal considerations in other areas of political science, see Kim Yi Dionne, "The Role of Executive Time Horizons in State Response to AIDS in Africa," *Comparative Political Studies* 44, no. 1 (2011): 55–77; Alan M. Jacobs, "Policy Making for the Long Term in Advanced Democracies," *Annual Review of Political Science* 19 (2016): 433–54, doi:10.1146/annurev-polisci-110813-034103; Andrew Healy and Neil Malhotra, "Myopic Voters and Natural Disaster Policy," *American Political Science Review* 103 (2009): 387–406; Alan M. Jacobs, *Governing for the Long Term: Democracy and the Politics of Investment* (New York: Cambridge University Press, 2011); Alan M. Jacobs, "The Politics of When: Redistribution, Investment, and Policy Making for the Long Term," *British Journal of Political Science* 38, no. 2 (2008): 193–220; Andrea H. Kendall-Taylor, "Political Insecurity and Oil: The Effect of Time Horizons on Oil Revenue Management in Azerbaijan and Kazakhstan," *Problems of Post-Communism* 58, no. 1 (2011): 44–57; Andrea Kendall-Taylor, "Instability and Oil: How Political Time Horizons Affect Oil Revenue Management," *Studies in Comparative International Development* 46, no. 3 (2011): 321–48.

4. For an approach to time in international politics that differs from mine, see Christopher McIntosh, "Theory across Time: The Privileging of Time-less Theory in International Relations," *International Theory* 7, no. 3 (2015): 464–500; Andrew Hom, Christopher McIntosh, Alasdair McKay, and Liam Stockdale, eds., *Time, Temporality, and Global Politics* (Bristol, U.K.: E-International Relations, 2016), http://www.e-ir.info/2016/07/15/edited-collection-time-temporality-and-global-politics.

5. Dale C. Copeland, *Economic Interdependence and War* (Princeton, N.J.: Princeton University Press, 2014).

6. Norrin M. Ripsman and Jack S. Levy, "Wishful Thinking or Buying Time? The Logic of British Appeasement in the 1930s," *International Security* 33, no. 2 (2008): 148–81.

7. Anne E. Sartori, *Deterrence by Diplomacy* (Princeton, N.J.: Princeton University Press, 2005).

8. For a sense of the debate over reputation, see Jonathan Mercer, *Reputation and International Politics* (Ithaca, N.Y.: Cornell University Press, 1996); Daryl G. Press, *Calculating Credibility: How Leaders Assess Military Threats* (Ithaca, N.Y.: Cornell University Press, 2005); Michael Tomz, *Reputation and International Cooperation: Sovereign Debt across Three Centuries* (Princeton, N.J.: Princeton University Press, 2007); Alex Weisiger and Keren Yarhi-Milo, "Revisiting Reputation: How Past Actions Matter in International Politics," *International Organization* 69, no. 2 (2015): 473–95, doi:10.1017/S0020818314000393.

9. Joshua D. Kertzer, *Resolve in International Politics* (Princeton, N.J.: Princeton University Press, 2016), 39–40.

10. The seminal neoliberal institutionalist work is Robert O. Keohane, *After Hegemony: Cooperation and Discord in the World Political Economy* (Princeton, N.J.: Princeton University Press, 1984).

11. On the challenges of time inconsistency, see Kyle Beardsley, "Agreement without Peace? International Mediation and Time Inconsistency Problems," *American Journal of Political Science* 52, no. 4 (2008): 723–40; Finn E. Kydland and Edward C. Prescott, "Rules Rather than Discretion: The Inconsistency of Optimal Plans," *Journal of Political Economy* 85, no. 3 (1977): 473–92.

12. Robert Powell, *In the Shadow of Power: States and Strategies in International Politics* (Princeton, N.J.: Princeton University Press, 1999), 69–73. Notably, Branislav L. Slantchev makes a similar argument about the willingness of governments to negotiate settlements to wars. See Branislav L. Slantchev, "The Principle of Convergence in Wartime Negotiations," *American Political Science Review* 97, no. 4 (2004): 621–32.

13. James D. Fearon, "Bargaining, Enforcement, and International Cooperation," *International Organization* 52, no. 2 (1998): 269–305.

14. For a test of this argument, see Dustin H. Tingley, "The Dark Side of the Future: An Experimental Test of Commitment Problems in Bargaining," *International Studies Quarterly* 55, no. 2 (2011): 521–44.

15. For general examples, see William Ascher, *Bringing in the Future: Strategies for Farsightedness and Sustainability in Developing Countries* (Chicago: University of Chicago Press, 2009); Ola Svenson and Gunnar Karlsson, "Decision-Making, Time Horizons, and Risk in the Very Long-Term Perspective," *Risk Analysis* 9, no. 3 (1989): 385–99.

16. One exception is shadow-of-the-future arguments. Robert Axelrod and Robert O. Keohane, "Achieving Cooperation under Anarchy: Strategies and Institutions," *World Politics* 38, no. 1 (1985): 226–54.

17. For discussions of time in the social sciences, see Andrew Abbott, *Time Matters: On Theory and Method* (Chicago: University of Chicago Press, 2001); Robert Bates and Kenneth A. Shepsle, "Intertemporal Institutions," in *The Frontiers of New Institutional Economics*, ed. John Drobak and John V. C. Nye (New York: Academic Press, 1997), 197–211; Tim Büthe, "Taking Temporality Seriously: Modeling History and the Use of Narratives as Evidence," *American Political Science Review* 96, no. 3 (2002): 481–93; Stephen Kern, *The Culture of Time and Space, 1880–1918* (Cambridge, Mass.: Harvard University Press, 2003); Paul Pierson, "Increasing Returns, Path Dependence, and the Study of Politics," *American Political Science Review* 94, no. 2 (2000): 251–67; Paul Pierson, *Politics in Time: History, Institutions, and Social Analysis* (Princeton, N.J.: Princeton University Press, 2004).

18. General discussions of human time horizons are widespread, including Jon Elster, *Explaining Social Behavior: More Nuts and Bolts for the Social Sciences* (Cambridge: Cambridge University Press, 2007), 115–19; Jean-Jacques Rousseau, *The Basic Political Writings*, trans. Donald A. Cress (Indianapolis: Hackett, 1987), 62; Jacob Viner, "Power versus Plenty as Objectives of Foreign Policy in the Seventeenth and Eighteenth Centuries," *World Politics* 1, no. 1 (1948): 10.

19. Pierson, *Politics in Time*, 41–42.

20. Jeremy R. Gray, "A Bias toward Short-Term Thinking in Threat-Related Negative Emotional States," *Personality and Social Psychology Bulletin* 25, no. 1 (1999): 65–75; George Loewen-

stein, Daniel Read, and Roy F. Baumeister, *Time and Decision: Economic and Psychological Perspectives on Intertemporal Choice* (New York: Russell Sage Foundation, 2003); George Loewenstein and Jon Elster, *Choice over Time* (New York: Russell Sage Foundation, 1992); Paul R. Portney and John P. Weyant, *Discounting and Intergenerational Equity* (New York: Resources for the Future, 1999). For behavioral economics, see George A. Akerlof and Robert J. Shiller, *Animal Spirits: How Human Psychology Drives the Economy, and Why It Matters for Global Capitalism* (Princeton, N.J.: Princeton University Press, 2010).

21. For a psychology-based argument drawing on "construal theory," see Ronald R. Krebs and Aaron Rapport, "International Relations and the Psychology of Time Horizons," *International Studies Quarterly* 56, no. 3 (2012): 530–43. Relatedly, see Nira Liberman and Yaacov Trope, "The Psychology of Transcending the Here and Now," *Science* 322, no. 5905 (2008): 1201–5; Nira Liberman, Michael D. Sagristano, and Yaacov Trope, "The Effect of Temporal Distance on Level of Mental Construal," *Journal of Experimental Social Psychology* 38, no. 6 (2002): 523–34; Yaacov Trope and Nira Liberman, "Temporal Construal," *Psychological Review* 110, no. 3 (2003): 403–20.

22. Paul A. Samuelson, "A Note on Measurement of Utility," *Review of Economic Studies* 4, no. 2 (1937): 155–61; Philip Streich and Jack S. Levy, "Time Horizons, Discounting, and Intertemporal Choice," *Journal of Conflict Resolution* 51, no. 2 (2007): 199–226.

23. Daniel W. Drezner, *Avoiding Trivia: The Role of Strategic Planning in American Foreign Policy* (Washington, D.C.: Brookings Institution Press, 2009).

24. There have been efforts to connect prospect theory with actor time horizons. On prospect theory, see Daniel Kahneman and Amos Tversky, "Prospect Theory: An Analysis of Decision Making under Risk," *Econometrica* 47 (1979): 263–92. For applications to the issue of time horizons, see Shlomo Benartzi and Richard H. Thaler, "Myopic Loss Aversion and the Equity Premium Puzzle," *Quarterly Journal of Economics* 110, no. 1 (1995): 73–92, doi:10.2307/2118511; Richard H. Thaler, Amos Tversky, Daniel Kahneman, and Alan Schwartz, "The Effect of Myopia and Loss Aversion on Risk Taking: An Experimental Test," *Quarterly Journal of Economics* 112, no. 2 (1997): 647–61.

25. Emilie M. Hafner-Burton, D. Alex Hughes, and David G. Victor, "The Cognitive Revolution and the Political Psychology of Elite Decision Making," *Perspectives on Politics* 11, no. 2 (2013): 368–86.

26. Michael Horowitz, Rose McDermott, and Allan C. Stam, "Leader Age, Regime Type, and Violent International Relations," *Journal of Conflict Resolution* 49, no. 5 (2005): 667–69.

27. Tingley, "Dark Side of the Future."

28. International relations has identified a number of advantages that democracies may enjoy. Shorter time horizons would not be one of them. For a critical review of the arguments about democratic credibility, see Alexander B. Downes and Todd S. Sechser, "The Illusion of Democratic Credibility," *International Organization* 66, no. 3 (2012): 457–89.

29. On democratic audience costs, see James D. Fearon, "Domestic Political Audiences and the Escalation of International Disputes," *American Political Science Review* 88, no. 3 (1994): 577–92. See also Thomas J. Christensen, *Useful Adversaries: Grand Strategy, Domestic Mobilization, and Sino-American Conflict, 1947–1958* (Princeton, N.J.: Princeton University Press, 1996); Margaret Levi, *Of Rule and Revenue* (Berkeley: University of California Press, 1988), 32–33, 178–79.

30. George F. Kennan, *American Diplomacy* (Chicago: University of Chicago Press, 1951), 93.

31. Randall L. Schweller, *Unanswered Threats: Political Constraints on the Balance of Power* (Princeton, N.J.: Princeton University Press, 2006).

32. For a study of the effect of authoritarian time horizons, see Joseph Wright, "To Invest or Insure? How Authoritarian Time Horizons Impact Foreign Aid Effectiveness," *Comparative Political Studies* 41, no. 7 (2008): 971–1000.

33. On tyrannies, see Stephen Peter Rosen, *War and Human Nature* (Princeton, N.J.: Princeton University Press, 2004), 135–78.

34. Jessica L. Weeks, "Autocratic Audience Costs: Regime Type and Signaling Resolve," *International Organization* 62, no. 1 (2008): 35–64.

35. On the consequences of losing power in non-democracies, see H. E. Goemans, *War and Punishment: The Causes of War Termination and the First World War* (Princeton, N.J.: Princeton University Press, 2000).

36. Alexis de Tocqueville, *Democracy in America*, trans. Harvey Mansfield and Delba Winthrop (Chicago: University of Chicago Press, 2002), 500–503. See also Rasmus Karlsson, "Why the Far-Future Matters to Democracy Today," *Futures* 37, no. 10 (2005): 1095–1103.

37. For a similar argument on the effect of religion, see Monica D. Toft, "Issue Indivisibility and Time Horizons as Rationalist Explanations for War," *Security Studies* 15 (Winter 2006): 34–69.

38. Katherine Barbieri, *The Liberal Illusion: Does Trade Promote Peace?* (Ann Arbor: University of Michigan Press, 2009); Katherine Barbieri and Jack S. Levy, "Sleeping with the Enemy: The Impact of War on Trade," *Journal of Peace Research* 36, no. 4 (1999): 463–79.

39. Robert D. Blackwill and Ashley J. Tellis, "Revising U.S. Grand Strategy toward China" (Washington, D.C.: Council on Foreign Relations, 2015), 18, http://www.cfr.org/china/revising-us-grand-strategy-toward-china/p36371.

40. Put differently, responding to a threat sooner rather than later is likely to have feedback effects that only make the threat more real. See Robert Jervis, *System Effects: Complexity in Political and Social Life* (Princeton, N.J.: Princeton University Press, 1998).

41. In this sense, there might be a Marxist explanation for cooperation with a rising great power. To the extent that the United States and China both benefit from the current global international system, it may be pursuit of economic benefit above all that has driven Sino-U.S. cooperation. I thank Alexander Wendt for suggesting this logic. For a related logic, see Matthew D. Stephen, "Rising Powers, Global Capitalism, and Liberal Global Governance: A Historical Materialist Account of the BRICs Challenge," *European Journal of International Relations* 20, no. 4 (2014): 912–38.

42. This addressing of threats is related to the notion of temporal construal, which suggests that more immediate issues are treated differently than more temporally distant ones. For an application to international relations, see Krebs and Rapport, "Psychology of Time Horizons."

43. Jacques deLisle, "9/11 and U.S.-China Relations," Foreign Policy Research Institute, September 3, 2011, http://www.fpri.org/articles/2011/09/911-and-us-china-relations.

44. On the notion of geopolitical "slack," see Peter Trubowitz, *Politics and Strategy: Partisan Ambition and American Statecraft* (Princeton, N.J.: Princeton University Press, 2011).

45. Copeland, *Economic Interdependence and War.*

46. Frank H. Knight, *Risk, Uncertainty, and Profit*, Hart, Schaffner, and Marx Prize Essays, no. 31 (Boston: Houghton Mifflin, 1921), 19.

47. For discussion of Knight's distinction between risk and uncertainty, see Allan H. Meltzer, "Rational Expectations, Risk, Uncertainty, and Market Responses" (Carnegie Mellon University, Tepper School of Business, 1982), http://repository.cmu.edu/tepper/751; Yasuhiro Sakai, "J. M. Keynes and F. H. Knight: How to Deal with Risk, Probability, and Uncertainty," Center for Risk Research (CRR) Discussion Paper Series A: General (Shiga University, Faculty of Economics, CRR, 2016), https://ideas.repec.org/p/shg/dpapea/15.html.

48. For a general discussion of risk and national security, see Michael J. Mazarr, *Rethinking Risk in National Security: Lessons of the Financial Crisis for Risk Management* (New York: Palgrave Macmillan, 2016). For an application to the issue of nuclear energy and the risk of nuclear proliferation, see Jon Elster, "Risk, Uncertainty and Nuclear Power," reprinted as Appendix 1 in Jon Elster, *Explaining Technical Change: A Case Study in Philosophy of Science* (New York: Cambridge University Press, 1983), 185–208.

49. This game is similar to the "Ellsberg Paradox" described in Daniel Ellsberg, "Risk, Ambiguity, and the Savage Axioms," *Quarterly Journal of Economics* 75, no. 4 (1961): 650–56.

50. Stephen C. Nelson and Peter J. Katzenstein, "Uncertainty, Risk, and the Financial Crisis of 2008," *International Organization* 68, no. 2 (2014): 361–92.

51. For a debate over uncertainty about intentions, see Sebastian Rosato, "The Inscrutable Intentions of Great Powers," *International Security* 39, no. 3 (2014): 48–88; see also the rejoinders to Rosato by Charles L. Glaser and Andrew Kydd and by Mark Haas and John Owen in *International Security* 40, no. 3 (2015–16): 197–215.

52. Jennifer Mitzen and Randall L. Schweller make the related argument that it is misplaced certainty, rather than uncertainty, that is particularly dangerous in international politics. Jennifer Mitzen and Randall L. Schweller, "Knowing the Unknown Unknowns: Misplaced Certainty and the Onset of War," *Security Studies* 20, no. 1 (2011): 2–35.

53. Robert Jervis, *American Foreign Policy in a New Era* (New York: Routledge, 2005), 86.

54. Eric Grynaviski argues that uncertainty—or the absence of intersubjective beliefs—may facilitate cooperation. My argument relies less on the need for intersubjective understandings to explain cooperation, but the implications are similar. Eric Grynaviski, *Constructive Illusions: Misperceiving the Origins of International Cooperation* (Ithaca, N.Y.: Cornell University Press, 2014).

55. Perhaps most famously, the logic of the security dilemma traces competition to uncertainty about why a state chooses to arm itself. Robert Jervis, "Cooperation under the Security Dilemma," *World Politics* 30, no. 2 (1978): 167–214.

56. For a discussion of the various uses of the concept of uncertainty in international relations, see Brian C. Rathbun, "Uncertain about Uncertainty: Understanding the Multiple Meanings of a Crucial Concept in International Relations Theory," *International Studies Quarterly* 51, no. 3 (2007): 533–57. See also Patrick Porter, "Taking Uncertainty Seriously: Classical Realism and National Security," *European Journal of International Security* 1, no. 2 (2016): 239–60.

57. On the notion of "irreversibility" as developed in the financial investment context, see Ben S. Bernanke, "Irreversibility, Uncertainty, and Cyclical Investment," *Quarterly Journal of Economics* 98, no. 1 (1983): 85–106, and Claude Henry, "Investment Decisions under Uncertainty: The 'Irreversibility Effect,'" *American Economic Review* 64, no. 6 (1974): 1006–12.

58. For a discussion of the implications of irreversibility applied to the question of nuclear energy, see Elster, "Risk, Uncertainty and Nuclear Power," 205–6.

59. On the 1 percent doctrine, see Ron Suskind, *One Percent Doctrine: Deep Inside America's Pursuit of Its Enemies since 9/11* (New York: Simon and Schuster, 2006).

60. For a critique of offense-defense theory, see Keir A. Lieber, "Grasping the Technological Peace: The Offense-Defense Balance and International Security," *International Security* 25, no. 1 (2000): 71–104.

61. On uncertainty about material capabilities, see Charles L. Glaser, *Rational Theory of International Politics: The Logic of Competition and Cooperation* (Princeton, N.J.: Princeton University Press, 2010), 105–8.

62. For an account of how leaders form beliefs about intentions, see Keren Yarhi-Milo, *Knowing the Adversary: Leaders, Intelligence, and Assessment of Intentions in International Relations* (Princeton, N.J.: Princeton University Press, 2014). More generally on the role of beliefs about intentions, see David M. Edelstein, "Managing Uncertainty: Beliefs about Intentions and the Rise of Great Powers," *Security Studies* 12, no. 1 (2002): 1–40.

63. On the logic of costly signals, see Fearon, "Signaling Foreign Policy Interests."

64. On the distinction between costly "signals" and "indices," see Robert Jervis, *The Logic of Images in International Relations* (New York: Columbia University Press, 1970). For an alternative approach, see Marcus Holmes, "The Force of Face-to-Face Diplomacy: Mirror Neurons and the Problem of Intentions," *International Organization* 67, no. 4 (2013): 829–61.

65. Victor D. Cha introduces the related concept of "hawk engagement." Hawk engagement involves offering cooperation with a potential threat. If a state cheats on any cooperative agreement, then that can be taken as an indicator of malign intent. See Victor D. Cha, "Hawk Engagement and Preventive Defense on the Korean Peninsula," *International Security* 27, no. 1 (2002): 40–78.

66. James D. Fearon, "Signaling Foreign Policy Interests: Tying Hands versus Sinking Costs," *Journal of Conflict Resolution* 41 (February 1997): 68–90.

67. John Maynard Keynes, *A Treatise on Probability* (London: Macmillan, 1921), 78.

68. Adam J. Tooze, *The Wages of Destruction: The Making and Breaking of the Nazi Economy* (New York: Viking, 2007), 97.

69. Jakub J. Grygiel and A. Wess Mitchell discuss such actions as "probing behavior." Jakub J. Grygiel and A. Wess Mitchell, *The Unquiet Frontier: Rising Rivals, Vulnerable Allies, and the Crisis of American Power* (Princeton, N.J.: Princeton University Press, 2016).

70. International Crisis Group, "Dangerous Waters: China-Japan Relations on the Rocks" (Brussels: International Crisis Group, 2013), 12, https://www.crisisgroup.org/asia/north-east -asia/china/dangerous-waters-china-japan-relations-rocks.

71. Some have questioned the extent to which China is newly assertive. See Alastair I. Johnston, "How New and Assertive Is China's New Assertiveness?," *International Security* 37, no. 4 (2013): 7–48.

72. Jessica Chen Weiss, *Powerful Patriots: Nationalist Protest in China's Foreign Relations* (New York: Oxford University Press, 2014).

73. This argument is made in Aaron L. Friedberg, *A Contest for Supremacy: China, America, and the Struggle for Mastery in Asia* (New York: W. W. Norton, 2011).

74. On hegemonic war, see Robert Gilpin, *War and Change in World Politics* (New York: Cambridge University Press, 1981); A. F. K. Organski and Jacek Kugler, *The War Ledger* (Chicago: University of Chicago Press, 1980).

75. Dale C. Copeland, *The Origins of Major War* (Ithaca, N.Y.: Cornell University Press, 2000).

76. On the "shadow of the future," see Robert Axelrod, *The Evolution of Cooperation* (New York: Basic Books, 1984); Axelrod and Keohane, "Achieving Cooperation under Anarchy."

77. John J. Mearsheimer, "Structural Realism," in *International Relations Theory: Discipline and Diversity*, 3rd ed., ed. Tim Dunne, Milja Kurki, and Steve Smith (New York: Oxford University Press, 2013), 75.

78. John J. Mearsheimer, *The Tragedy of Great Power Politics* (New York: W. W. Norton, 2001), 45–46.

79. On time horizons in offensive realism, see Gerald Geunwook Lee, "To Be Long or Not to Be Long—That Is the Question: The Contradiction of Time-Horizon in Offensive Realism," *Security Studies* 12 (2006): 196–217.

80. For a similar treatment of uncertainty about intentions, see Rosato, "Inscrutable Intentions of Great Powers."

81. Mearsheimer, *Tragedy of Great Power Politics*, 345.

82. For an argument that emphasizes contingency and political processes in realism, see Jonathan Kirshner, "Gilpin Approaches *War and Change*: A Classical Realist in Structural Drag," in *Power, Order, and Change in World Politics*, ed. G. John Ikenberry (New York: Cambridge University Press, 2014), 131–61.

83. Glaser, *Rational Theory of International Politics*, 146–49.

84. Mearsheimer, *Tragedy of Great Power Politics*, 157–58.

85. Ibid., 158.

86. On the ability of leaders to measure capabilities, see William C. Wohlforth, *The Elusive Balance: Power and Perceptions during the Cold War* (Ithaca, N.Y.: Cornell University Press, 1993).

87. G. John Ikenberry, *After Victory: Institutions, Strategic Restraint, and the Rebuilding of Order after Major Wars* (Princeton, N.J.: Princeton University Press, 2001).

88. Note that not all of these emerging threats are necessarily new great powers. For example, interwar Germany is illustrative of a case of an emerging threat that was not a new great power.

89. Of course, the notable exception is Paul M. Kennedy, *The Rise and Fall of the Great Powers* (New York: Vintage Books, 1987). As a historian, Kennedy is less interested in theoretical generalization than I am.

2. The Arrival of Imperial Germany

1. For another analysis of this case that attempts to derive lessons from it for understanding the rise of China, see Avery Goldstein, "An Emerging China's Emerging Grand Strategy: A Neo-Bismarckian Turn?," in *International Relations Theory and the Asia-Pacific*, ed. G. John Ikenberry and Michael Mastanduno (New York: Columbia University Press, 2003), 57–106.

2. Robert I. Giesberg, *The Treaty of Frankfort* (Philadelphia: University of Pennsylvania Press, 1966).

3. For an account of how Bismarck legitimated Prussia's rise in the 1860s, see Stacie E. Goddard, "When Right Makes Might: How Prussia Overturned the European Balance of Power," *International Security* 33, no. 3 (2008): 110–42.

4. Hansard's *Parliamentary Debates*, 3rd ser., vol. 204 (London: Cornelius Buck, 1871), 81–82.

5. On the immediate reaction to the Treaty of Frankfurt, see Deryck Schreuder, "Gladstone as 'Troublemaker': Liberal Foreign Policy and the German Annexation of Alsace-Lorraine, 1870–1871," *Journal of British Studies* 17 (1978): 106–35; Paul W. Schroeder, "The Lost Intermediaries: The Impact of 1870 on the European System," *International History Review* 6 (1984): 1–27.

6. Quoted in Gordon A. Craig, *Germany, 1866–1945* (New York: Oxford University Press, 1978), 115.

7. According to Michael Howard, "During the campaign [in the summer of 1870] Bismarck had been enthusiastic in his demands for [the annexation of Metz] as part of Germany's new protective belt against French attack; but during the autumn his ardor cooled as he realized the problems which this purely French enclave would raise in an empire whose political structure would be complicated enough without it." Michael Howard, *The Franco-Prussian War: The German Invasion of France, 1870–1871* (New York: Routledge, 1961), 447. Also see Herman von Petersdorff, *Bismarck, die gesammelten Werke* (Berlin: O. Stollberg, 1923), 6b:500.

8. Petersdorff, *Bismarck, die gesammelten Werke*, 6b:316–17, quoted in Otto Pflanze, *Bismarck and the Development of Germany*, vol. 2, *The Period of Consolidation, 1871–1880* (Princeton, N.J.: Princeton University Press, 1990), 249.

9. Pflanze, *Bismarck*, 2:252.

10. On the specific provisions of the Schönbrunn Convention, see William A. Gauld, "The 'Dreikaiserbundnis' and the Eastern Question, 1871–6," *English Historical Review* 40, no. 158 (1925): 207–21.

11. Pflanze, *Bismarck*, 2:260–61.

12. See Lothar Gall, *Bismarck, the White Revolutionary*, vol. 2, *1871–1898*, trans. J. A. Underwood (London: Unwin Hyman, 1986), 45. France paid off the last of its war indemnity a month before the league was consummated, leading to the withdrawal of the German occupation force from France. Paris feared that the league was a way for Germany to reposition itself for future aggression.

13. The best study of the crisis is James Stone, *The War Scare of 1875: Bismarck and Europe in the Mid-1870s* (Stuttgart: Steiner, 2010).

14. William L. Langer, *European Alliances and Alignments, 1871–1890* (New York: Vintage Books, 1950), 21.

15. For documents relating to the War in Sight crisis, see W. N. Medlicott and Dorothy K. Coveney, eds., *Bismarck and Europe* (New York: St. Martin's Press, 1971), 88–91.

16. While the French estimated the effect of the law would be to add 28,000 troops, German leaders feared 144,000 new soldiers. See Joseph V. Fuller, "The War-Scare of 1875," *American Historical Review* 24, no. 2 (1919): 200; Langer, *European Alliances and Alignments*, 44.

17. Stone argues that the roots of the crisis ultimately lay in domestic politics and opposition to French republicanism. See Stone, *War Scare of 1875*.

18. Bismarck's actual involvement in the editorial remains somewhat disputed. See Fuller, "War-Scare of 1875," 200–201; Allan Mitchell, *The German Influence in France after 1870* (Chapel Hill: University of North Carolina Press, 1979), 127; Pflanze, *Bismarck*, 2:267.

19. Message from Gontaut-Biron to Louis Decazes, April 21, 1875, quoted in Fuller, "War-Scare of 1875," 203.

20. William Flavelle Monypenny and George Earle Buckle, *The Life of Benjamin Disraeli* (New York: Macmillan, 1913), 2:421–22. See also Allan Mitchell, "Bonapartism as a Model for Bismarckian Politics," *Journal of Modern History* 49 (1977): 181–99.

21. Gorchakov resented the growth of Germany, which had reduced both Russian influence and his personal influence throughout Europe. See Langer, *European Alliances and Alignments*, 49.

22. The most acrimonious of these meetings was between Gorchakov and Bismarck. Gorchakov told the German chancellor: "My dear Bismarck, now don't get nervous. You have in you two Bismarcks—one that is really you and that I like, and the other a nervous and excitable Bismarck." Quoted in Fuller, "War-Scare of 1875," 216.

23. Gorchakov to Orloff, May 13, 1875, in Ministère des Affaires Éstrangères, *Documents diplomatiques français*, (Paris: Imprimerie Imperiale, 1930), 1: 456.

24. Lord Derby on the low likelihood of war during the crisis: "We did not think that France was contemplating a renew of the war, neither did we believe that the German Government were contemplating an act so entirely repugnant to the moral sense of Europe as that of rushing into an unprovoked war with the intentions of completing the destruction of her former opponent." Hansard's *Parliamentary Debates*, 3rd ser., vol. 224, p. 1098.

25. Austria-Hungary was not as concerned as others by the crisis. Vienna hoped that Russo-German tension would push Berlin toward an alliance with Austria. Nicholas Der Bagdasarian, *The Austro-German Rapprochement, 1870–1879* (Rutherford, N.J.: Fairleigh Dickinson University Press, 1976), 180.

26. Otto von Bismarck, *Bismarck, the Man and the Statesman*, trans. A. J. Butler (New York: Harper and Brothers, 1899), 2:192.

27. Pflanze, *Bismarck*, 2:272.

28. Quoted in Jonathan Steinberg, *Bismarck: A Life* (New York: Oxford University Press, 2011), 352.

29. George F. Kennan, *The Decline of Bismarck's European Order: Franco-Russian Relations, 1875–1890* (Princeton, N.J.: Princeton University Press, 1979), 23.

30. Bismarck was dismayed that Gorchakov took credit for mediating a resolution to the crisis. See Gall, *Bismarck, the White Revolutionary*, 2:47. In his memoirs, Bismarck accuses Gorchakov of staging a "circus performance." Petersdorff, *Bismarck, die gesammelten Werke*, 15:364.

31. The National Material Capabilities data set is available from the Correlates of War Project, http://cow.dss.ucdavis.edu/data-sets/national-material-capabilities/national-material-capabilities-v4-0.

32. See David Harris, "Bismarck's Advance to England, January, 1876," *Journal of Modern History* 3 (1931): 441–56. On the English decision to decline, see Kenneth Bourne, *The Foreign Policy of Victorian England, 1830–1902* (Oxford: Clarendon Press, 1970), 127.

33. Derby to Russell, February 16, 1876, dispatch no. 117, reprinted in Harold Temperley and Lillian Penson, *Foundations of British Foreign Policy: From Pitt (1792) to Salisbury (1902)* (London: Frank Cass, 1966), 356.

34. The central points of the Kissingen Diktat are excerpted and translated in Medlicott and Coveney, *Bismarck and Europe*, 102–3. For the original text, see Johannes Lepsius, Albrecht Mendelssohn-Bartholdy, and Friedrich Thimme, *Die Grosse Politik Der Europaischen Kabinette, 1871–1914* (Berlin: Deutsche Verlagsgesellschaft fur Politik und Geschichte, 1922), 2:294.

35. On the Russian reaction to the Kissingen Diktat, see James Y. Simpson, *The Saburov Memoirs; or, Bismarck and Russia; Being Fresh Light on the League of the Three Emperors, 1881* (New York: Macmillan, 1929), 50–62.

36. Quoted in Medlicott and Coveney, *Bismarck and Europe*, 103.

37. For background on this particular crisis, see David Harris, *A Diplomatic History of the Balkan Crisis of 1875–1878: The First Year* (Stanford, Calif.: Stanford University Press, 1936).

38. On Russian interests, see B. H. Sumner, *Russia and the Balkans, 1870–1880* (London: Archon Books, 1962). On Austrian interests, see F. R. Bridge, *From Sadowa to Sarajevo: The Foreign Policy of Austria-Hungary, 1866–1914* (London: Routledge and Kegan Paul, 1972). In general, see Vaso Trivanovitch, "Serbia, Russia, and Austria during the Rule of Milan Obrenovich, 1868–78," *Journal of Modern History* 3 (1931): 414–40.

39. On British interests, see Richard Millman, *Britain and the Eastern Question, 1875–1878* (Oxford: Clarendon Press, 1979); R. W. Seton-Watson, *Disraeli, Gladstone, and the Eastern Question* (London: Macmillan, 1935). On concerns about British access to the Black Sea, see Arthur J. Marder, "British Naval Policy in 1878," *Journal of Modern History* 12 (1940): 367–73.

40. William L. Langer writes, "European peace, [Bismarck's] greatest interest, could best be preserved by satisfying the interested powers at the expense of Turkey, a state which was hardly worth preserving." Langer, *European Alliances and Alignments*, 101.

41. On the Andrassy Note, see Bagdasarian, *Austro-German Rapprochement*, 192; Harris, *History of the Balkan Crisis*, 165ff.; Langer, *European Alliances and Alignments*, 75.

42. On the Berlin Memorandum, see Gauld, "Eastern Question, 1871–6," 213–14.

43. These months included efforts like the Reichstadt Agreement and the Treaty of Budapest, none of which succeeded. For the text of the Reichstadt Agreement, see Alfred Franzis Pribram, *The Secret Treaties of Austria-Hungary, 1879–1914* (Cambridge, Mass.: Harvard University Press, 1920), 2:188–91. Also see George Hoover Rupp, "The Reichstadt Agreement," *American Historical Review* 30 (1925): 503–10. On the Treaty of Budapest, see Langer, *European Alliances and Alignments*, 113–14.

44. On Plevna, see Rupert Furneaux, *The Siege of Plevna* (London: Anthony Blond, 1958).

45. On the Treaty of San Stefano, see William A. Gauld, "The 'Dreikaiserbundnis' and the Eastern Question, 1877–8," *English Historical Review* 42, no. 168 (1927): 565–66.

46. W. N. Medlicott, *The Congress of Berlin and After: A Diplomatic History of the Near Eastern Settlement, 1878–1880* (London: Frank Cass, 1963).

47. On Tunis, see William L. Langer, "The European Powers and the French Occupation of Tunis, 1878–1881," pts 1 and 2, *American Historical Review* 31, no. 1 (1925): 55–78; 31, no. 2 (1926): 251–65.

48. Langer, *European Alliances and Alignments*, 163.

49. The "honest broker" speech is translated and excerpted in Medlicott and Coveney, *Bismarck and Europe*, 103–4. The original text is available in Petersdorff, *Bismarck, die gesammelten Werke*, 11:526.

50. Gall, *Bismarck, the White Revolutionary*, 2:54–55.

51. For data on trade, see B. R. Mitchell, *International Historical Statistics: Europe, 1750–1988* (New York: Stockton Press, 1992), 635–730. The trade data from this period reveal nothing of particular interest, suggesting that trade persists even between states that may have other sources of tension. Katherine Barbieri, *The Liberal Illusion: Does Trade Promote Peace?* (Ann Arbor: University of Michigan Press, 2009).

52. W. N. Medlicott, "Diplomatic Relations after the Congress of Berlin," *Slavonic Review* 8 (1929): 66–79; Bruce Waller, *Bismarck at the Crossroads: The Reorientation of German Foreign Policy after the Congress of Berlin, 1878–1880* (London: Athlone Press, 1974).

53. On Wilhelm's objections, see Pflanze, *Bismarck*, 2:502.

54. For the text of the treaty, see Pribram, *Secret Treaties of Austria-Hungary*, 1:24–35.

55. Hans Lothar von Schweinitz, *Denkwürdigkeiten des Botschafters General von Schweinitz* (Berlin: R. Hobbing, 1927), 2:60.

56. Pearl Boring Mitchell, *The Bismarckian Policy of Conciliation with France, 1875–1885* (Philadelphia: University of Pennsylvania Press, 1935).

57. Monypenny and Buckle, *Life of Benjamin Disraeli*, 6:489–90.

58. Simpson, *Saburov Memoirs*, 60–61.

59. On Gladstone's views, see Bourne, *Foreign Policy of Victorian England*, 138; W. N. Medlicott, *Bismarck, Gladstone, and the Concert of Europe* (New York: Greenwood Press, 1969). As Pflanze writes, "Gladstone's 'idealistic' vision of a federative Europe . . . was diametrically opposed to Bismarck's 'realistic' appraisal of the European balance of power system as composed of competing states, whose natural inclination was the pursuit of self-interest, producing frictions the exploitation of which was the key to German security and, coincidentally, to the preservation of peace." Otto Pflanze, *Bismarck and the Development of Germany*, vol. 3, *The Period of Fortification, 1880–1898* (Princeton, N.J.: Princeton University Press, 1990), 86.

60. Russell to Charles Abbott, October 4, 1880, quoted in Paul M. Kennedy, *The Rise of the Anglo-German Antagonism, 1860–1914* (London: Ashfield Press, 1980), 157.

61. For the text of the treaty, see Pribram, *Secret Treaties of Austria-Hungary*, 1:36–49.

62. Langer, *European Alliances and Alignments*, 211–12.

63. On the origins of the Triple Alliance, see Archibald Cary Coolidge, *The Origins of the Triple Alliance*, 2nd ed. (New York: Charles Scribner's Sons, 1926). For the text, see Pribram, *Secret Treaties of Austria-Hungary*, 1:64–73.

64. On concerns about France's relations with Russia, especially after the rise of the government of Léon Gambetta in France in November 1881, see A. J. P. Taylor, *The Struggle for Mastery in Europe, 1848–1918* (Oxford: Oxford University Press, 1954), 274–75.

65. Quoted in Chlodwig of Hohenlohe-Schillingsfürst, *Denkwürdigkeiten* (Stuttgart, 1906), 2:174.

66. Emile Bourgeois and Georges Pagès, *Les origines et responsabilités de la Grande Guerre* (Paris: Hachette, 1921), 202.

67. Langer, "French Occupation of Tunis," pts. 1 and 2.

68. Ministère des Affaires Éstrangères, *Documents diplomatiques français*, ser. 1, vol. 2, nos. 368, 369.

69. Reported by Saint-Vallier, ibid., ser. 1, vol. 4, no. 294.

70. Mitchell, *Bismarckian Policy of Conciliation*, 168–200; G. N. Sanderson, "The Anglo-German Agreement of 1890 and the Upper Nile," *English Historical Review* 78 (1963): 49–72.

71. Lepsius, Mendelssohn-Bartholdy, and Thimme, *Die grosse Politik*, vol. 4, no. 727.

72. As Gall notes, "Colonial policy was always, for [Bismarck], merely a function of the situation in Europe, and it was this that guided his every step in this field." Gall, *Bismarck, the White Revolutionary*, 2:143. See also Hans-Ulrich Wehler, "Bismarck's Imperialism, 1862–1890," in *Imperial Germany*, ed. James Sheehan (New York: New Viewpoints, 1976), 180–222.

73. Bismarck interview with Eugen Wolf, December 5, 1888, in Petersdorff, *Bismarck, die gesammelten Werke*, 8:646.

74. For summaries of Germany's forays into colonialism, see William Osgood Aydelotte, *Bismarck and British Colonial Policy: The Problem of South West Africa, 1883–1885* (Philadelphia: University of Pennsylvania Press, 1937); A. J. P. Taylor, *Germany's First Bid for Colonies, 1884–1885: A Move in Bismarck's European Policy* (Hamden, Conn.: Archon Books, 1967).

75. Kennedy, *Anglo-German Antagonism*, 177.

76. David Calleo, *The German Problem Reconsidered: Germany and the World Order, 1870 to the Present* (Cambridge: Cambridge University Press, 1978), 9–25; Craig, *Germany, 1866–1945*, 116–24.

77. Pflanze, *Bismarck*, 3:122.

78. Prosser Gifford and William Roger Louis, *Britain and Germany in Africa: Imperial Rivalry and Colonial Rule* (New Haven, Conn.: Yale University Press, 1967).

79. E. Malcolm Carroll, *Germany and the Great Powers, 1866–1914* (Hamden, Conn.: Archon Books, 1966), 174–85; Langer, *European Alliances and Alignments*, 289–96; Pflanze, *Bismarck*, 3:122–42.

80. Edmond George Petty-Fitzmaurice Fitzmaurice, *The Life of Granville George Leveson Gower, Second Earl Granville* (New York: Longmans, Green, 1905), 2:431.

81. G. P. Gooch and Harold Temperley, *British Documents on the Origins of the War* (London: Her Majesty's Stationery Office, 1928), 3:408–9.

82. Hans-Ulrich Wehler, *The German Empire, 1871–1918*, trans. Kim Traynor (Dover, N.H.: Berg, 1985), 183.

83. Horst Kohl, *Die politischen Reden des Fürsten Bismarck* (Stuttgart: Cotta, 1892), 10:413.

84. The immediate cause of the fall of Ferry's government was French colonial failures in Asia, but the détente policy lapsed with Ferry's demise. See Frederick L. Schuman, *War and Diplomacy in the French Republic: An Inquiry into Political Motivations and the Control of Foreign Policy* (New York: Howard Fertig, 1969), 80–95.

85. Charles de Freycinet, *Souvenirs* (Paris: Charles Delagrave, 1913), 2:297–98.

86. Frederic H. Seager, *The Boulanger Affair: Political Crossroad of France, 1886–1889* (Ithaca, N.Y.: Cornell University Press, 1969).

87. The increase in manpower was consistent with a German constitutional principle that the size of the military should be 1 percent of the total population. See Pflanze, *Bismarck*, 3:228–29.

88. Quoted in Serge Goriainov, "The End of the Alliance of the Emperors," *American Historical Review* 23 (1918): 331. For the original text, see Petersdorff, *Bismarck, die gesammelten Werke*, 13:212–13.

89. The new parliament passed the Septennat easily by a vote of 227 to 31. See Pflanze, *Bismarck*, 3:240.

90. On the negotiations, see Pribram, *Secret Treaties of Austria-Hungary*, 2:44–81.

91. Report of Salisbury to the Queen, February 10, 1887, in George Earle Buckle, *The Letters of Queen Victoria*, 3rd ser. (London: John Murray, 1930), 1:272–73.

92. Goriainov, "End of the Alliance."

93. For the text of the Reinsurance Treaty, see Lepsius, Mendelssohn-Bartholdy, and Thimme, *Die grosse Politik*, vol. 5, no. 1092.

94. Goriainov, "End of the Alliance," 334–35.

95. W. N. Medlicott, "The Mediterranean Agreements of 1887," *Slavonic Review* 5 (1926): 66–88.

96. Pflanze, *Bismarck*, 3:252.

97. Ibid., 269–70; Kennan, *Decline of Bismarck's European Order*, 342–44.

98. On the effect of the Lombard-Verbot, see Laurence B. Packard, "Russia and the Dual Alliance," *American Historical Review* 25 (1920): 400; Schuman, *War and Diplomacy*, 135–36; Wehler, *German Empire*, 190.

99. Bismarck to Salisbury, November 22, 1887, in Lepsius, Mendelssohn-Bartholdy, and Thimme, *Die grosse Politik*, vol. 4, no. 930.

100. On the discussion of preemptive war, see Langer, *European Alliances and Alignments*, 426–52.

101. On the war scare of late 1887 into early 1888, see Kennan, *Decline of Bismarck's European Order*, 362–63.

102. Taylor, *Struggle for Mastery in Europe*, 323.

103. For the text of the speech, see Medlicott and Coveney, *Bismarck and Europe*, 173.

104. On Moltke's and Waldersee's influence on Wilhelm II, see William L. Langer, *The Franco-Russian Alliance, 1890–1894* (New York: Octagon Books, 1967), 28.

105. Pflanze, *Bismarck*, 3:310–12.

106. Schuman, *War and Diplomacy*, 135–36.

107. Bismarck to Paul von Hatzfeldt, January 11, 1889, in Lepsius, Mendelssohn-Bartholdy, and Thimme, *Die grosse Politik*, vol. 4, no. 943.

108. Quoted in Medlicott and Coveney, *Bismarck and Europe*, 175–76.

109. On the Naval Defense Act, see Bourne, *Foreign Policy of Victorian England*, 149.

110. For Salisbury's rejection, see Lepsius, Mendelssohn Bartholdy, and Thimme, *Die grosse Politik*, vol. 4, no. 945. On British views of the proposed alliance, see C. J. Lowe, *The Reluctant Imperialists: British Foreign Policy, 1878–1902* (London: Routledge and Kegan Paul, 1967), 1:153.

111. Pflanze, *Bismarck*, 3:312–13.

112. Buckle, *Letters of Queen Victoria*, 1:526.

113. Pflanze, *Bismarck*, 3:316.

114. Langer speculates that Wilhelm offered his initial support either because he did not see it as a particularly costly commitment or because he lacked any reasonable alternative to offer. Langer, *European Alliances and Alignments*, 498.

115. Otto von Bismarck, *Gedanken und Erinnerungen* (Stuttgart: Cotta, 1898), 3:88ff.; Lepsius, Mendelssohn-Bartholdy, and Thimme, *Die grosse Politik*, vol. 6, nos. 1360–62.

116. Importantly, Bismarck's resignation was the result of more than just disagreement over policy toward Russia. The chancellor faced considerable domestic problems. The divide over Russian policy was perhaps the last straw. On the domestic issues, see Pflanze, *Bismarck*, 3:350–73.

117. Bismarck, *Gedanken und Erinnerungen*, 3:92.

118. Goriainov, "End of the Alliance," 348–49.

119. Packard, "Russia and the Dual Alliance," 403–4.

120. Freycinet, *Souvenirs*, 2:100; Langer, *Franco-Russian Alliance*, 70.

121. Langer, *Franco-Russian Alliance*, 119–20.

122. Quoted in Kennedy, *Anglo-German Antagonism*, 204.

123. General Schweinitz was sent to St. Petersburg to convey the news. He tried to convince the Russians that Germany was still interested in friendly relations with Russia, just on more transparent terms. The Russians were skeptical. Goriainov, "End of the Alliance," 344.

124. Quoted in Langer, *European Alliances and Alignments*, 502–3.

125. Ibid., 506.

126. Wilhelm first referred to his approach to foreign policy as the "New Course" in a speech on April 21, 1890. Carroll, *Germany and the Great Powers*, 286.

127. Kennedy, *Anglo-German Antagonism*, 205–9.

128. For background on the Heligoland Treaty, see D. R. Gillard, "Salisbury's African Policy and the Heligoland Offer of 1890," *English Historical Review* 75 (1960): 631–53; Sanderson,

"Anglo-German Agreement of 1890"; D. R. Gillard, "Salisbury's Heligoland Offer: The Case against the 'Witu Thesis,'" *English Historical Review* 80 (1965): 538–52.

129. Taylor, *Struggle for Mastery in Europe*, 329.

130. Quoted in Langer, *Franco-Russian Alliance*, 80–81.

131. George F. Kennan, *The Fateful Alliance: France, Russia, and the Coming of the First World War* (New York: Pantheon Books, 1984), 37–51; William L. Langer, *The Diplomacy of Imperialism, 1890–1902* (New York: Alfred A. Knopf, 1956), 8–9.

132. The empress's visit was a poorly planned disaster that included a visit to the ruins of Saint-Cloud, a monument to the German invasion of 1870. See Langer, *Franco-Russian Alliance*, 142; Schuman, *War and Diplomacy*, 139.

133. Note the change in Giers's views of Germany following the decision not to renew the Reinsurance Treaty. Quoted and translated in Schuman, *War and Diplomacy*, 139.

134. Pribram, *Secret Treaties of Austria-Hungary*, 1:150–63.

135. Langer, *Franco-Russian Alliance*, 173–75.

136. Packard, "Russia and the Dual Alliance," 407.

137. Ministère des Affaires Éstrangères, *Documents diplomatiques français*, July 24, 1891, vol. 8, no. 438.

138. For the text of the notes, see Kennan, *Fateful Alliance*, 259–62.

139. Langer, *Franco-Russian Alliance*, 221.

140. Ibid., 225–32.

141. According to Langer, "Through the winter of 1892–1893, the Germans made efforts to draw the Russians from France and to the side of the Triple Alliance, but . . . these efforts were bound to remain barren of results so long as such important issues as the commercial agreement and the military law hung in the balance." Ibid., 310.

142. Arthur Vagts, "William II and the Siam Episode," *American Historical Review* 45 (1940): 834–41.

143. For the text of the alliance, see Kennan, *Fateful Alliance*, 269–72.

144. Packard, "Russia and the Dual Alliance," 410.

145. Taylor, *Struggle for Mastery in Europe*, 339.

146. Schuman, *War and Diplomacy*, 142.

147. Lepsius, Mendelssohn-Bartholdy, and Thimme, *Die grosse Politik*, vol. 4, no. 930.

148. Calleo, *German Problem Reconsidered*, 11.

149. Quoted in G. P. Gooch, *Franco-German Relations, 1871–1914* (London: Longmans, Green, 1923), 16.

150. Quoted in Mitchell, *Bismarckian Policy of Conciliation*, 167.

151. A. A. W. Ramsay, *Idealism and Foreign Policy: A Study of the Relations of Great Britain with Germany and France, 1860–1878* (London: John Murray, 1925), 355.

152. For an overview of British views of Germany's rise, see Paul M. Kennedy, "Idealists and Realists: British Views of Germany, 1864–1939," *Transactions of the Royal Historical Society*, 5th ser., 25 (1975): 137–56; Bernadotte Everly Schmitt, *England and Germany, 1740–1914* (Princeton, N.J.: Princeton University Press, 1918).

153. Gwendolen Cecil, *Life of Salisbury* (London: Hodder and Stoughton, 1921), 2:373.

154. For a review of the economic relations between the two, see Wilfried Feldenkirchen, *Werner von Siemens: Inventor and International Entrepreneur* (Columbus: Ohio State University Press, 1994), chap. 1.

155. See Salisbury's letter concerning the Mediterranean Agreement written on November 2, 1887, reprinted in Bourne, *Foreign Policy of Victorian England*, 427–28.

156. Kennedy, *Anglo-German Antagonism*, 204.

157. Pflanze, *Bismarck*, 3:436.

158. Feldenkirchen, *Werner von Siemens*, 24.

159. As I noted above, this is not intended to be a "great man" argument about Bismarck. Rather, it is a claim about the strategies he adopted. On Bismarck as a great man, see Daniel L. Byman and Kenneth M. Pollack, "Let Us Now Praise Great Men: Bringing the Statesman Back In," *International Security* 25, no. 4 (2001): 107–46; Henry A. Kissinger, "The White Revolutionary: Reflections on Bismarck," *Daedalus* 97 (1968): 888–924.

3. The Rise of the United States

1. For background on the United States' rise, see Charles S. Campbell, *The Transformation of American Foreign Relations, 1865–1900*, New American Nation Series (New York: Harper and Row, 1976); John M. Dobson, *America's Ascent: The United States Becomes a Great Power, 1880–1914* (DeKalb: Northern Illinois University Press, 1978); Nell Irvin Painter, *Standing at Armageddon: The United States, 1877–1919* (New York: W.W. Norton, 1987).

2. League of Nations, *Industrialization and Foreign Trade* (Geneva: League of Nations, 1945), 13; Aaron L. Friedberg, *The Weary Titan: Britain and the Experience of Relative Decline, 1895–1905* (Princeton, N.J.: Princeton University Press, 1988), 26; Ernest R. May, *Imperial Democracy: The Emergence of America as a Great Power* (New York: Harcourt, Brace and World, 1961), 6. On the more general growth of U.S. power, see Bradford Perkins, *The Great Rapprochement: England and the United States, 1895–1914* (New York: Atheneum, 1968), 9; Fareed Zakaria, *From Wealth to Power: The Unusual Origins of America's World Role* (Princeton, N.J.: Princeton University Press, 1998), 131. On the development of the U.S. military, see B. Franklin Cooling, *Gray Steel and Blue Water Navy: The Formative Years of America's Military-Industrial Complex, 1881–1917* (Hamden, Conn.: Archon Books, 1979).

3. For another attempt that employs time horizons to explain earlier European reactions to the emergence of the United States, see Chad E. Nelson, " 'My Foresight Does Not Embrace Such Remote Fears': Time Horizons and the Response to the Rise of the United States," unpublished manuscript, September 2016.

4. On the earlier roots of U.S. aggressive expansion, see Colin Elman, "Extending Offensive Realism: The Louisiana Purchase and America's Rise to Regional Hegemony," *American Political Science Review* 98, no. 4 (2004): 563–76; Zakaria, *From Wealth to Power*.

5. For useful histories, see William Archibald Dunning, *The British Empire and the United States: A Review of Their Relations during the Century of Peace following the Treaty of Ghent* (New York: Charles Scribner's Sons, 1914); Robert Balmain Mowat, *The Diplomatic Relations of Great Britain and the United States* (New York: Longmans, Green, 1925); Stephen R. Rock, *Why Peace Breaks Out: Great Power Rapprochement in Historical Perspective* (Chapel Hill: University of North Carolina Press, 1989), 24–26.

6. Roger Brown, *The Republic in Peril: 1812* (New York: Columbia University Press, 1964); Reginald Horsman, *The Causes of the War of 1812* (Philadelphia: University of Pennsylvania Press, 1962); Bradford Perkins, *Prologue to War: England and the United States, 1805–1812* (Berkeley: University of California Press, 1961); J. A. C. Stagg, *Mr. Madison's War: Politics, Diplomacy, and Warfare in the Early American Republic, 1783–1830* (Princeton, N.J.: Princeton University Press, 1983).

7. On the Oregon crisis, see Frederick Merk, *The Oregon Question* (Cambridge, Mass.: Harvard University Press, 1967); David M. Pletcher, *The Diplomacy of Annexation: Texas, Oregon, and the Mexican War* (Columbia: University of Missouri Press, 1973); Donald A. Rakestraw, *For Honor or Destiny: The Anglo-American Crisis over the Oregon Territory* (New York: Peter Lang, 1995).

8. On British involvement in the U.S. Civil War, see Ephraim Douglass Adams, *Great Britain and the American Civil War* (Gloucester, Mass.: Peter Smith, 1957); Brian Jenkins, *Britain and the War for the Union* (Montreal: McGill-Queen's University Press, 1974); Howard Jones, *Union in Peril: The Crisis over British Intervention in the Civil War* (Chapel Hill: University of North Carolina Press, 1992). On the Trent Affair, see Charles Francis Adams, *The Trent Affair: An Historical Retrospect* (Boston: Massachusetts Historical Society, 1912); Norman B. Ferris, *The "Trent" Affair: A Diplomatic Crisis* (Knoxville: University of Tennessee Press, 1977); Gordon H. Warren, *Fountain of Discontent: The Trent Affair and Freedom of the Seas* (Boston: Northeastern University Press, 1981).

9. Kenneth Bourne, "British Preparations for War with the North, 1861–1862," *English Historical Review* 76 (1961): 600–632; Kenneth Bourne, *Britain and the Balance of Power in North America, 1815–1908* (Berkeley: University of California Press, 1967), 257; Paul M. Kennedy, *The War Plans of the Great Powers, 1880–1914* (Boston: Unwin Hyman, 1979), 75–98.

10. Donald F. Warner, *The Idea of Continental Union: Agitation for the Annexation of Canada to the United States, 1849–1893* (Lexington: University of Kentucky Press, 1960).

11. Bourne, "British Preparations for War," 302.

12. Charles S. Campbell, *From Revolution to Rapprochement: The United States and Great Britain, 1783–1900* (New York: John Wiley and Sons, 1974), 121–25; Goldwin Smith, *The Treaty of Washington, 1871: A Study in Imperial History* (Ithaca, N.Y.: Cornell University Press, 1941).

13. Marshall Bertram, *The Birth of Anglo-American Friendship: The Prime Facet of the Venezuela Boundary Dispute; A Study of the Interreaction of Diplomacy and Public Opinion* (Lanham, Md.: University Press of America, 1992), 3.

14. Marcus Baker, "The Venezuelan Boundary Controversy and Its Work," *National Geographic Magazine* 8 (1897): 193–201; Joseph J. Matthews, "Informal Diplomacy in the Venezuelan Crisis of 1896," *Mississippi Valley Historical Review* 50 (1963): 195–212.

15. On Grover Cleveland's policy toward Venezuela, see Nelson M. Blake, "Background of Cleveland's Venezuelan Policy," *American Historical Review* 47 (1942): 259–77.

16. On Scruggs, see Campbell, *From Revolution to Rapprochement*, 176; J. A. S. Grenville and George B. Young, *Politics, Strategy, and American Diplomacy: Studies in Foreign Policy, 1873–1917* (New Haven, Conn.: Yale University Press, 1966), 127–33.

17. See *Congressional Record*, 53rd Congress, 3rd Session, 837 (January 10, 1895), 2113 (February 13, 1895), and 2642 (February 23, 1895).

18. Gerald G. Eggert, *Richard Olney: Evolution of a Statesman* (University Park: Pennsylvania State University Press, 1974); Henry James, *Richard Olney and His Public Service* (New York: Da Capo Press, 1971).

19. May, *Imperial Democracy*, 39–40.

20. On Cleveland's diplomacy, see Walter LaFeber, "The Background of Cleveland's Venezuelan Policy: A Reinterpretation," *American Historical Review* 66 (1961): 947–67.

21. George B. Young, "Intervention under the Monroe Doctrine: The Olney Corollary," *Political Science Quarterly* 57 (1942): 279. See also Grenville and Young, *Politics, Strategy, and American Diplomacy*, 178.

22. For the full text of Olney's note, see *Foreign Relations of the United States* (Washington, D.C., Government Printing Office) (hereinafter cited as *FRUS*), 1895, 1:552–62.

23. James D. Richardson, *A Compilation of the Messages and the Papers of the Presidents, 1789–1897* (Washington, D.C., 1899), 9:632.

24. Salisbury to Lord Pauncefote, November 26, 1895. See *Parliamentary Papers*, 1896, XCVII, State Papers, United States, no. 1 (1896), (C-7926), nos. 11, 15, 16.

25. J. A. S. Grenville, *Lord Salisbury and Foreign Policy: The Close of the Nineteenth Century* (London: Athlone Press, 1964), 63.

26. For the text of Cleveland's message, see *FRUS*, 1895, 1:542–45.

27. May, *Imperial Democracy*, 38.

28. Bertram, *Birth of Anglo-American Friendship*, 25–26.

29. A. E. Campbell, *Great Britain and the United States, 1895–1903* (London: Longmans, 1960), 16.

30. Quoted ibid., 31.

31. On the Kruger telegram, see Campbell, *From Revolution to Rapprochement*, 107; William L. Langer, *The Diplomacy of Imperialism, 1890–1902* (New York: Alfred A. Knopf, 1956), 237.

32. On the shift in British strategy, see Grenville, *Lord Salisbury and Foreign Policy*, 68.

33. Matthews, "Venezuelan Crisis of 1896."

34. Bertram, *Birth of Anglo-American Friendship*, 117; Campbell, *From Revolution to Rapprochement*, 186.

35. Venezuela was compelled to accept an agreement that it did not actively participate in negotiating. According to Charles S. Campbell, "Venezuela . . . was incensed at being told to sign a treaty in the negotiation of which she had not participated. She was only slightly mollified when London and Washington decided to let her appoint one of the arbitrators originally designated for American appointment, provided he was not a Venezuelan." Campbell, *From Revolution to Rapprochement*, 187.

36. Bourne, *Balance of Power*, 319.

37. Grenville, *Lord Salisbury and Foreign Policy*, 55.

38. Campbell, *Great Britain and the United States*, 34.

39. For background, see Dwight C. Minder, *The Fight for the Panama Route* (New York: Columbia University Press, 1940); Thomas Schoonover, *The United States in Central America, 1860–1911* (Durham, N.C.: Duke University Press, 1991); Mary Wilhelmine Williams, *Anglo-American Isthmian Diplomacy, 1815–1915* (Washington, D.C.: American Historical Association, 1916).

40. On the timing of McKinley's remarks, see J. A. S. Grenville, "Great Britain and the Isthmian Canal, 1898–1901," *American Historical Review* 61 (1955): 54–55.

41. For the text of McKinley's address, see *FRUS*, 1898, lxxi–ii.

42. For the text of the Clayton-Bulwer Treaty, see United States, *Treaties, Conventions, International Acts, Protocols, and Agreements between the United States of America and Other Powers, 1776–1909* (Washington, D.C.: Government Printing Office, 1910), 1:659–63. For discussion of the treaty, see Charles S. Campbell, *Anglo-American Understanding, 1898–1903* (Baltimore: Johns Hopkins University Press, 1957), 63–64.

43. Hay's proposal can be found in *The British Blue Book*, "United States No. 1 (1900)," Cd. 30.

44. Campbell, *Great Britain and the United States*, 63.

45. Salisbury to Pauncefote, February 2, 1899, telegram no. 22, F.O. 55/392, quoted in Grenville, "Isthmian Canal," 59.

46. The week of December 9–15, 1899, is commonly referred to as "Black Week," as the British suffered significant military setbacks in the Boer War. Stuart Anderson, *Race and Rapprochement: Anglo-Saxonism and Anglo-American Relations, 1895–1904* (Rutherford, N.J.: Fairleigh Dickinson University Press, 1981), 135–36.

47. John Henry Ferguson, *American Diplomacy and the Boer War* (Philadelphia: University of Pennsylvania Press, 1939); Lionel M. Gelber, *The Rise of Anglo-American Friendship: A Study in World Politics, 1898–1906* (New York: Oxford University Press, 1938), 71–72.

48. Pauncefote to Salisbury, January 19, 1900, quoted in Campbell, *Anglo-American Understanding*, 190.

49. Pauncefote to Salisbury, January 21, 1900, cited in Grenville, "Isthmian Canal," 61.

50. For the text of the eventual agreement, see *FRUS*, 1901, 517–19.

51. Gelber, *Rise of Anglo-American Friendship*, 91.

52. Grenville, "Isthmian Canal," 48.

53. Gelber, *Rise of Anglo-American Friendship*, 103.

54. Useful surveys include C. C. Eldridge, *Kith and Kin: Canada, Britain, and the United States from the Revolution to the Cold War* (Cardiff: University of Wales Press, 1997); Lawrence Martin, *The Presidents and the Prime Ministers: Washington and Ottawa Face to Face; the Myth of Bilateral Bliss, 1867–1982* (Toronto: Doubleday, 1982); Lester Burrell Shippee, *Canadian-American Relations, 1849–1874* (New Haven, Conn.: Yale University Press; Toronto: Ryerson Press, 1939); Charles Callan Tansill, *Canadian-American Relations, 1875–1911* (New Haven, Conn.: Yale University Press, 1943).

55. Tansill, *Canadian-American Relations*, 121–38.

56. Grenville, *Lord Salisbury and Foreign Policy*, 373.

57. Bourne, *Balance of Power*, 251–312.

58. Campbell, *Anglo-American Understanding*, 2–3.

59. Ibid., 65.

60. On the Spanish-American War, see Philip S. Foner, *The Spanish-Cuban-American War and the Birth of American Imperialism, 1895–1902*, 2 vols. (New York: Monthly Review Press, 1972); David F. Healy, *The United States in Cuba, 1898–1902: Generals, Politicians, and the Search for Policy* (Madison: University of Wisconsin Press, 1963); John L. Offner, *An Unwanted War: The Diplomacy of the United States and Spain over Cuba, 1895–1898* (Chapel Hill: University of North Carolina Press, 1992); David F. Trask, *The War with Spain in 1898* (New York: Macmillan, 1981).

61. Quoted in Campbell, *Anglo-American Understanding*, 31.

62. Anderson, *Race and Rapprochement*, 112. See also Campbell, *Anglo-American Understanding*, 86.

63. For the agreement creating the Joint High Commission, see United States, *Treaties, Conventions, International Acts*, 1:770–73.

64. Quoted in Campbell, *Anglo-American Understanding*, 106.

65. Ibid., 116.

66. The modus vivendi established provisional lines at the summits of Chilkoot and White Passes and at a point near the Dalton Trail. See *FRUS*, 1899, 320–32.

67. Campbell, *Anglo-American Understanding*, 149–50.

68. Howard K. Beale, *Theodore Roosevelt and the Rise of America to World Power* (Baltimore: Johns Hopkins University Press, 1956); David H. Burton, *Theodore Roosevelt: Confident Imperialist* (Philadelphia: University of Pennsylvania Press, 1968).

69. Campbell, *Great Britain and the United States*, 108.

70. Gelber, *Rise of Anglo-American Friendship*, 51.

71. Campbell, *Anglo-American Understanding*, 240.

72. The more conciliatory Hay did not support Roosevelt's subterfuge. Campbell, *Great Britain and the United States*, 114–15; Gelber, *Rise of Anglo-American Friendship*, 144–45.

73. Gelber, *Rise of Anglo-American Friendship*, 152–53.

74. Roosevelt to Lodge, July 16, 1903, in *Selections from the Correspondence of Theodore Roosevelt and Henry Cabot Lodge, 1884–1918* (New York: Charles Scribner's Sons, 1925), 2:39.

75. For the text of the boundary settlement, see United States, *Treaties, Conventions, International Acts*, 1:787–94.

76. To provide one illustration of a Canadian grievance, the United States was ultimately granted control over two of the four islands at the mouth of the Portland Channel. Up until a week before the agreement was signed, all four islands were to be given to Canada, but the U.S. representative indicated that this was unacceptable. The arbitrators granted two islands to the United States. Gelber, *Rise of Anglo-American Friendship*, 159–60.

77. Grenville, *Lord Salisbury and Foreign Policy*, 372.

78. Campbell, *Anglo-American Understanding*, 240.

79. Henry Cabot Lodge, "Memoir of Henry Cabot Lodge," *Proceedings of the Massachusetts Historical Society* 58 (1925): 342.

80. Robert G. Neale, "British-American Relations during the Spanish-American War: Some Problems," *Historical Studies* 6 (1953): 86.

81. Anderson, *Race and Rapprochement*, 160.

82. Campbell, *Great Britain and the United States*, 182.

83. Thomas A. Bailey, "Dewey and the Germans at Manila Bay," *American Historical Review* 45 (1939): 59–81; Lester Burrell Shippee, "Germany and the Spanish-American War," *American Historical Review* 30 (1925): 754–77.

84. The laws of neutrality dictated that the United States could not be docked in the port of a neutral during the war. Hong Kong was a British colony at the time.

85. Bailey, "Dewey and the Germans"; Robert G. Neale, *Great Britain and United States Expansion: 1898–1900* (East Lansing: Michigan State University Press, 1966), 60; Shippee, "Germany and the Spanish-American War."

86. On the British reaction to Dewey's arrival in Manila, see Campbell, *Anglo-American Understanding*, 40–41.

87. On the terms of the armistice, see *FRUS*, 1898, 819.

88. On the debate over annexing Hawaii, see May, *Imperial Democracy*, 13–24; Thomas J. Osborne, *Empire Can Wait: American Opposition to Hawaiian Annexation, 1893–1898* (Kent, Ohio: Kent State University Press, 1981); Julius W. Pratt, "The 'Large Policy' of 1898," *Mississippi Valley Historical Review* 19 (1932): 219–42.

89. May, *Imperial Democracy*, 243–62.

90. Neale, *Expansion*, 137.

91. Neale, "British-American Relations," 86; Neale, *Expansion*, 117–18.

92. Hay to Roosevelt, July 28, 1898, in Tyler Dennett, *John Hay: From Poetry to Politics* (Port Washington, N.Y.: Kennikat Press, 1933), 191.

93. Kenton J. Clymer, *John Hay: The Gentleman as Diplomat* (Ann Arbor: University of Michigan Press, 1975), 143–56.

94. For the text of the first Open Door note, see *FRUS*, 1899, 131–33.

95. For the text of the second Open Door note, see *FRUS*, 1900, 299.

96. Clymer, *John Hay*, 150–51.

97. Speech at Lord Mayor's banquet, as quoted in the *Times* (London), November 10, 1898, 8.

98. Lansdowne to Claude MacDonald, January 7, 1902, in G. P. Gooch and Harold Temperley, *British Documents on the Origins of the War* (London: Her Majesty's Stationery Office, 1928), vol. 2, no. 120, 109–10.

99. Rising Anglo-German antagonism during this period has been covered at length elsewhere. For two of the best studies, see Paul M. Kennedy, *The Rise of the Anglo-German Antagonism, 1860–1914* (London: Ashfield Press, 1980); David Stevenson, *Armaments and the Coming of War: Europe, 1904–1914* (New York: Oxford University Press, 1996).

100. Charles A. Kupchan, *How Enemies Become Friends: The Sources of Stable Peace* (Princeton, N.J.: Princeton University Press, 2010), 73–111.

101. Admiralty to Foreign Office, January 5, 1901, F.O. 55, 405, reprinted in Campbell, *Anglo-American Understanding*, app. 4, 357–60.

102. Bourne, *Balance of Power*, 342.

103. Friedberg also details British military discussions of alternative, more competitive strategies that could have been pursued. Friedberg, *Weary Titan*, 187–88.

104. Anne Orde, *The Eclipse of Great Britain: The United States and British Imperial Decline, 1895–1956* (New York: St. Martin's Press, 1996), 27–28.

105. Quoted in May, *Imperial Democracy*, 32.

106. On Chamberlain, see James L. Garvin, *The Life of Joseph Chamberlain*, 3 vols. (London: Macmillan, 1932–34).

107. Anderson, *Race and Rapprochement*, 89.

108. For discussion, see ibid., 122–23; Grenville, *Lord Salisbury and Foreign Policy*, 169–70. For the text of Chamberlain's speech, see the *Times* (London), May 14, 1898.

109. On international reaction to Chamberlain's remarks, see Neale, *Expansion*, 102.

110. Joseph Chamberlain, "Recent Developments of Policy in the United States and Their Relation to an Anglo-American Alliance," *Scribner's Magazine*, December 1898.

111. Stephen R. Rock, "Anglo-U.S. Relations, 1845–1930: Did Shared Liberal Values and Democratic Institutions Keep the Peace?," in *Paths to Peace: Is Democracy the Answer?*, ed. Miriam Fendius Elman (Cambridge, Mass.: MIT Press, 1997), 137–38; Rock, *Why Peace Breaks Out*, 48, 54–55.

112. Anderson, *Race and Rapprochement*, 37–38, 45.

113. Ibid., 89–91.

114. On Balfour's speech, see Blanche E. C. Dugdale, *Arthur James Balfour, First Earl of Balfour* (London: Hutchinson and Company, 1936), 1:225–27.

115. Edward Dicey, "The New American Imperialism," *Nineteenth Century* 44 (1898): 501.

116. Kupchan reaches a similar conclusion about the influence of shared identity on Anglo--U.S. rapprochement. See Kupchan, *How Enemies Become Friends*, 73–111.

117. H. C. Allen, *Great Britain and the United States: A History of Anglo-American Relations (1783–1952)* (New York: St. Martin's Press, 1955), 541.

118. Rock, *Why Peace Breaks Out*, 59.

119. Here it is worth considering Ido Oren's argument that whether or not a state is viewed as a democracy may be driven by other power politics concerns. See Ido Oren, "The Subjectivity of the 'Democratic' Peace: Changing U.S. Perceptions of Imperial Germany," *International Security* 20 (1995): 147–84.

120. *Times* (London), February 14, 1903, quoted in Bourne, *Balance of Power*, 350.

121. Campbell, *Great Britain and the United States*, 149.

122. Anderson, *Race and Rapprochement*, 128.

123. Gelber, *Rise of Anglo-American Friendship*, 36, 103, 274–75.

124. On the influence of U.S. power on British behavior, see Campbell, *Great Britain and the United States*, 122.

125. Kennedy, *Anglo-German Antagonism*.

126. Canadian prime minister Wilfrid Laurier remained concerned by U.S. encroachment into what Canada viewed as its territory. Campbell, *Anglo-American Understanding*, 262.

127. Campbell, *Great Britain and the United States*, 195, 208–11.

4. The Resurgence of Interwar Germany

1. For a similarly framed discussion that pays some attention to temporal dynamics, see Mark R. Brawley, "Neoclassical Realism and Strategic Calculations: Explaining Divergent British, French, and Soviet Strategies toward Germany between the World Wars (1919–1939)," in *Neoclassical Realism, the State, and Foreign Policy*, ed. Steven E. Lobell, Norrin M. Ripsman, and Jeffrey W. Taliaferro (New York: Cambridge University Press, 2009), 75–98.

2. For useful surveys, see Edward Hallett Carr, *International Relations between the Two World Wars (1919–1939)* (London: Macmillan, 1947); Martin Kitchen, *Europe between the Wars* (New York: Longman, 1988); Richard Overy, *The Inter-war Crisis, 1919–1939* (New York: Longman, 1994); R. A. C. Parker, *Europe, 1919–45* (London: Weidenfeld and Nicolson, 1969). For a collection of useful documents, see Anthony Adamthwaite, *The Lost Peace: International Relations in Europe, 1918–1939* (New York: St. Martin's Press, 1981).

3. John J. Mearsheimer, *The Tragedy of Great Power Politics* (New York: W. W. Norton, 2001), 305–7.

4. For a useful review of the historiography of this period, see Jon Jacobson, "Is There a New International History of the 1920s?," *American Historical Review* 88 (1983): 617–45.

5. Norrin M. Ripsman and Jack S. Levy, "Wishful Thinking or Buying Time? The Logic of British Appeasement in the 1930s," *International Security* 33, no. 2 (2008): 148–81.

6. For general background, see Michael Howard, *The Continental Commitment: The Dilemma of British Defence Policy in the Era of the Two World Wars* (London: Ashfield Press, 1989).

7. On Anglo-German relations, see Paul W. Doerr, *British Foreign Policy, 1919–1939* (Manchester: Manchester University Press, 1998); Martin Gilbert, *Britain and Germany between the Wars* (London: Longmans, 1964); W. N. Medlicott, *British Foreign Policy since Versailles, 1919–1963* (London: Methuen, 1968); P. A. Reynolds, *British Foreign Policy in the Inter-war Years* (London: Longmans, Green, 1954).

8. On Versailles, see Manfred F. Boemeke, Gerald D. Feldman, and Elisabeth Gläser, eds., *The Treaty of Versailles: A Reassessment after Seventy-Five Years*, Publications of the German Historical Institute (Washington, D.C.: German Historical Institute; Cambridge: Cambridge University Press, 1998).

9. Arnold Wolfers, *Britain and France between Two Wars: Conflicting Strategies of Peace since Versailles* (New York: Harcourt, Brace, 1940), 11–12.

10. Erik Goldstein, "The Evolution of British Diplomatic Strategy for the Locarno Pact, 1924–1925," in *Diplomacy and World Power: Studies in British Foreign Policy, 1890–1950*, ed. Michael Dockrill and Brian McKercher (Cambridge: Cambridge University Press, 1996), 119.

11. On British military planning during this period, see Talbot C. Imlay, "Strategic and Military Planning, 1919–39," in *The Fog of Peace and War Planning: Military and Strategic Planning under Uncertainty*, ed. Talbot C. Imlay and Monica Duffy Toft (New York: Routledge, 2006), 139–58.

12. Quoted in Goldstein, "British Diplomatic Strategy," 123.

13. Anne Orde, *Great Britain and International Security, 1920–1926* (London: Royal Historical Society, 1978), 93.

14. Chamberlain to D'Abernon, July 29, 1925, Austen Chamberlain Papers, University of Birmingham, AC 52/289, quoted ibid., 112–13.

15. Germany refused to join the league due to the requirement in the Versailles settlement that limited German armaments but not those of other countries. Germany would not enter the league if it was not permitted to arm itself like any other member. On German reluctance to join the league, see Jon Jacobson, *Locarno Diplomacy: Germany and the West, 1925–1929* (Princeton, N.J.: Princeton University Press, 1972), 47–68; Christopher M. Kimmich, *Germany and the League of Nations* (Chicago: University of Chicago Press, 1976); Orde, *Great Britain and International Security*, 140.

16. For a skeptical view of Locarno, see George A. Grun, "Locarno: Idea and Reality," *International Affairs* 31 (1955): 477–85.

17. The best historical study of Locarno is Jacobson, *Locarno Diplomacy*. The treaties are reprinted in William J. Newman, *The Balance of Power in the Interwar Years, 1919–1939*, Studies in Political Science, PS60 (New York: Random House, 1968), 205–27.

18. Germany applied for league membership in February 1926 and was formally admitted in September of that same year.

19. On Stresemann, see Hajo Holborn, "Diplomats and Diplomacy in the Early Weimar Republic," in *The Diplomats, 1919–1939*, ed. Gordon A. Craig and Felix Gilbert (Princeton, N.J.: Princeton University Press, 1953), 123–71.

20. Zara S. Steiner, *The Lights That Failed: European International History, 1919–1933*, Oxford History of Modern Europe (Oxford: Oxford University Press, 2005), 397.

21. Jacobson, *Locarno Diplomacy*, 9. Stresemann's quotation is from Gustav Stresemann, *Vermächtnis: Der Nachlass in drei Bänden* (Berlin: Ullstein, 1932), 2:67–68.

22. Lord Robert Cecil et al., *The Locarno Treaties: Their Importance, Scope, and Possible Consequences* (New York: Farmers' Loan and Trust Company, 1925).

23. For a critical assessment of Stresemann's policies, see Hans W. Gatzke and Otto Pflanze, *Stresemann and the Rearmament of Germany* (New York: W. W. Norton, 1954).

24. Jonathan Wright, *Gustav Stresemann: Weimar's Greatest Statesman* (New York: Oxford University Press, 2002), 435.

25. Jonathan Wright, "Stresemann: A Mind Map," in *Locarno Revisited: European Diplomacy, 1920–1929*, ed. Gaynor Johnson (New York: Routledge, 2004), 122.

26. A. J. P. Taylor, *The Origins of the Second World War* (New York: Simon and Schuster, 1961), 54.

27. F. S. Northedge, *The Troubled Giant: Britain among the Great Powers, 1916–1939* (London: George Bell and Sons, 1966), 267.

28. Quoted in Steiner, *Lights That Failed*, 565.

29. Richard S. Grayson, *Austen Chamberlain and the Commitment to Europe: British Foreign Policy, 1924–29* (London: Frank Cass, 1997), 121.

30. Orde, *Great Britain and International Security*, 128.

31. Jacobson, *Locarno Diplomacy*, 202–3.

32. John Maynard Keynes, "The Report of the Young Commission," *Nation and Athenaeum* 45 (1929): 359–61.

33. On Henderson, see Henry R. Winkler, "Arthur Henderson," in Craig and Gilbert, *Diplomats*, 311–43.

34. By the middle of 1930, all foreign troops, including the French, had withdrawn from the Rhineland. See Jacobson, *Locarno Diplomacy*, 282–86.

35. F. G. Stambrook, "The German-Austrian Customs Union Project of 1931: A Study of German Methods and Motives," in *European Diplomacy between Two Wars, 1919–1939*, ed. Hans W. Gatzke (Chicago: Quadrangle Books, 1972), 94–124.

36. P. M. H. Bell, *France and Britain, 1900–1940: Entente and Estrangement* (London: Longman, 1996), 105.

37. Adam Adamthwaite, *The Making of the Second World War* (London: Allen and Unwin, 1977), 42.

38. On British views of communism, see Gabriel Gorodetsky, *The Precarious Truce: Anglo-Soviet Relations, 1924–27* (Cambridge: Cambridge University Press, 1977); David Carlton, *Churchill and the Soviet Union* (Manchester: Manchester University Press, 2000); Maurice Baumont, *The Origins of the Second World War* (New Haven, Conn.: Yale University Press, 1978), 139.

39. On reactions to Hitler, see Maurice Cowling, *The Impact of Hitler: British Politics and British Policy, 1933–1940*, Cambridge Studies in the History and Theory of Politics (Cambridge: Cambridge University Press, 1975), 68–69.

40. Quoted in Edward W. Bennett, *German Rearmament and the West, 1932–1933* (Princeton, N.J.: Princeton University Press, 1979), 203.

41. Winston Churchill, *While England Slept: A Survey of World Affairs, 1932–1938* (New York: Putnam's, 1938), 62–63.

42. Quoted in Bennett, *German Rearmament and the West*, 91.

43. Wolfers, *Britain and France*, 212–22.

44. Quoted in Michael I. Handel, *The Diplomacy of Surprise: Hitler, Nixon, Sadat* (Cambridge, Mass.: Center for International Affairs, Harvard University, 1981), 33.

45. Bennett, *German Rearmament and the West*, 89.

46. On the Saar situation, see C. J. Hill, "Great Britain and the Saar Plebiscite of 13 January 1935," *Contemporary History* 9 (1974): 121–42; B. T. Reynolds, *The Saar and Franco-German Problem* (London: Edward Arnold, 1934).

47. On Stresa, see Nicholas Rostow, *Anglo-French Relations, 1934–36* (London: Macmillan Press, 1984).

48. Quoted in Handel, *Diplomacy of Surprise*, 44.

49. Baumont, *Second World War*, 136–37.

50. Hines H. Hall III, "The Foreign Policy-Making Process in Britain, 1934–35, and the Origins of the Anglo-German Naval Agreement," *Historical Journal* 19 (1976): 496.

51. On Western contempt for Bolshevism, see Michael Jabara Carley, *1939: The Alliance That Never Was and the Coming of World War II* (Chicago: Ivan R. Dee, 1999).

52. Donald Cameron Watt, "The Anglo-German Naval Agreement of 1935: An Interim Judgment," *Journal of Modern History* 28 (1956): 16–62; Charles Bloch, "Great Britain, German Rearmament, and the Naval Agreement of 1935," in Gatzke, *European Diplomacy between Two Wars*, 125–51; Éva H. Haraszti, *Treaty-Breakers or "Realpolitiker"? The Anglo-German Naval Agreement of June 1935*, trans. Sándor Simon (Boppard am Rhein: Harald Boldt, 1974).

53. On this balancing act, see Christopher Layne, "Security Studies and the Use of History: Neville Chamberlain's Grand Strategy Revisited," *Security Studies* 17, no. 3 (2008): 397–437, doi:10.1080/09636410802319628.

54. Henderson B. Braddick, "The Hoare-Laval Plan: A Study in International Politics," *Journal of Politics* 24, no. 3 (1962): 342–64; W. N. Medlicott, "The Hoare-Laval Pact Reconsidered," in *Retreat from Power: Studies in Britain's Foreign Policy of the Twentieth Century*, vol. 1, *1906–1939*, ed. David Dilks (London: Macmillan, 1981), 118–38.

55. According to Jacques Néré, "That Hitler was resolved sooner or later to rid himself of the Locarno Agreements could hardly be doubted; his program could not otherwise be carried out. The Ethiopian affair gave him an exceptional opportunity, since the Locarno guarantors, Italy and Britain, were openly in conflict." Jacques Néré, *The Foreign Policy of France from 1914 to 1945* (London: Routledge and Kegan Paul, 1975), 184.

56. Adam J. Tooze, *The Wages of Destruction: The Making and Breaking of the Nazi Economy* (New York: Viking, 2007), 283.

57. On the Rhineland remilitarization, see Gerhard L. Weinberg, *The Foreign Policy of Hitler's Germany: Diplomatic Revolution in Europe, 1933–1936* (Chicago: University of Chicago Press, 1970), 257; Arnold J. Toynbee, *Documents on International Affairs, 1936* (London: Oxford University Press, 1937), 57–61; George Ward Price, *I Know These Dictators* (New York: Henry Holt, 1938), 179.

58. Weinberg, *Foreign Policy of Hitler's Germany*, 254–61.

59. Ripsman and Levy, "Wishful Thinking or Buying Time?"

60. Haraszti, *Treaty-Breakers or "Realpolitiker"?*, 50.

61. Watt, "Anglo-German Naval Agreement," 171–73.

62. In Thomas Jones, *A Diary with Letters, 1931–1950* (London: Oxford University Press, 1954), 129.

63. On the Ten Year Rule, see Brian Bond, *British Military Policy between the Two World Wars* (New York: Oxford University Press, 1980), 23–27, 94–97; Orde, *Great Britain and International Security*, 162–63.

64. Bennett, *German Rearmament and the West*, 79.

65. Bond, *British Military Policy*; Michael Howard, "British Military Preparations for the Second World War," in Dilks, *Retreat from Power*, 1:102–17; Stephen W. Roskill, *Naval Policy between the Wars* (New York: Walker, 1968); Robert Paul Shay Jr., *British Rearmament in the Thirties: Politics and Profits* (Princeton, N.J.: Princeton University Press, 1977); Wesley K. Wark, *The Ultimate Enemy: British Intelligence and Nazi Germany, 1933–1939* (Ithaca, N.Y.: Cornell University Press, 1985).

66. On the German air threat, see Uri Bialer, *The Shadow of the Bomber: The Fear of Air Attack and British Politics, 1932–1939* (London: Royal Historical Society, 1980); Howard, *Continental Commitment*, 80; Wolfers, *Britain and France*, 202.

67. W. N. Medlicott, "Britain and Germany: The Search for Agreement, 1930–37," in Dilks, *Retreat from Power*, 1:78.

68. For an argument with a similar logic applied to the 1930s, see Ripsman and Levy, "Wishful Thinking or Buying Time?"

69. On the historical legacy, see, in particular, Walter A. McDougall, *France's Rhineland Diplomacy, 1914–1924: The Last Bid for a Balance of Power in Europe* (Princeton, N.J.: Princeton University Press, 1978).

70. For an overview of French policy, see Jon Jacobson, "Strategies of French Foreign Policy after World War I," *Journal of Modern History* 55 (1983): 78–95.

71. Quoted in Orde, *Great Britain and International Security*, 62.

72. Wolfers, *Britain and France*, 11.

73. Piotr S. Wandycz, *The Twilight of French Eastern Alliances, 1926–1936: French-Czechoslovak-Polish Relations from Locarno to the Remilitarization of the Rhineland* (Princeton, N.J.: Princeton University Press, 1988).

74. Quote from Anthony Adamthwaite, *Grandeur and Misery: France's Bid for Power in Europe, 1914–1940* (London: Edward Arnold, 1995), 122.

75. Sally Marks, *The Illusion of Peace: International Relations in Europe, 1918–1933* (New York: St. Martin's Press, 1976), 80.

76. On the Thoiry conversations, see Néré, *Foreign Policy of France*, 76–78; Jacobson, *Locarno Diplomacy*, 84–90.

77. On Briand's hope for a general rapprochement, see Jacobson, *Locarno Diplomacy*, 86.

78. On the objections of French military leaders, see ibid., 104; Steiner, *Lights That Failed*, 461.

79. Foch to Government, March 8, 1926, quoted in Adamthwaite, *Grandeur and Misery*, 123.

80. Néré, *Foreign Policy of France*, 85–87.

81. Marks, *Illusion of Peace*, 85; Néré, *Foreign Policy of France*, 89.

82. Wolfers, *Britain and France*, 61.

83. Quoted in Baumont, *Second World War*, 21.

84. For a detailed discussion of various factors affecting French attitudes toward disarmament, see Adamthwaite, *Grandeur and Misery*, 191; Martin S. Alexander, *The Republic in Danger: General Maurice Gamelin and the Politics of French Defence, 1933–1940* (Cambridge: Cambridge University Press, 1992); Robert Allan Doughty, *The Seeds of Disaster: The Development of French Army Doctrine, 1919–1939* (Hamden, Conn.: Archon Books, 1985); Robert J. Young, *In Command of France: French Foreign Policy and Military Planning, 1933–1940* (Cambridge, Mass.: Harvard University Press, 1978).

85. Taylor, *Second World War*, 68.

86. Adamthwaite, *Grandeur and Misery*, 187.

87. As reported by the French Ambassador to Germany André François-Poncent and quoted in Maurice Vaisse, "Against Appeasement: French Advocates of Firmness, 1933–38," in *The Fascist Challenge and the Policy of Appeasement*, ed. Wolfgang J. Mommsen and Lothar Kettenacker (London: Allen and Unwin, 1983), 231.

88. On French reactions to National Socialism, see Robert Michael, *The Radicals and Nazi Germany: The Revolution in French Attitudes toward Foreign Policy, 1933–1939* (Washington, D.C.: University Press of America, 1982).

89. Adamthwaite, *Grandeur and Misery*, 193; Néré, *Foreign Policy of France*, 128–30.

90. Barthou to Campbell, April 17, 1934, quoted in Young, *In Command of France*, 55.

91. On the French view of Stresa, see Néré, *Foreign Policy of France*, 153–54.

92. Adamthwaite, *Making of the Second World War*, 48; Young, *In Command of France*, 82–85.

93. William Evans Scott, *Alliance against Hitler: The Origins of the Franco-Soviet Pact* (Durham, N.C.: Duke University Press, 1962).

94. Joseph Stalin sought a more comprehensive agreement, but Laval resisted attempts to make the pact into a more formal alliance. Laval's reluctance was rooted primarily in concerns about domestic reactions to an alliance with the communist Soviet Union. Adamthwaite, *Grandeur and Misery*, 197.

95. Of course, German gross national product was also larger than French gross national product. Statistics from Anthony Adamthwaite, *France and the Coming of the Second World War, 1936–1939* (London: Frank Cass, 1977), 164.

96. For discussions of French military doctrine in the interwar period, see Elizabeth Kier, *Imagining War: French and British Military Doctrine between the Wars* (Princeton, N.J.: Princeton University Press, 1997); Barry R. Posen, *The Sources of Military Doctrine: France, Britain, and Germany between the World Wars* (Ithaca, N.Y.: Cornell University Press, 1984).

97. The French army had 340,000 troops compared to the 100,000 that Germany was limited to by Versailles. Young, *In Command of France*, 36.

98. Paul Beaudry and Franck Portier, "The French Depression in the 1930s," *Review of Economic Dynamics* 5, no. 1 (2002): 73–99.

99. Weinberg, *Foreign Policy of Hitler's Germany*, 245–47; Taylor, *Second World War*, 97.

100. Jacobson, *Locarno Diplomacy*, 110.

101. For background, see Gabriel Gorodetsky, *Soviet Foreign Policy, 1917–1991: A Retrospective* (London: Frank Cass, 1994); Caroline Kennedy-Pipe, *Russia and the World, 1917–1991* (London: Edward Arnold, 1998), 11–55; Adam B. Ulam, *Expansion and Coexistence: The History of Soviet Foreign Policy, 1917–67* (New York: Praeger, 1968), 76–279.

102. On the Soviet view of Versailles, see Theodore H. von Laue, "Soviet Diplomacy: G. V. Chicherin, Peoples Commissar for Foreign Affairs, 1918–1930," in Craig and Gilbert, *Diplomats*, 234–81.

103. On the Soviet emergence into world politics, see Jon Jacobson, *When the Soviet Union Entered World Politics* (Berkeley: University of California Press, 1994).

104. Hans W. Gatzke, "Russo-German Military Collaboration during the Weimar Republic," *American Historical Review* 63, no. 3 (1958): 565–97.

105. For an interesting comment on Rapallo, see Ian Johnson, "Sowing the Wind: The First Soviet-German Military Pact and the Origins of World War II," War on the Rocks, June 7, 2016, http://warontherocks.com/2016/06/sowing-the-wind-the-first-soviet-german-military-pact-and-the-origins-of-world-war-ii.

106. On these relations, see Harvey Leonard Dyck, *Weimar Germany and Soviet Russia, 1926–1933: A Study in Diplomatic Instability* (New York: Columbia University Press, 1966); Kurt Rosenbaum, *Community of Fate: German-Soviet Diplomatic Relations, 1922–1928* (Syracuse, N.Y.: Syracuse University Press, 1965).

107. Aleksandr M. Nekrich, *Pariahs, Partners, Predators: German-Soviet Relations, 1922–1941*, trans. Gregory L. Freeze (New York: Columbia University Press, 1997), 11.

108. Ibid., 12.

109. On Soviet views of capitalism, see John Erickson, "Threat Identification and Strategic Appraisal by the Soviet Union, 1930–1941," in *Knowing One's Enemies: Intelligence Assessment before the Two World Wars*, ed. Ernest R. May (Princeton, N.J.: Princeton University Press, 1984), 383–84.

110. Gorodetsky, *Precarious Truce*, 76.

111. On the Treaty of Berlin, see Gatzke, "Russo-German Military Collaboration," 581; Graham Ross, *The Great Powers and the Decline of the European State System* (New York: Longman, 1983), 60–61.

112. For a review of the various crises that arose, see Nekrich, *Pariahs, Partners, Predators*, 25–29.

113. Quoted ibid., 72.

114. Ibid., 64.

115. Adolf Hitler, *Mein Kampf*, trans. Ralph Manheim (Boston: Houghton Mifflin, 1962), 641–67.

116. Nekrich, *Pariahs, Partners, Predators*, 79.

117. Quoted ibid., 263n69.

118. Jonathan Haslam, *The Soviet Union and the Struggle for Collective Security in Europe, 1933–39* (New York: St. Martin's Press, 1984), 12–13; Jiri Hochman, *The Soviet Union and the Failure of Collective Security, 1934–1938* (Ithaca, N.Y.: Cornell University Press, 1984).

119. According to Aleksandr M. Nekrich, "Moscow interpreted the persecution of German communists as a signal that Berlin was deliberately seeking to raise tension between the two countries and that it no longer had an interest in better relations." Nekrich, *Pariahs, Partners, Predators*, 74.

120. Quoted in Haslam, *Struggle for Collective Security*, 26.
121. On the Hugenberg memo, see ibid., 19; Geoffrey Roberts, *The Soviet Union and the Origins of the Second World War: Russo-German Relations and the Road to War, 1933–1941* (New York: St. Martin's Press, 1995), 12. For Soviet reaction, see Jane Degras, *Soviet Documents on Foreign Policy* (London: Oxford University Press, 1951), 21–23.
122. Watt, "Anglo-German Naval Agreement," 160.
123. Edward Hallett Carr, *German-Soviet Relations between the Two World Wars, 1919–1939* (Baltimore: Johns Hopkins University Press, 1951), 111.
124. Haslam, *Struggle for Collective Security*, 36. On the Danzig issue and its significance to both Germany and Poland, see Weinberg, *Foreign Policy of Hitler's Germany*, 63–64.
125. Haslam, *Struggle for Collective Security*, 36–37.
126. Nekrich, *Pariahs, Partners, Predators*, 81.
127. Haslam, *Struggle for Collective Security*, 40.
128. On the effect of German behavior on the Soviet decision, see Carr, *German-Soviet Relations*, 115–16; Haslam, *Struggle for Collective Security*, 40.
129. Ingeborg Plettenberg, "The Soviet Union and the League of Nations," in *The League of Nations in Retrospect: Proceedings of the Symposium* (New York: Walter de Gruyter, 1983), 144–81.
130. Haslam, *Struggle for Collective Security*, 45.
131. Nekrich, *Pariahs, Partners, Predators*, 90.
132. On the Eastern Locarno idea, see Scott, *Alliance against Hitler*, esp. chap. 9, "Eastern Locarno."
133. Haslam, *Struggle for Collective Security*, 49–51; Roberts, *Soviet Union*, 18–19.
134. Haslam, *Struggle for Collective Security*, 51.
135. Roberts, *Soviet Union*, 24.
136. Ibid., 21–23.
137. Haslam, *Struggle for Collective Security*, 85–86; Nekrich, *Pariahs, Partners, Predators*, 91; Roberts, *Soviet Union*, 26–28; Young, *In Command of France*, 154–55.
138. Haslam, *Struggle for Collective Security*, 82.
139. Roberts, *Soviet Union*, 1–8.
140. Nekrich, *Pariahs, Partners, Predators*, 92; Roberts, *Soviet Union*, 36.
141. Quoted in Haslam, *Struggle for Collective Security*, 98.
142. Erickson, "Threat Identification and Strategic Appraisal," 189.
143. On Soviet involvement in the Spanish Civil War, see Edward Hallett Carr, *The Comintern and the Spanish Civil War* (London: Macmillan, 1984); David Tredwell Cattell, *Soviet Diplomacy and the Spanish Civil War* (Berkeley: University of California Press, 1957); Erickson, "Threat Identification and Strategic Appraisal," 391; Haslam, *Struggle for Collective Security*, 107–28; José Manuel Martinez Bande, *Communist Intervention in the Spanish Civil War, 1936–1939* (Madrid: Spanish Information Service, 1966); R. Dan Richardson, *Comintern Army: The International Brigades and the Spanish Civil War* (Lexington: University Press of Kentucky, 1982).
144. Roberts, *Soviet Union*, 42.
145. Nekrich, *Pariahs, Partners, Predators*, 98; Jonathan Haslam, *The Soviet Union and the Threat from the East, 1933–41: Moscow, Tokyo, and the Prelude to the Pacific War* (Pittsburgh: University of Pittsburgh Press, 1992).
146. There is a voluminous literature on the non-aggression pact, which is beyond the scope of this chapter. See Nekrich, *Pariahs, Partners, Predators*, 103–41; Anthony Read and David Fisher, *The Deadly Embrace: Hitler, Stalin, and the Nazi-Soviet Pact, 1939–1941* (London: Michael Joseph, 1988); Geoffrey Roberts, *The Unholy Alliance: Stalin's Pact with Hitler* (London: Tauris, 1989).
147. On the cooperative, institutional approach of the 1920s, see Maarten L. Pereboom, *Democracies at the Turning Point: Britain, France, and the End of the Postwar Order, 1928–1933* (New York: Peter Lang, 1995); Martin Thomas, *Britain, France, and Appeasement: Anglo-French Relations in the Popular Front Era* (New York: Berg, 1996).
148. Ulam, *Expansion and Coexistence*, 217.
149. Handel, *Diplomacy of Surprise*, 35.
150. Orde, *Great Britain and International Security*, 210.
151. Ripsman and Levy, "Wishful Thinking or Buying Time?"

152. On the balance of power in Europe, see Williamson Murray and Allan Reed Millett, *Calculations: Net Assessment and the Coming of World War II* (New York: Free Press, 1992); Williamson Murray, *The Change in the European Balance of Power, 1938–1939* (Princeton, N.J.: Princeton University Press, 1984).

153. Bennett, *German Rearmament and the West*, 506.

154. Taylor, *Second World War*, 42.

155. Ibid., 119.

156. Bennett, *German Rearmament and the West*, 509.

157. Taylor, *Second World War*, xxiv. See also Alexander J. Groth, *Democracies against Hitler: Myth, Reality, and Prologue* (Brookfield, Vt.: Ashgate, 1999); Richard Overy, "Misjudging Hitler: A. J. P. Taylor and the Third Reich," in *"The Origins of the Second World War" Reconsidered: A. J. P. Taylor and the Historians*, ed. Gordon Martel (London: Routledge, 1999), 93–115.

158. Adamthwaite, *Coming of the Second World War*, 22.

5. The Origins of the Cold War

1. On the instinct of the United States to leave Europe after the war, see Mark S. Sheetz, "Exit Strategies: American Grand Designs for Postwar European Security," *Security Studies* 8, no. 4 (1999): 1–43.

2. For largely practical reasons, this chapter will focus primarily on U.S. policy during the period when the Cold War began. Despite the post–Cold War opening of some Soviet archives, the available evidence is still mostly from the U.S. side. Notable studies of the origins of the Cold War from the Soviet perspective include Caroline Kennedy-Pipe, *Stalin's Cold War: Soviet Strategies in Europe, 1943 to 1956* (New York: St. Martin's Press, 1995); Vojtech Mastny, *The Cold War and Soviet Insecurity: The Stalin Years* (New York: Oxford University Press, 1996); Vojtech Mastny, *Russia's Road to the Cold War* (New York: Columbia University Press, 1979); Vladimir O. Pechatnov, "The Big Three after World War II: New Documents on Soviet Thinking about Post-War Relations with the United States and Great Britain," Cold War International History Project, Working Paper 13 (Washington, D.C.: Woodrow Wilson International Center for Scholars, 1995), http://www.wilsoncenter.org/publication/the-big-three-after-world-war-ii-new-documents-soviet-thinking-about-post-war-relations; Vladislav Zubok and Constantine Pleshakov, *Inside the Kremlin's Cold War: From Stalin to Khrushchev* (Cambridge, Mass.: Harvard University Press, 1996).

3. John J. Mearsheimer, *The Tragedy of Great Power Politics* (New York: W. W. Norton, 2001), 338–44.

4. For an argument more critical of the U.S. role, see Christopher Layne, *The Peace of Illusions: American Grand Strategy from 1940 to the Present*, Cornell Studies in Security Affairs (Ithaca, N.Y.: Cornell University Press, 2006).

5. This chapter does not comment directly on the extensive and voluminous historical debate over who "started" the Cold War. To be clear, though, I find myself most convinced by those arguments that recognize that both the United States and the Soviet Union perceived threats from each other regarding their security and their allies' security. Mutual fear contributed greatly to the origins of the Cold War. On this historical debate, see John Lewis Gaddis, "The Emerging Post-Revisionist Synthesis on the Origins of the Cold War," *Diplomatic History* 7 (1983): 171–90; Anders Stephanson, "The United States," in *The Origins of the Cold War in Europe: International Perspectives*, ed. David Reynolds (New Haven, Conn.: Yale University Press, 1994), 23–52. For a traditionalist approach, see Arthur Schlesinger, "Origins of the Cold War," *Foreign Affairs* 46 (1967): 22–52. For a revisionist approach, see Lloyd Gardner, *Architects of Illusion: Men and Ideas in American Foreign Policy, 1941–1949* (Chicago: Quadrangle Books, 1970) and William Appleman Williams, *The Tragedy of American Diplomacy* (Cleveland: World Publishing, 1959). For the post-revisionist argument, see John Lewis Gaddis, *The United States and the Origins of the Cold War, 1941–1947* (New York: Columbia University Press, 1972).

6. On Barbarossa, see Alan Clark, *Barbarossa: The Russian-German Conflict, 1941–45* (New York: William Morrow, 1965).

7. George F. Kennan, *Soviet-American Relations*, vol. 2, *The Decision to Intervene* (Princeton, N.J.: Princeton University Press, 1958); David W. McFadden, *Alternative Paths: Soviets and Americans, 1917–1920* (New York: Oxford University Press, 1993); John Swettenham, *Allied Intervention in Russia, 1918–1919* (London: Allen and Unwin, 1967); Richard H. Ullman, *Anglo-Soviet Relations, 1917–1921*, vol. 1, *Intervention and War* (Princeton, N.J.: Princeton University Press, 1961); Stephen M. Walt, *Revolution and War* (Ithaca, N.Y.: Cornell University Press, 1996), 138–40.

8. The United States resisted recognition of the Soviet Union until various domestic and economic pressures convinced Roosevelt to recognize the new regime in 1933. On the rationale behind the eventual recognition, see Edward M. Bennett, *Recognition of Russia: An American Foreign Policy Dilemma* (Waltham, Mass.: Blaisdell, 1970); Robert Dallek, *Franklin D. Roosevelt and American Foreign Policy, 1932–1945* (New York: Oxford University Press, 1979), 78–80; John Lewis Gaddis, *The Long Peace: Inquiries into the History of the Cold War* (New York: Oxford University Press, 1987), 12–15.

9. Earlier in 1941, the "moral embargo" on the sale of arms to the Soviet Union had been lifted, but the March lend-lease act only authorized assistance to Great Britain. Roosevelt still had to convince a wary Congress to provide assistance to the Soviet Union. On the decision to extend lend-lease to the Soviet Union, see George C. Herring, *Aid to Russia, 1941–1946: Strategy, Diplomacy, the Origins of the Cold War* (New York: Columbia University Press, 1973), 1–24; Leon Martel, *Lend-Lease, Loans, and the Coming of the Cold War: A Study of the Implementation of Foreign Policy* (Boulder, Colo.: Westview Press, 1979).

10. Congress voted its approval on October 24, and aid was officially extended on November 7. For discussion of the issue, see *Foreign Relations of the United States* (Washington, D.C., Government Printing Office) (hereinafter cited as *FRUS*), 1941, 1:768–866.

11. On allied cooperation with the Soviet Union throughout the war, see John R. Deane, *The Strange Alliance: The Story of Our Efforts at Wartime Co-operation with Russia* (New York: Viking, 1947); Ralph Levering, *American Opinion and the Russian Alliance, 1939–1945* (Chapel Hill: University of North Carolina Press, 1976).

12. Roosevelt to William Leahy, U.S. Ambassador to France, June 26, 1941, in Elliott Roosevelt, ed., *F.D.R.: His Personal Letters, 1882–1945* (New York: Duell, Sloan and Pearce, 1950), 2:1177–78. See also Arnold A. Offner, "Uncommon Ground: Anglo-American-Soviet Diplomacy, 1941–42," *Soviet Union / Union Soviétique* 18 (1991): 237–57.

13. The best study of Roosevelt's wartime diplomacy is Warren F. Kimball, *The Juggler: Franklin Roosevelt as Wartime Statesman* (Princeton, N.J.: Princeton University Press, 1991).

14. On Roosevelt's ideas for the postwar order, see James MacGregor Burns, *Roosevelt: The Soldier of Freedom* (New York: Harcourt, Brace, Jovanovich, 1970); Gaddis, *Origins of the Cold War*, 10–13; Willard D. Range, *Franklin D. Roosevelt's World Order* (Athens: University of Georgia Press, 1959). See also the following speeches in Samuel I. Rosenman, comp., *The Public Papers and Addresses of Franklin D. Roosevelt*, 13 vols. (New York: Russell and Russell, 1938–50): annual message to Congress, January 6, 1941, 9:672.; radio address, May 27, 1941, 10:181–94; address to the annual dinner of the White House Correspondents' Association, March 15, 1941, 10:60–69.

15. On the four policemen concept, see Robert A. Divine, *Roosevelt and World War II* (Baltimore: Johns Hopkins University Press, 1969), 57–58; Gaddis, *Origins of the Cold War*, 24–25; Range, *Franklin D. Roosevelt's World Order*, 172–76; Forest Davies, "Roosevelt's World Blueprint," *Saturday Evening Post*, April 10, 1943, 20–21, 109–10.

16. Warren I. Cohen, *The Cambridge History of American Foreign Relations*, vol. 4, *America in the Age of Soviet Power, 1945–1991* (Cambridge: Cambridge University Press, 1993), 8.

17. Rosenman, *Addresses of Franklin D. Roosevelt*, 13:32–42.

18. For the negotiations over the second front, see Roosevelt to Stalin, April 11, 1942, *FRUS*, 1942, 3:542–43; Roosevelt conversations with Molotov, May 30 and June 1, 1942, *FRUS*, 1942, 3:576–77, 582–83. See also Mark A. Stoler, *The Politics of the Second Front: American Military Planning and Diplomacy, 1941–1943* (Westport, Conn.: Greenwood Press, 1977).

19. *FRUS*, 1943, 1:605, 620–21, 664–65, 710–11, 751, 756–57, 800.

20. Rosenman, *Addresses of Franklin D. Roosevelt*, 12:553–63.

21. On the Tehran conference, see *FRUS*, Tehran, 459–62. See also Keith Eubank, *Summit at Tehran* (New York: William Morrow, 1985); Warren F. Kimball, *Forged in War: Roosevelt, Churchill,*

and the Second World War (New York: William Morrow, 1997), 121–55; Paul D. Mayle, *Eureka Summit: Agreement in Principle and the Big Three at Tehran, 1943* (Newark: University of Delaware Press, 1987).

22. Vladislav Zubok, *A Failed Empire: The Soviet Union in the Cold War from Stalin to Gorbachev* (Chapel Hill: University of North Carolina Press, 2007), 25.

23. Geir Lundestad, *The American Non-policy toward Eastern Europe, 1943–1947: Universalism in an Area Not of Essential Interest to the United States* (New York: Humanities Press, 1975); Eduard Mark, "American Policy toward Eastern Europe and the Origins of the Cold War, 1941–46: An Alternative Interpretation," *Journal of American History* 68 (1981): 313–36.

24. George V. Kacewicz, *Great Britain, the Soviet Union, and the Polish Government in Exile, 1939–1945* (Boston: Martinus Nijhoff, 1979); R. C. Lukas, *The Strange Allies: The United States and Poland, 1941–1945* (Knoxville: University of Tennessee Press, 1978); Antony Polonsky, *The Great Powers and the Polish Question: A Documentary Study of Cold War Origins* (London: Orbis Books, 1976).

25. Stalin's unhappiness with the exiled Polish government and his inclination to create a new, pro-Soviet government instead is reported in a memo from Ambassador W. Averill Harriman to Secretary of State Cordell Hull, January 11, 1944, *FRUS*, 1944, 3:1218–20. On broken relations between Moscow and the exiled Polish government, see *FRUS*, 1943, 3:389–93.

26. Churchill to Roosevelt, January 28, 1944, in Francis L. Loewenheim, Harold D. Langley, and Manfred Jonas, eds., *Roosevelt and Churchill: Their Secret Wartime Correspondence* (New York: E. P. Dutton, 1975), 423. Also see *FRUS*, 1944, 3:1216–20, 1226, 1228–30.

27. At Tehran, the Allies had agreed to negotiate the postwar borders of Poland on the basis of the 1921 Curzon Line. See *FRUS*, Tehran, 510, 512, 594, 598–604.

28. On optimism regarding Poland, see *FRUS*, 1944, 3:1300–1301, 1305–13.

29. On the effect of the Warsaw uprising, see Deborah Welch Larson, *Origins of Containment: A Psychological Explanation* (Princeton, N.J.: Princeton University Press, 1985), 92–106; Kimball, *Forged in War*, 273–74. For general background, see Jan M. Ciechanowski, *The Warsaw Rising of 1944* (New York: Cambridge University Press, 1974); Jan T. Gross, *Revolution from Abroad: The Soviet Conquest of Poland's Western Ukraine and Western Belorussia* (Princeton, N.J.: Princeton University Press, 1988).

30. *FRUS*, 1944, 3:1379–81, 1384.

31. Harriman to Harry Hopkins, September 10, 1944, *FRUS*, 1944, 4:988–90; Harriman to Hull, September 20, 1944, ibid., 992–98.

32. On Harriman's thinking, see W. Averell Harriman and Elie Abel, *Special Envoy to Churchill and Stalin, 1941–1946* (New York: Random House, 1975).

33. Harriman to Hull, September 29, 1944, *FRUS*, 1944, 4:1001–2. See also Dallek, *Roosevelt and American Foreign Policy*, 466; Herring, *Aid to Russia*, 135–36; Martel, *Coming of the Cold War*, 76–83.

34. On discussions about the postwar Germany, see John Morton Blum, *Roosevelt and Morgenthau* (Boston: Houghton Mifflin, 1970); Gaddis, *Origins of the Cold War*, 118–25; Warren F. Kimball, *Swords or Ploughshares? The Morgenthau Plan for Defeated Nazi Germany, 1943–1946* (Philadelphia: Lippincott, 1976).

35. On the Quebec conference, see *FRUS*, Quebec, 1944; David B. Woolner, *The Second Quebec Conference Revisited: Waging War, Formulating Peace; Canada, Great Britain, and the United States in 1944–1945* (New York: St. Martin's Press, 1998).

36. Stalin insisted that all sixteen Soviet states be individually represented in the organization and that the permanent members of the executive council of the body have complete veto power. On Dumbarton Oaks, see Robert A. Divine, *Second Chance: The Triumph of Internationalism in America during World War II* (New York: Atheneum, 1967), 215–16, 220–22, 225–28; Gaddis, *Origins of the Cold War*, 27–29; Robert C. Hilderbrand, *Dumbarton Oaks: The Origins of the United Nations and the Search for Postwar Security* (Chapel Hill: University of North Carolina Press, 1990); Ernest R. May and Angeliki E. Laiou, *The Dumbarton Oaks Conversations and the United Nations, 1944–1994* (Cambridge, Mass.: Harvard University Press, 1988); George Schild, *Bretton Woods and Dumbarton Oaks: American Economic and Political Postwar Planning in the Summer of 1944* (New York: St. Martin's Press, 1995).

37. Winston Churchill, *Triumph and Tragedy* (Boston: Houghton Mifflin, 1953), 179–82, 186–91.

38. For Roosevelt's endorsement of the meeting, see *FRUS*, 1944, 4:1002.

39. On the spheres-of-influence agreement, see Dallek, *Roosevelt and American Foreign Policy*, 479–80; Warren F. Kimball, "Naked Reverse Right: Roosevelt, Churchill, and Eastern Europe from TOLSTOY to Yalta—and a Little Beyond," *Diplomatic History* 9 (1985): 1–24; Larson, *Origins of Containment*, 107–12; Albert Reiss, "The Churchill-Stalin 'Percentages Agreement' on the Balkans, Moscow, October 1944," *American Historical Review* 83 (1978): 368–87; Marc Trachtenberg, *A Constructed Peace: The Making of the European Settlement, 1945–1963* (Princeton, N.J.: Princeton University Press, 1999), 5–6; Joseph M. Siracusa, "The Meaning of TOLSTOY: Churchill, Stalin, and the Balkans, Moscow, October 1944," *Diplomatic History* 3 (1979): 443–63.

40. Quoted in Churchill, *Triumph and Tragedy*, 201; Herbert Feis, *Churchill, Roosevelt, Stalin: The War They Waged and the Peace They Sought* (Princeton, N.J.: Princeton University Press, 1957). See also *FRUS*, 1944, 4:1005–10.

41. Churchill, *Triumph and Tragedy*, 186, 206, 210.

42. Joseph Stalin, *Stalin's Correspondence with Churchill, Atlee, Roosevelt, and Truman, 1941–1945* (London: Lawrence and Wishart, 1958), 2:165. For Roosevelt's reaction, see *FRUS*, Quebec, 1944, 368.

43. Henry L. Stimson, manuscript diary, December 31, 1944, quoted in Dallek, *Roosevelt and American Foreign Policy*, 507.

44. For a good summary, see R. C. Raack, *Stalin's Drive to the West, 1938–1945: The Origins of the Cold War* (Stanford, Calif.: Stanford University Press, 1995), 73–101.

45. Dallek, *Roosevelt and American Foreign Policy*, 506.

46. Yalta has been extensively examined. Among the best studies are Russell D. Buhite, *Decisions at Yalta: An Appraisal of Summit Diplomacy* (Wilmington, Del.: Scholarly Resources, 1986); Diane Shaver Clemens, *Yalta* (New York: Oxford University Press, 1970); Dallek, *Roosevelt and American Foreign Policy*, 506–25; Richard F. Fenno, *The Yalta Conference* (Boston: Heath, 1955); Jonathan L. Snell, *The Meaning of Yalta: Big Three Diplomacy and the New Balance of Power* (Baton Rouge: Louisiana State University Press, 1956); Fraser J. Harbutt, *Yalta 1945: Europe and America at the Crossroads* (New York: Cambridge University Press, 2010); Edward R. Stettinius, *Roosevelt and the Russians: The Yalta Conference* (Garden City, N.Y.: Doubleday, 1949); S. M. Plokhy, *Yalta: The Price of Peace* (New York: Penguin Books, 2011); Athan G. Theoharis, "Roosevelt and Truman on Yalta: The Origins of the Cold War," *Political Science Quarterly* 87 (1972): 210–41; Athan G. Theoharis, *The Yalta Myths: An Issue in U.S. Politics, 1945–1955* (Columbia: University of Missouri Press, 1970).

47. For an exchange of notes between Stalin and Roosevelt regarding Poland, see "President Roosevelt's Letter to Stalin, February 6, 1945, on the Acceptable Compromise regarding the Composition of the Post-War Polish Government," available from the Cold War International History Project, Woodrow Wilson International Center for Scholars, Washington, D.C.

48. For discussions of Poland at Yalta, see *FRUS*, Yalta, 667–71, 677–81, 709, 711, 716–21, 726–28, 776–82, 786–91, 792–93, 803–7, 903, 905–7, 911, 938. See also Stettinius, *Roosevelt and the Russians*, 183, 270–71; Dallek, *Roosevelt and American Foreign Policy*, 513–19.

49. For the text of the declaration, see *FRUS*, Yalta, 971–73.

50. According to the Atlantic Charter, the signatories "respect the right of all peoples to choose the form of government under which they will live; and they wish to see sovereign rights and self-government restored to those who have been forcibly deprived of them." On the Atlantic Charter, see Douglas Brinkley and David R. Facey-Crowther, *The Atlantic Charter* (New York: St. Martin's Press, 1994); Theodore Wilson, *The First Summit: Roosevelt and Churchill at Placentia Bay, 1941* (Lawrence: University Press of Kansas, 1991). Also see *FRUS*, 1941, 1:341–79.

51. For Roosevelt's views of the declaration, see Dallek, *Roosevelt and American Foreign Policy*, 516; Gaddis, *Origins of the Cold War*, 163–73.

52. Bruce Kuklick, *American Policy and the Division of Germany: The Clash with Russia over Reparations* (Princeton, N.J.: Princeton University Press, 1962); Bruce Kuklick, "The Division of Germany and American Policy on Reparations," *Western Political Quarterly* 23 (1970): 276–93; E. F. Penrose, *Economic Planning for Peace* (Princeton, N.J.: Princeton University Press, 1953); Jacob Viner, "German Reparations Once More," *Foreign Affairs* 21 (1943): 659–73. See also the Yalta

briefing paper "Reparation and Restitution Policy toward Germany," January 16, 1945, *FRUS*, Yalta, 194–97.

53. Stettinius, *Roosevelt and the Russians*, 299.

54. The Soviet proposal for reparations is in "Basic Principles of Exaction and Reparations from Germany," submitted to the foreign ministers at Yalta on February 7, 1945, in *FRUS*, Yalta, 707.

55. On the first charge principle, see Trachtenberg, *Constructed Peace*, 24; Daniel Yergin, *Shattered Peace: The Origins of the Cold War and the National Security State* (Boston: Houghton Mifflin, 1977), 96.

56. For discussion, see Ernest R. May, "The United States, the Soviet Union, and the Far Eastern War, 1941–1945," *Pacific Historical Review* 24 (1955): 153–63; Louis Morton, "Soviet Intervention in the War with Japan," *Foreign Affairs* 40 (1962): 53–62.

57. This pact included control over the southern Sakhalin Island, the naval base at Port Arthur on the Liaotung Peninsula, the Kurile Islands, and Outer Mongolia as well as international control over the port at Dairen, joint control of the Chinese Eastern and Southern Mongolian railways. See Dallek, *Roosevelt and American Foreign Policy*, 515–19; Gaddis, *Origins of the Cold War*, 78–79; Marc S. Gallicchio, *The Cold War Begins in Asia: American East Asian Policy and the Fall of the Japanese Empire* (New York: Columbia University Press, 1988), 2–3. See also "Agreement regarding the Entry of the Soviet Union into the War against Japan," February 11, 1945, in *FRUS*, Yalta, 984.

58. Quoted in Dallek, *Roosevelt and American Foreign Policy*, 520.

59. For the text of the speech, see Rosenman, *Addresses of Franklin D. Roosevelt*, 13:570–86.

60. On the need to cultivate public support of the United Nations, see Dallek, *Roosevelt and American Foreign Policy*, 520–25; Gaddis, *Origins of the Cold War*, 49–50.

61. For background on the Romania situation, see Elizabeth W. Hazard, *Cold War Crucible: United States Foreign Policy and the Conflict in Romania, 1943–1953* (New York: Columbia University Press, 1996); Ghita Ionescu, *Communism in Rumania, 1944–1962* (New York: Oxford University Press, 1964). For the U.S. position, see "Recommended Policy on the Question of Establishing Diplomatic Relations and Concluding Peace Treaties with the Former Axis Satellite States," June 29, 1945, *FRUS*, Potsdam, 1:357–62.

62. Walter LaFeber, *America, Russia, and the Cold War*, 7th ed. (New York: McGraw-Hill, 1993), 15; Melvyn P. Leffler, *A Preponderance of Power: National Security, the Truman Administration, and the Cold War* (Stanford, Calif.: Stanford University Press, 1992), 34–36.

63. Quoted in LaFeber, *Cold War*, 16.

64. Harry S. Truman, *Memoirs*, vol. 1, *Year of Decisions* (Garden City, N.Y.: Doubleday, 1955), 79–82.

65. There is a historical debate over whether the suspension of aid unnecessarily aggravated Soviet-U.S. relations. George C. Herring argues that the decision led to Soviet suspicions about U.S. intentions, as the United States was attempting to gain short-term leverage over Stalin. Herring, *Aid to Russia*, 180–211. On subsequent discussions within the U.S. government about extending a postwar reconstruction loan to the Soviet Union, see *FRUS*, 1945, 5:937–1053, in particular, Crowley to Truman, May 11, 1945, 999–1000.

66. On the Hopkins mission, see Robert Sherwood, *Roosevelt and Hopkins* (New York: Grosset and Dunlap, 1950), 885–87; Truman, *Memoirs*, 1:257–58.

67. On Truman's thinking, see Truman, *Memoirs*, 1:211–17.

68. For background on Potsdam, see Herbert Feis, *Between War and Peace: The Potsdam Conference* (Princeton, N.J.: Princeton University Press, 1960); James L. Gormly, *From Potsdam to the Cold War: Big Three Diplomacy, 1945–1947* (Wilmington, Del.: Scholarly Resources, 1990); Charles L. Mee, *Meeting at Potsdam* (New York: M. Evans, 1975).

69. On Secretary of War Stimson's assurance to Truman that Soviet assistance would no longer be necessary to defeat Japan, see Leffler, *Preponderance of Power*, 37. See also Robert H. Ferrell, ed., *Off the Record: The Private Papers of Harry S. Truman* (New York: Harper and Row, 1980), 53–54.

70. On the London conference, see Gaddis, *Origins of the Cold War*, 263–67; Jonathan Knight, "Russia's Search for Peace: The London Council of Foreign Ministers, 1945," *Journal of Con-*

temporary History 13 (1978): 137–63; Robert L. Messer, *The End of an Alliance: James F. Byrnes, Roosevelt, Truman, and the Origins of the Cold War* (Chapel Hill: The University of North Carolina Press, 1982), 115–36; Patricia Dawson Ward, *The Threat of Peace: James F. Byrnes and the Council of Foreign Ministers* (Kent, Ohio: Kent State University Press, 1979).

71. On the use of atomic diplomacy and economic tools to gain leverage in London, see Ward, *Threat of Peace*, 18–49; Leffler, *Preponderance of Power*, 38–39. On atomic diplomacy, in general, see Gar Alperovitz, *Atomic Diplomacy: Hiroshima and Nagasaki* (New York: Vintage, 1965); Barton J. Bernstein, "The Quest for Security: American Foreign Policy and International Control of Atomic Energy, 1942–1946," *Journal of American History* 60 (1974): 1003–44.

72. On the failure of the London conference, see Leffler, *Preponderance of Power*, 38–40.

73. Byrnes's speech can be found in "Neighboring Nations in One World," U.S. Department of State, *Bulletin* 13, no. 333 (1945): 709–11. See also Eduard Mark, "Charles E. Bohlen and the Acceptable Limits of Soviet Hegemony in Eastern Europe: A Memorandum of 18 October 1945," *Diplomatic History* 3 (1979): 201–13.

74. On this split, see Gaddis, *Origins of the Cold War*, 273–80; Mark, "Soviet Hegemony in Eastern Europe"; Robert L. Messer, "Paths Not Taken: The U.S. Department of State and Alternatives to Containment," *Diplomatic History* 1 (1977): 297–319. Also see two articles in the *New York Times* by James Reston: "Two Views in the Capital on U.S.-Russian Relations," September 30, 1945, and "Washington Back as 'Hard Approach' to Russia," October 14, 1945.

75. For the speech, see *The Public Papers of Harry S. Truman: Containing the Public Messages, Speeches, and Statements of the President, 1945* (Washington, D.C.: Government Printing Office, 1961), 431–38.

76. On the Navy Day speech and the ambivalence surrounding it, see Gaddis, *Origins of the Cold War*, 268–69; Leffler, *Preponderance of Power*, 45–46.

77. The Bohlen-Robinson report is reprinted in *Diplomatic History* 1, no. 4 (1977): 389–99; quotation at 399.

78. Messer, "Paths Not Taken," 311.

79. Leffler, *Preponderance of Power*, 100.

80. On the Moscow conference, see Gaddis, *Origins of the Cold War*, 280–81; Messer, *End of an Alliance*, 137–55; Ward, *Threat of Peace*, 50–77.

81. Robert J. Donovan, *Conflict and Crisis: The Presidency of Harry S Truman, 1945–1948* (Columbia: University of Missouri Press, 1977), 158–61.

82. For Ethridge's report, see "Summary Report on Soviet Policy in Romania and Bulgaria," December 7, 1945, *FRUS*, 1945, 5:633–37. See also Mark Ethridge and C. E. Black, "Negotiating on the Balkans, 1945–1947," in *Negotiating with the Russians*, ed. Raymond Dennett and Joseph E. Johnson (Boston: World Peace Foundation, 1951), 184–203.

83. For a full description of this meeting, see Truman, *Memoirs*, 1:546–53.

84. For the text of the speech, see Joseph Stalin, "9 February 1946 Election Speech," *Vital Speeches of the Day* 12 (1946): 300–304. The reaction of the U.S. State Department is in *FRUS*, 1945, 6:695. On the importance of the speech, see Gaddis, *Origins of the Cold War*, 299–301; Leffler, *Preponderance of Power*, 103–4.

85. See *Time*, February 18, 1946. Douglas's comment is reported in James Forrestal, *The Forrestal Diaries* (New York: Viking, 1951), 134–35.

86. Gaddis, *Origins of the Cold War*, 301.

87. Trachtenberg, *Constructed Peace*, 203.

88. Useful reviews of the crisis in Iran in include Richard W. Cottam, *Iran and the United States: A Cold War Case Study* (Pittsburgh: University of Pittsburgh Press, 1988); Louise L'Estrange Fawcett, *Iran and the Cold War: The Azerbaijan Crisis of 1946* (New York: Cambridge University Press, 1992); James F. Goode, *The United States and Iran, 1946–51: The Diplomacy of Neglect* (New York: St. Martin's Press, 1989); Gary R. Hess, "The Iranian Crisis of 1945–46 and the Cold War," *Political Science Quarterly* 89 (1974): 117–46; Bruce Robellet Kuniholm, *The Origins of the Cold War in the Near East: Great Power Conflict and Diplomacy in Iran, Turkey, and Greece* (Princeton, N.J.: Princeton University Press, 1980); Fred H. Lawson, "The Iranian Crisis of 1945–1946 and the Spiral Model of International Conflict," *International Journal of Middle East Studies* 21 (1989): 307–26; Mark Hamilton Lytle, *The Origins of the Iranian-American Alliance* (London: Holmes and

Meier, 1987); Stephen L. McFarland, "A Peripheral View of the Origins of the Cold War: The Crisis in Iran, 1941–1947," *Diplomatic History* 4 (1980): 333–51; Eduard Mark, "The War Scare of 1946 and Its Consequences," *Diplomatic History* 21 (1997): 383–416; Richard Pfau, "Containment in Iran, 1946," *Diplomatic History* 1 (1977): 359–72.

89. The United States declined to join in the alliance with Iran. See *FRUS*, 1941, 3:468–77 and *FRUS*, 1942, 4:263. On the extension of lend-lease assistance to Iran, see *FRUS*, 1942, 4:289–300. See also Kuniholm, *Cold War in the Near East*, 145–46.

90. On the treaty, see U.S. Department of State, *Bulletin* 6, no. 143 (1942): 249–52.

91. After the Soviet defeat of the Germans at Stalingrad during the winter of 1943, concern about Soviet intentions grew. With the Germans defeated, the necessity of using Iran to transport supplies declined, so continuing Soviet interest in Iran had to have some other motivation.

92. On the Tehran Declaration, see Barry Rubin, *The Great Powers in the Middle East, 1941–1947: The Road to the Cold War* (London: Frank Cass, 1980), 88–89; Kuniholm, *Cold War in the Near East*, 166–67. See also *FRUS*, 1943, 4:413–14.

93. In response, the central Iranian government refused the Soviet demand for an oil concession and announced that it would not grant anymore outside oil concessions until the war was over and its territory had been evacuated. See Yergin, *Shattered Peace*, 182.

94. On Stalin's interests, see Walter Bedell Smith, *My Three Years in Moscow* (Philadelphia: Lippincott, 1950), 52; Natalia I. Yegorova, "The 'Iran Crisis' of 1945–1946: A View from the Russian Archives," Cold War International History Project, Working Paper 15 (Washington, D.C.: Woodrow Wilson International Center for Scholars, 1996).

95. Clemens, *Yalta*, 246; Kuniholm, *Cold War in the Near East*, 213–16.

96. "Memorandum concerning Iran," Briefing Book Paper, January 6, 1945, in *FRUS*, Yalta, 340.

97. Though Tehran wanted all foreign forces to leave, it appears to have been concerned more by Soviet forces than by British forces. U.S. ambassador Wallace Murray reported a conversation he had with Iranian prime minister Mohsen Sadr in which Sadr "stressed Iran is caught in an Anglo-Soviet vise and cannot extricate herself by her own efforts. He spoke more emphatically of Russian interference in internal affairs but also indicated fear and resentment of British activities." Memo from Murray to Acting Secretary of State Joseph Grew, July 20, 1945, quoted in Rubin, *Great Powers in the Middle East*, 164.

98. Henderson to Byrnes, December 11, 1945, quoted in Rubin, *Great Powers in the Middle East*, 169.

99. In the 1921 treaty, the Russians renounced their interests in Iran as long as the region remained stable. See Günther Nollau and Hans Jürgen Wiehe, *Russia's South Flank: Soviet Operations in Iran, Turkey, and Afghanistan* (New York: Praeger, 1963), 21; Rouhollah Ramazani, *The Foreign Policy of Iran: A Developing Nation in World Affairs, 1500–1941* (Charlottesville: University Press of Virginia, 1966), 139–67, 186–92.

100. Quoted in Rubin, *Great Powers in the Middle East*, 171.

101. Ibid., 171–72.

102. Fawcett, *Iran and the Cold War*, 53.

103. For the text of the "long telegram," see Kennan to Byrnes, February 22, 1946, *FRUS*, 1946, 6:696–709; quotation at 701–2.

104. On the effect of Kennan's telegram, see John H. Backer, *The Decision to Divide Germany: American Foreign Policy in Transition* (Durham, N.C.: Duke University Press, 1978), 152–55; Walter Isaacson and Evan Thomas, *The Wise Men: Six Friends and the World They Made* (New York: Simon and Schuster, 1986), 352–56; Larson, *Origins of Containment*, 255–57.

105. For the text of the speech, see *New York Times*, March 1, 1946. Analysis is in Messer, *End of an Alliance*, 88–91.

106. Rossow to Byrnes, March 5, 1946, *FRUS*, 1946, 7:340.

107. Fraser J. Harbutt, *The Iron Curtain: Churchill, America, and the Origins of the Cold War* (New York: Oxford University Press, 1986), 183–208; Henry B. Ryan, "A New Look at Churchill's 'Iron Curtain' Speech," *Historical Journal* 22 (1979): 895–920.

108. Byrnes's remark is in *FRUS*, 1946, 7:347. See Hess, "Iranian Crisis," 360; Pfau, "Containment in Iran, 1946," 360. For additional reports of ominous Soviet behavior in Iran, see "Memo-

randum on Events Relative to Iran," March 1946, *FRUS*, 7:346–48, and Rossow to Byrnes, *FRUS*, 1946, 7:344–45.

109. *New York Times*, March 14, 1946.

110. Walter Lippmann, *Toledo Blade*, March 12, 1946.

111. Discussions about bringing the Iran issue before the United Nations Security Council had been continuous since January. On March 18, Iran finally formally requested that the Security Council consider Soviet behavior in Iran. Byrnes offered U.S. support: "The United States is committed to support the Charter of the United Nations. Should the occasion arise, our military strength will be used to support the purposes and principles of the Charter." Quoted in Joseph Marion Jones, *The Fifteen Weeks (February 21–March 5, 1947)* (New York: Harcourt, Brace, and World, 1955), 55.

112. See Murray to Byrnes, March 22, 1946, *FRUS*, 1946, 7:369–71; Murray to Byrnes, March 23, 1946, ibid., 373–75.

113. The U.S. insistence on Security Council approval so angered Soviet representative Andrei Gromyko that he walked out of the debate in protest. See Andrei Gromyko, *Memoirs* (New York: Doubleday, 1989), 237–38.

114. For the U.S. position on Turkey at Potsdam, see *FRUS*, Potsdam, 2:303–4, 313–14, 366–67.

115. Quoted in Leffler, *Preponderance of Power*, 78. From expanded draft of letter from the Secretary of War to the Secretary of State, "U.S. Position re Soviet Proposals of Kiel Canal and Dardanelles," July 8, 1945.

116. Kuniholm, *Cold War in the Near East*, 265.

117. Truman, *Memoirs*, 1:412.

118. Harriman to Byrnes, October 23, 1945, *FRUS*, 1945, 5:902.

119. On these conflicting assessments, see Melvyn P. Leffler, "Strategy, Diplomacy, and the Cold War: The United States, Turkey, and NATO, 1945–1952," *Journal of American History* 71 (1985): 807–25.

120. Quoted in Rubin, *Great Powers in the Middle East*, 204–6.

121. Wilson to Byrnes, March 18, 1946, *FRUS*, 1946, 7:818–19.

122. Kuniholm, *Cold War in the Near East*, 335–37.

123. Rubin, *Great Powers in the Middle East*, 213–15.

124. On the immediate U.S. reaction, see the Central Intelligence Group's "Weekly Summary, 16 August 1946," in Woodrow J. Kuhns, *Assessing the Soviet Threat: The Early Cold War Years* (Washington, D.C.: Central Intelligence Agency, 1997), 70–71.

125. There is a historical debate over how significant and real the Soviet threat to Turkey was. Various intelligence sources reported that the Soviet Union was neither interested in nor prepared for war over the issue. For the argument that the threat was legitimate, see Mark, "War Scare of 1946." For the counterargument, see Leffler, "Strategy, Diplomacy, and the Cold War."

126. Leffler, *Preponderance of Power*, 123–24; Leffler, "Strategy, Diplomacy, and the Cold War," 815; Rubin, *Great Powers in the Middle East*, 217; Gaddis, *Origins of the Cold War*, 336–37.

127. Memorandum by Henderson, "The Present Situation in the Near East—a Danger to World Peace," *FRUS*, 1946, 7:1–6. On Henderson, see Kuniholm, *Cold War in the Near East*, 237–41.

128. Henderson to Byrnes, August 15, 1946, *FRUS*, 1946, 7:840–42. See also Henderson, "Memorandum on Turkey Prepared in the Division of Near Eastern Affairs," October 21, 1946, *FRUS*, 1946, 7:894–97.

129. Yergin, *Shattered Peace*, 235.

130. On the consequences of the Turkey crisis, see Kuniholm, *Cold War in the Near East*, 62–63; Leffler, *Preponderance of Power*, 123–24; Mark, "War Scare of 1946," 411–12.

131. The text of the treaty is available in *FRUS*, 1946, 2:190–3. For discussion, see Carolyn Eisenberg, *Drawing the Line: The American Decision to Divide Germany, 1944–1949* (New York: Cambridge University Press, 1996), 228–29.

132. On Byrnes's view of the demilitarization proposal, see Eduard Mark, "October or Thermidor? Interpretations of Stalinism and the Perception of Soviet Foreign Policy in the United States, 1927–1947," *American Historical Review* 49 (1989): 953; Yergin, *Shattered Peace*, 224–25. See

also *FRUS*, 1946, 2:267–68. On Soviet behavior in Germany as a litmus test, see Eisenberg, *Drawing the Line*, 229; Leffler, *Preponderance of Power*, 34.

133. Memorandum of Conversation between Byrnes and Molotov, by Charles E. Bohlen, Assistant to the Secretary of State, April 28, 1946, *FRUS*, 2: 146–47.

134. Arthur H. Vandenberg Jr., ed., *Private Papers of Senator Vandenberg* (Boston: Houghton Mifflin, 1952), 268.

135. On U.S. reactions to Molotov's rejection, see Eisenberg, *Drawing the Line*, 234–48. See also U.S. Delegation Minutes of the Thirty-Eighth Meeting of the Council of Foreign Ministers, July 9, 1946, *FRUS*, 2:843–47.

136. Eisenberg, *Drawing the Line*, 233–76; Leffler, *Preponderance of Power*, 119–21; Trachtenberg, *Constructed Peace*, 41–55.

137. David Reynolds, "The Origins of the Cold War: The European Dimension, 1944–1951," *Historical Journal* 28 (1985): 497–515. On fears of communism, see John Lamberton Harper, *America and the Reconstruction of Italy, 1945–1948* (New York: Cambridge University Press, 1986); John O. Iatrides, *Revolt in Athens: The Greek Communist Second Round, 1944–1945* (Princeton, N.J.: Princeton University Press, 1972); James Edward Miller, "The Search for Stability: An Interpretation of American Policy in Italy, 1943–46," *Journal of Italian History* 1 (1978): 264–86; Lawrence S. Wittner, *American Intervention in Greece, 1943–1949* (New York: Columbia University Press, 1982).

138. On the Clifford-Elsey report, see Clark Clifford, *Counsel to the President* (New York: Random House, 1991), 45–76, 109–29; Eisenberg, *Drawing the Line*, 256; Gaddis, *Origins of the Cold War*, 321–22, 337; Leffler, *Preponderance of Power*, 130–38.

139. Melvyn P. Leffler, "Adherence to Agreements: Yalta and the Experiences of the Early Cold War," *International Security* 11 (1986): 88–123; Larson, *Origins of Containment*, 135–36, 150–212; J. Philipp Rosenberg, "The Belief System of Harry S. Truman and Its Effect on Foreign Policy Decision-Making during His Administration," *Presidential Studies Quarterly* 12 (1982): 226–38.

140. Leffler, *Preponderance of Power*, 131.

141. The complete Clifford-Elsey report, titled "American Relations with the Soviet Union," is in Arthur Krock, *Memoirs: Sixty Years on the Firing Line* (New York: Funk and Wagnalls, 1968), 417–82; quotation at 431.

142. Ibid., 477.

143. Further, the report failed to mention U.S. violations of various agreements that might have aroused suspicions in Moscow. For example, the United States had not withdrawn its own troops from Iceland and Panama. For a discussion of the unbalanced nature of the report, see Leffler, *Preponderance of Power*, 130–38.

144. On the necessary time for rebuilding the Soviet military, see ibid., 133–34.

145. Ibid., 138. See also Eisenberg, *Drawing the Line*, 228–29; Mark, "October or Thermidor?," 951–62.

146. For another report on U.S. beliefs about Soviet intentions, see the Central Intelligence Group's "Special Study No. 3, August 24, 1946," in Kuhns, *Assessing the Soviet Threat*, 77–80.

147. Herring, *Aid to Russia*, 233.

148. On the Soviet requests and the U.S. considerations, see ibid., 237–75; Martel, *Coming of the Cold War*, 169–221; Thomas G. Patterson, "The Abortive American Loan to Russia and the Origins of the Cold War," *Journal of American History* 56 (1969): 70–92.

149. On the U.S. conditions, see Secretary of State to Charge of the Soviet Union, February 21, 1946, *FRUS*, 1946, 6:828–29. The conditions went beyond Iran to include issues such as U.S. property rights in liberated nations, intellectual property matters, economic freedom in Eastern Europe, freedom of navigation, civil aviation, and final settlement of lend-lease obligations.

150. Herring, *Aid to Russia*, 270. See also Byrnes to William L. Clayton, September 24, 1946, *FRUS*, 1946, 7:223.

151. On U.S. military planning for the postwar era, see Steven T. Ross, *American War Plans, 1945–1950* (New York: Garland, 1988); Michael S. Sherry, *Preparing for the Next War: America Plans for Postwar Defense, 1941–45* (New Haven, Conn.: Yale University Press, 1977).

152. Mastny, *Cold War and Soviet Insecurity*, 21.

153. Zubok and Pleshakov, *Inside the Kremlin's Cold War*, 34–35.

154. Zubok, *Failed Empire*, 25.
155. Zubok and Pleshakov, *Inside the Kremlin's Cold War*, 17.
156. Quoted in Mastny, *Cold War and Soviet Insecurity*, 23.
157. John Lewis Gaddis, *Strategies of Containment: A Critical Appraisal of Postwar American National Security Policy* (New York: Oxford University Press, 1982), 16.
158. Making the case that ideology played a more significant role is Douglas J. Macdonald, "Communist Bloc Expansion in the Early Cold War: Challenging Realism, Refuting Revisionism," *International Security* 20 (1995): 152–88.
159. Leffler, *Preponderance of Power*, 34–36.
160. For the argument that Washington incorrectly viewed Poland as a litmus test, see Yergin, *Shattered Peace*, 85.
161. Zubok and Pleshakov, *Inside the Kremlin's Cold War*, 47–50. See also "Memorandum from G. Zhukov to Stalin, May 24, 1946" and the "Memorandum from M. Litvinov to Stalin, May 25, 1946," both available through the Cold War International History Project; Pechatnov, "Big Three after World War II"; R. C. Raack, "Stalin Plans His Post-War Germany," *Journal of Contemporary History* 28 (1993): 53–73.
162. Paul M. Kennedy, *The Rise and Fall of the Great Powers* (New York: Vintage Books, 1987), 353–72.
163. Geoffrey A. Hosking, *A History of the Soviet Union* (London: Fontana, 1985), 296.
164. Kennedy, *Rise and Fall*, 363.
165. On the Soviet military, see Matthew A. Evangelista, "Stalin's Postwar Army Reappraised," *International Security* 3 (1982): 110–38. Also see the "Assessing the Soviet Threat to Western Europe" roundtable in *Diplomatic History* 22, no. 3 (1998), including Phillip A. Karber and Jerald A. Combs, "The United States, NATO, and the Soviet Threat to Western Europe: Military Estimates and Policy Options, 1945–1963," 399–430; John S. Duffield, "Progress, Problems, and Prospects," 431–38; and Matthew A. Evangelista, "The 'Soviet Threat': Intentions, Capabilities, and Context," 439–50.
166. Quoted in Gaddis, *Strategies of Containment*, 40. See also Leffler, *Preponderance of Power*, 6; Cohen, *History of American Foreign Relations*, 4:35.
167. William C. Wohlforth, *The Elusive Balance: Power and Perceptions during the Cold War* (Ithaca, N.Y.: Cornell University Press, 1993), 60.

6. Conclusion and the Contemporary Rise of China

1. James Freeman Clarke, "Wanted, a Statesman!," *Old and New* 2 (December 1870): 644. Paul Pierson paraphrases the contemporaneous German chancellor Otto von Bismarck expressing an identical sentiment, but Pierson provides no citation and I have been unable to locate any source attributing this quotation to Bismarck. See Paul Pierson, *Politics in Time: History, Institutions, and Social Analysis* (Princeton, N.J.: Princeton University Press, 2004), 42.
2. Jonathan M. DiCicco and Jack S. Levy, "Power Shifts and Problem Shifts: The Evolution of the Power Transition Research Program," *Journal of Conflict Resolution* 43, no. 6 (1999): 675–704; Woosang Kim, "Power Transitions and Great Power War from Westphalia to Waterloo," *World Politics* 45 (1992): 153–72; Richard Ned Lebow and Benjamin Valentino, "Lost in Transition: A Critical Analysis of Power Transition Theory," *International Relations* 23, no. 3 (2009): 389–410; Douglas Lemke and Ronald L. Tammen, "Power Transition Theory and the Rise of China," *International Interactions* 29, no. 4 (2003): 269–71; David Rapkin and William Thompson, "Power Transition, Challenge, and the (Re)Emergence of China," *International Interactions* 29, no. 4 (2003): 315–42; Ronald L. Tammen, *Power Transitions: Strategies for the Twenty-First Century* (New York: Chatham House, 2000).
3. Charles F. Doran and Wes Parsons, "War and the Cycle of Relative Power," *American Political Science Review* 74, no. 4 (1980): 947–65; Charles F. Doran, *Systems in Crisis: New Imperatives of High Politics at Century's End* (New York: Cambridge University Press, 1991); Brock F. Tessman and Steve Chan, "Power Cycles, Risk Propensity, and Great-Power Deterrence," *Journal of Conflict Resolution* 48, no. 2 (2004): 131–53.

4. William C. Wohlforth, *The Elusive Balance: Power and Perceptions during the Cold War* (Ithaca, N.Y.: Cornell University Press, 1993).

5. John J. Mearsheimer, *The Tragedy of Great Power Politics* (New York: W. W. Norton, 2001), 33–34.

6. Stephen M. Walt, *The Origins of Alliances* (Ithaca, N.Y.: Cornell University Press, 1987).

7. For an argument about the sources of beliefs about intentions, see Keren Yarhi-Milo, *Knowing the Adversary: Leaders, Intelligence, and Assessment of Intentions in International Relations* (Princeton, N.J.: Princeton University Press, 2014).

8. David M. Edelstein, "Managing Uncertainty: Beliefs about Intentions and the Rise of Great Powers," *Security Studies* 12, no. 1 (2002): 1–40.

9. On time inconsistency problems more generally, see Kyle Beardsley, *The Mediation Dilemma* (Ithaca, N.Y.: Cornell University Press, 2011).

10. Stephen G. Brooks, "Dueling Realisms," *International Organization* 51, no. 3 (1997): 445–77.

11. Kenneth N. Waltz, "Structural Realism after the Cold War," *International Security* 25, no. 1 (2000): 39–41.

12. John J. Mearsheimer, "Reckless States and Realism," *International Relations* 23 (2009): 244.

13. Brian C. Rathbun, "Uncertain about Uncertainty: Understanding the Multiple Meanings of a Crucial Concept in International Relations Theory," *International Studies Quarterly* 51, no. 3 (2007): 533–57.

14. For the argument that problems in international relations arise from misplaced certainty rather than from uncertainty, see Jennifer Mitzen and Randall L. Schweller, "Knowing the Unknown Unknowns: Misplaced Certainty and the Onset of War," *Security Studies* 20, no. 1 (2011): 2–35.

15. George Loewenstein and Jon Elster, *Choice over Time* (New York: Russell Sage Foundation, 1992); George Loewenstein, Daniel Read, and Roy F. Baumeister, *Time and Decision: Economic and Psychological Perspectives on Intertemporal Choice* (New York: Russell Sage Foundation, 2003).

16. Andrew Abbott, *Time Matters: On Theory and Method* (Chicago: University of Chicago Press, 2001).

17. Anuj K. Shah, Sendhil Mullainathan, and Eldar Shafir, "Some Consequences of Having Too Little," *Science* 338, no. 6107 (2012): 682–85.

18. Pierson, *Politics in Time.*

19. Stephen Kern, *The Culture of Time and Space, 1880–1918* (Cambridge, Mass.: Harvard University Press, 2003).

20. Gary Goertz, *International Norms and Decision Making: A Punctuated Equilibrium Model* (Lanham, Md.: Rowman and Littlefield, 2003); Stephen Jay Gould, *Punctuated Equilibrium* (Cambridge, Mass.: Harvard University Press, 2007); Albert Somit and Steven A. Peterson, *The Dynamics of Evolution: The Punctuated Equilibrium Debate in the Natural and Social Sciences* (Ithaca, N.Y.: Cornell University Press, 1992); Laura L. Carstensen, "The Influence of a Sense of Time on Human Development," *Science* 312, no. 5782 (2006): 1913–15, doi:10.1126/science.1127488.

21. For one treatment of time horizons in a very different context, see Alan M. Jacobs, *Governing for the Long Term: Democracy and the Politics of Investment* (New York: Cambridge University Press, 2011).

22. Among the many studies of the rise of China are Michael Beckley, "China's Century? Why America's Edge Will Endure," *International Security* 36, no. 3 (2011): 41–78; Steve Chan, *Looking for Balance: China, the United States, and Power Balancing in East Asia* (Stanford, Calif.: Stanford University Press, 2012); Elizabeth C. Economy and Michel C. Oksenberg, eds., *China Joins the World: Progress and Prospects* (New York: Council on Foreign Relations Press, 1999); Aaron L. Friedberg, *A Contest for Supremacy: China, America, and the Struggle for Mastery in Asia* (New York: W. W. Norton, 2011); Avery Goldstein, *Rising to the Challenge: China's Grand Strategy and International Security* (Stanford, Calif.: Stanford University Press, 2005); Alastair I. Johnston, "Is China a Status Quo Power?," *International Security* 27, no. 4 (2003): 5–56; Andrew J. Nathan and Andrew Scobell, *China's Search for Security* (New York: Columbia University Press, 2012); Robert S. Ross and Zhu Feng, *China's Ascent : Power, Security, and the Future of International Politics* (Ithaca,

N.Y.: Cornell University Press, 2008); David Shambaugh, *China Goes Global: The Partial Power* (New York: Oxford University Press, 2013); Susan L. Shirk, *China: Fragile Superpower* (New York: Oxford University Press, 2007).

23. See Beckley, "China's Century?"; Friedberg, *Contest for Supremacy*.

24. For an exhaustive survey of China's military capabilities, see Roger Cliff, *China's Military Power: Assessing Current and Future Capabilities* (New York: Cambridge University Press, 2015).

25. See the concluding chapter of the 2001 edition of Mearsheimer, *Tragedy of Great Power Politics*. See also John J. Mearsheimer, "China's Unpeaceful Rise," *Current History* 105 (2006): 160–61.

26. Alastair I. Johnston, *Social States: China in International Institutions, 1980–2000* (Princeton, N.J.: Princeton University Press, 2008).

27. Beckley, "China's Century?"; Stephen G. Brooks and William C. Wohlforth, "The Rise and Fall of the Great Powers in the Twenty-First Century: China's Rise and the Fate of America's Global Position," *International Security* 40, no. 3 (2015): 7–53.

28. On economic statecraft within China, see William J. Norris, *Chinese Economic Statecraft: Commercial Actors, Grand Strategy, and State Control* (Ithaca, N.Y.: Cornell University Press, 2016).

29. Thomas J. Christensen, *The China Challenge: Shaping the Choices of a Rising Power* (New York: W. W. Norton, 2015), 298.

30. Shirley Kan, "U.S.-China Counter-Terrorism Cooperation: Issues for U.S. Policy," Congressional Research Service (CRS) Report for Congress, December 7 (Washington, D.C.: CRS, 2004); Shirley Kan, "U.S.-China Counterterrorism Cooperation: Issues for U.S. Policy," CRS Report for Congress, July 15 (Washington, D.C.: CRS, 2010).

31. U.S. Department of Defense, Air-Sea Battle Office, "Air-Sea Battle: Service Collaboration to Address Anti-Access and Area Denial Challenges" (Washington, D.C.: Department of Defense, May 2013), http://archive.defense.gov/pubs/ASB-ConceptImplementation-Summary-May -2013.pdf; Kurt Campbell and Brian Andrews, "Explaining the U.S. 'Pivot' to Asia" (London: Chatham House, August 2013).

32. For a discussion of this guidance, see M. Taylor Fravel, *Strong Borders, Secure Nation Cooperation and Conflict in China's Territorial Disputes* (Princeton, N.J.: Princeton University Press, 2008), 134–35; Dingding Chen and Jianwei Wang, "Lying Low No More? China's New Thinking on the Tao Guang Yang Hui Strategy," *China: An International Journal* 9, no. 2 (2011): 195–216.

33. Some have questioned just how newly assertive Chinese foreign policy has been. See Alastair I. Johnston, "How New and Assertive Is China's New Assertiveness?," *International Security* 37, no. 4 (2013): 7–48.

34. On the South China Sea disputes, see Bill Hayton, *The South China Sea: The Struggle for Power in Asia* (New Haven, Conn.: Yale University Press, 2014); International Crisis Group, "Stirring up the South China Sea (I)," April 23, 2012, http://www.crisisgroup.org/en/regions/asia /north-east-asia/china/223-stirring-up-the-south-china-sea-i.aspx; International Crisis Group, "Stirring up the South China Sea (II): Regional Responses," July 24, 2012, http://www .crisisgroup.org/en/regions/asia/north-east-asia/china/229-stirring-up-the-south-china-sea -ii-regional-responses.aspx; International Crisis Group, "Stirring up the South China Sea (III): A Fleeting Opportunity for Calm," May 7, 2015, http://www.crisisgroup.org/en/regions/asia /north-east-asia/china/267-stirring-up-the-south-china-sea-III-a-fleeting-opportunity-for -calm.aspx; Shannon Tiezzi, "Why China Is Stopping Its South China Sea Island-Building (For Now)," *Diplomat*, June 16, 2015, http://thediplomat.com/2015/06/why-china-is-stopping-its -south-china-sea-island-building-for-now.

35. Christensen, *China Challenge*, 265.

36. Ibid., 260.

37. Jessica Chen Weiss, *Powerful Patriots: Nationalist Protest in China's Foreign Relations* (New York: Oxford University Press, 2014), 248. For a more skeptical view of the supposed growth in Chinese nationalism, see Alastair Iain Johnson, "Is Chinese Nationalism Rising? Evidence from Bejing," *International Security* 41, no. 3 (2016/17): 7–43.

38. Andrew H. Kydd, "Trust, Reassurance, and Cooperation," *International Organization* 54, no. 2 (2000): 325–57.

39. Yarhi-Milo, *Knowing the Adversary*.

Index

Page numbers in italics indicate illustrations.

Calleo, David, 64
Campbell, A. E., 78, 92
Campbell, Charles S., 82, 84, 85
Campbell, Ronald, 108
Campenon Jean-Baptiste, 65
Canada, 74; Alaskan boundary dispute
  with, 80, 82–86
Caprivi, Georg von, 60–62
Carr, Edward Hallett, 113
Central American canal plans, 79–82, 84
Chamberlain, Austen, 98–100
Chamberlain, Joseph, 90–91
Cheney, Richard, 21
Chiang Kai-shek, 138
China, 1–4, 8–9, 122, 125, 157–161; colonial
  spheres of influence in, 86–88; Japan and,
  8, 103, 160; Roosevelt on, 126; Soviet
  Union and, 132, 138, 145; territorial
  claims of, 8, 25, 160; U.S. relations with,
  1–4, 8–9, 26–27, 122, 157–161; U.S. trade
  deficit with, 8. *See also* Manchuria
Christensen, Thomas J., 9, 160
Churchill, Winston, 99, 101; "iron curtain"
  speech by, 141; on Poland, 127–133; at
  Potsdam Conference, 134, 142, 147; at
  Tehran Conference, 126–127, 138, 147;
  at Yalta Conference, 130–135, 147
Clarke, James Freeman, 151
Clayton-Bulwer Treaty (1850), 79–80, 81
Cleveland, Grover, 75–79, 89
Clifford, Clark, 145–146, 148
Coburg, Prince of, 57
Cohen, Warren I., 126
Cold War, 23, 121–150, 159; Germany and,
  144; hardening of, 144–147; Iran and,
  138–141; Molotov on, 148; Poland and,
  127–130; Turkey and, 141–144
Concert of Europe, 49, 100
Congress of Berlin (1878), 47–48
cooperation/competition strategies, 15–28,
  28t, 33–34, 129, 151–154; active/passive,
  15; alternative arguments to, 28–34,
  39–40, 124; buck-passing and, 28–33;
  during Cold War, 121–127, 137, 147–150;
  engagement and, 32–34; by France with
  Nazis, 97–100, 105–110, 117–119; of
  imperial Germany, 4, 38–65; of interwar
  Germany, 94–120; Machiavelli on, 2–3;
  outcomes of, 27–28, 28t; Sino-U.S.
  relations and, 1–4, 8–9, 26–27, 122; by
  Soviet Union with Nazis, 110–119;
  Soviet-U.S. relations and, 121–123,
  129–130, 147–150; theoretical implications
  of, 154–157; types of, 14–15; by United
  Kingdom with Nazis, 97–105, 117–119; by
  United Kingdom with United States,
  71–75, 88–93; Yalta Conference and,
  130–134

Copeland, Dale C., 11
Crimean War, 49
Crowe, Eyre, 53
Cyprus, 47
Czechoslovakia, 130; Locarno treaties
  and, 98, 106; Soviet agreement with,
  115, 146

Decazes, Louis, 43
Declaration on Liberated Europe, 131–133,
  135
defensive realism, 155–156. *See also*
  offensive realism
Deng Xiaoping, 3, 160
Denmark, 40
Derby, Earl of (Frederick Stanley), 45
Dewey, George, 86–87
Dicey, Edward, 91
Disraeli, Benjamin, 40, 43, 48
Dollfuss, Engelbert, 114
Douglas, William O., 138

Eden, Anthony, 104
Egorov, Aleksandr I., 112
Egypt, 52, 54, 55
Elsey, George, 145–146, 148
emerging powers: engagement with, 33;
  now-or-later dilemma of, 23–28, 28t;
  provocation of, 24–25
engagement, logic of, 32–34; Anglo-U.S.
  relations and, 73–74, 92; imperial Germany
  and, 39–40; interwar Germany and, 96
Ethiopia, Italian invasion of, 103, 104
Ethridge, Mark, 137
European Advisory Commission, 127
existing powers, now-or-later dilemma of,
  16–23, 27–28, 28t

Fearon, James D., 11–12
Feldenkirchen, Wilfried, 69
Ferry, Jules, 53
Finland, 135
Foch, Ferdinand, 106–107
France, 43, 86, 109; German détente with,
  48, 50–51, 53, 65; interwar British
  relations with, 97, 98, 108, 117–118;
  interwar German relations with, 97–100,
  103, 105–110, 117–119; interwar military
  budgets of, 108–109; Locarno treaties and,
  98; Russian alliances with, 15, 58, 62–63;
  Soviet agreements with, 109, 115; Stresa
  Front and, 102, 103, 105, 108; Tunis
  occupied by, 47, 51; War Composite Index
  of, 70–71, 71; during War in Sight crisis,
  42–45
Franco-Prussian War, 40, 44, 47
Frankfurt, Treaty of (1871), 40
Frederick III, German kaiser, 58